TOMUS

Ron Pratt

Order this book online at www.trafford.com/07-0077
or email orders@trafford.com

Most Trafford titles are also available at major online book retailers.

© Copyright 2007 Ron Pratt.
All rights reserved. No part of this publication may be reproduced, stored in a retrieval system, or transmitted, in any form or by any means, electronic, mechanical, photocopying, recording, or otherwise, without the written prior permission of the author.

Note for Librarians: A cataloguing record for this book is available from Library and Archives Canada at www.collectionscanada.ca/amicus/index-e.html

Printed in Victoria, BC, Canada.

ISBN: 978-1-4251-1676-7

We at Trafford believe that it is the responsibility of us all, as both individuals and corporations, to make choices that are environmentally and socially sound. You, in turn, are supporting this responsible conduct each time you purchase a Trafford book, or make use of our publishing services. To find out how you are helping, please visit www.trafford.com/responsiblepublishing.html

Our mission is to efficiently provide the world's finest, most comprehensive book publishing service, enabling every author to experience success. To find out how to publish your book, your way, and have it available worldwide, visit us online at www.trafford.com/10510

 www.trafford.com

North America & international
toll-free: 1 888 232 4444 (USA & Canada)
phone: 250 383 6864 ♦ fax: 250 383 6804 ♦ email: info@trafford.com

The United Kingdom & Europe
phone: +44 (0)1865 722 113 ♦ local rate: 0845 230 9601
facsimile: +44 (0)1865 722 868 ♦ email: info.uk@trafford.com

10 9 8 7 6 5 4 3

TOMUS INDEX

Church of Education	2
The Reformation	29
The Renaissance	37
Church of Psychology/ Psychiatry	46
Church of Labour	58
Church of Politics/ Pr Flaks	68
Church of Multinational/ Global corps.	74
Church of Canada's Citizens	82
This Millennium: The Beginning of the End	87
Nominal Christianity; The Myth of Neutrality	90
God the Creator's Realm	106
Lucifer's realm	108
The Myths / Hooks of Lucifer	109
To Promote Unity	116
How do we Handle Being Wronged by Another	116
Backsliding / Indulging in wilful sin	120
Faith	123
Auto Suggestion	124
Sapiential Literature	126
Duty to God	127
Strong in Faith	128

The following was utilized as a lecture series and delivered 7 Feb 2001 at Fort Nelson, B.C. regarding the up-coming Provincial Election to be held 16 May 2001.

This is the most important, and significant election in the history of Canada; the most important Election of this epoch...and it is being slid by us as smooth as silk, and, as usual, we don't even know it.

Whether or not Canada will die as a Nation, will be decided with this Election. It seems the plan of the multinationals is to give the Liberal's THEIR "END" by making it possible for a Liberal Government to win British Columbia via a land-slide vote, thereby clearing the way for the multinationals to commence with the second and last stage of their deliberate plot to take control of the Canadian economy.

We are at the second and last stage of a deliberate plot that was born into STAGE 1, 56 years ago.

I don't know whether or not you realize it...Canada has not functioned as a Nation, since JUNE 1945, which is the date Democracy was murdered in Canada, and the two stage plot was born.

As Burdick Trestrail, 1945, and Diane Francis, 1999 so rightly stated : "Canadians are easy to scam". Trestrail added to his remark..."THEY'RE NOT OVERLY BRIGHT".

The end of stage one has brought about the anticipated, and worked for result, of those PR FLAKS: i.e. our Nation is dying, perishing because of a lack of PATRIOTISM'S VITAL OXYGEN. Cut off from the very source of her life, SLOWLY dying the death of the ASPHYXIATED, and we never even noticed her peril.

Therefore, no effort was made to go to the aid of our DYING NATION, while she was being RAPED and RAVAGED.

While her citizens have an opportunity to go to her aid and rescue her via this Election, it is highly unlikely her citizen's will see the peril of our dying nation, and she WILL die the death of the ASPHYXIATED.

The Liberals, in keeping with their usual "WHEELING AND DEALING" modus operendi, have been known to "THROW" an Election, when they know something BIG and BAD is coming "down the pike". (Any Government in power is in a position to KNOW that).

WHATEVER party deals with the "BIG AND BAD" issue, will end up in the electorate's bad books for a long time come, over that "BIG BAD ISSUE", and will be voted (thrown) out by the electorate.

The Liberal's then win will the next two or three elections, because the electorate is venting their anger on the party that "dealt" with the "BIG AND BAD" Issue, i.e.. A V ROE to NASA, at a time when Canada was the "AERONAUTICAL CHAMPIONS OF THE WORLD"...World Leaders in the field.

1 of 6 THE CHURCH OF EDUCATION/PR FLAKS

Because the realm of present day politics has been totally polluted by:
    THE CHURCH OF EDUCATION;
    THE CHURCH OF PSYCHOLOGY /PSYCHIATRY;
    THE CHURCH OF LABOUR;
    THE CHURCH OF POLITICS / PR FLAKS;
    THE CHURCH OF MULTI – NATIONALISM;

THE CHURCH OF CANADA'S CITIZENS;

THE CHURCH OF MEDICINE / HEALTH CARE will NOT be addressed via this Synthesis because that subject has been succinctly addressed by the late Dr. Robert Mendelson of Chicago Ill, and GARY BANNERMAN and DON NIXDORF, DC., via the book "SQUANDERING BILLIONS", Hancock House Publishers, 2005. This CHURCH was developed out of the FANATICISM of LUCIFER'S realm. This whole scenario MUST be brought down; taken off the stage; out of the wings; out of the 'building'; and SENT DOWN THE ROAD, along with their GNOSTICISM. Any that deny the Deity of Jesus Christ, or say that Jesus Christ was NOT who He said He was, WILL FAIL.

What does all this GOBBLEDEGOOK MEAN ??? For most of us, it is a GIVEN; many of us are quite CERTAIN; That during an election, we CANNOT BELIEVE WHAT THE POLITICIANS SAY...and that the elected members of Parliament and the legislature, sitting on the benches, don't HAVE ANYTHING TO SAY REGARDING PARTY POLITICS. PARTY POWER - BROKERS, SITTING IN THE "BACK ROOM", MAKE THE DECISIONS, and the Elected Members simply go along with that, and support the "BACK ROOM" FEW, like it or lump it; and to add insult to injury, THE CONSTITUENTS, (THAT'S US), HAVE EVEN LESS TO SAY.

How did this sad state of affairs come to be??? How was this slid by us, without us even REALIZING it, or RECOGNIZING it ???

Well, Let's start with THE CHURCH OF EDUCATION. I call it a "CHURCH" because it has MORE adherents that believe in, and follow it's teachings, and are willing to be led by it, and support it, and be taught by it, and are willing to follow it's teachings in faith/believing, feasting at it's communion table in reverential awe, than any religious congregation I know of... so it qualifies as a **CHURCH**.

Let's see how this CHURCH developed, and came into being... It started in 1830, headed by BRADLAUGH (an atheist) and HOLYOKE (an agnostic)...BOTH WERE PROPAGANDISTS (NOW KNOWN AS PR FLAKS).

By 1848 they had founded the "FREE THOUGHT FEDERATION" which consisted of many affiliated societies, who had by 1848, developed their platform of "THE 9 DEMANDS OF LIBERALISM". Five of these were:
- ALL RELIGIOUS TEACHING IN PUBLIC SCHOOLS MUST BE PROHIBITED;
- USE OF THE BIBLE IN PUBLIC SCHOOLS MUST BE PROHIBITED;
- THEOLOGICAL OATHS IN ALL GOVERNMENTAL DEPARTMENTS AND COURTS MUST BE PROHIBITED;
- LAWS TOWARD ENFORCEMENT OF CHRISTIAN MORALITY MUST BE ABROGATED;
- THERE MUST BE SEPARATION OF RELIGION AND EDUCATION.

Their thinking was, that if they were to control the minds of the general population, Christian morality had to be washed out of the minds of the general population, because Christian morality would bring their "NEW" educational philosophy, based on spurious speculations and gross theosophies and their theory of "SECULARISM", down.

The term "SECULARISM" came about in 1846, and coincides with the endeavours of HORACE MANN, a PROPAGANDIST, who became known as "THE FATHER OF AMERICAN PUBLIC SCHOOLS". In 1837 he worked perseveringly to establish public schools without Religious influence. Obviously, both HORACE MANN and JOHN DEWEY plagiarized the teachings of the pagan GREEK EMPIRE, passing them off as their OWN "WISDOM" and "NEW" FREE THOUGHT, by the grace and help of LUCIFER. It appears this "wisdom", secularism, and "NEW" thought theory had a TREMENDOUS influence on both FREUD and JUNG. (A drug addict and an occultist).

That their EXTREME PROGRAMME for Public Schools made rapid and CONSIDERABLE PROGRESS may be gathered from ABRAHAM LINCOLN'S PROCLAMATION (RE DIVORCE OF EDUCATION FROM RELIGION) issued in March, 1863, when he said "WE HAVE BEEN RECIPIENTS OF THE CHOICEST BOUNTIES OF HEAVEN; WE HAVE BEEN PRESERVED, THESE MANY YEARS, IN PEACE AND PROSPERITY ...BUT WE HAVE FORGOTTEN GOD. WE HAVE FORGOTTEN THE GRACIOUS HAND, WHICH PRESERVED US IN PEACE, AND ENRICHED AND MULTIPLIED US; WE HAVE VAINLY IMAGINED, IN THE DECEITFULNESS OF OUR HEARTS, THAT ALL THESE BLESSINGS WERE PRODUCED BY SOME SUPERIOR WISDOM AND VIRTUE OF OUR OWN. INTOXICATED WITH UNBROKEN SUCCESS, WE HAVE BECOME TOO SELF - SUFFICIENT TO FEEL THE NECESSITY OF REDEEMING AND PRESERVING GRACE; TOO PROUD TO PRAY TO THE GOD WHO MADE US".

This should remind US of the constant inclination of Canadians to turn away from God, and be immersed in MATERIALISTIC PURSUITS. In OUR day, widespread yielding to this TEMPTATION (from whom ??? (LUCIFER)), has given rise to an even GREATER danger – the way of life we call "SECULARISM".

Why this SHARP contradiction between CANADIAN TRADITION and our present day ALARMING condition of affairs??? The CHIEF contributing factor in this DEPLORABLE situation is UNDOUBTEDLY, the educational philosophy of JOHN

DEWEY – the man who, for over 50 years, had been accepted as THE PHILOSOPHER OF EDUCATION.

In Dewey's teachings, man is no more than a biological organism; he has no separate soul or mind; man's natural inclination, instincts, and impulses grow and develop under controlled and directed experiences. (THEIR/HIS CONTROLLED AND DIRECTED EXPERIENCES).
Dewey INSISTS traditional Religious and cultural values CANNOT be material for education. There are no absolutes in the philosophy of Dewey and his cronies. "Man MUST grow and develop individually and socially, SOLELY by meeting or adopting himself to his problems and environment". John Dewey, 1888.

Man has his OWN responses and behaviour patterns, and these are NOT to be interfered with, according to Dewey and his cronies, whose teachings are MONIST; (single...empirical). There is no place for GOD or for a separate SOUL - it is sheer, rampant, SECULARISM-HUMANISM-PAGANISM; GROSS THEOSOPHY and SPURIOUS SPECULATION.

These CORROSIVE INFLUENCES have made TREMENDOUS inroads into Canadian educational philosophy, and has produced for us, an educational philosophy that has gone so far awry, that it MUST be stamped out, or it will take our Nation down with it, as has been the history of the past regarding ANY Nation that has adopted the educational philosophies of past PAGAN empires, and particularly the empires of PAGAN GREECE and PAGAN ROME. It's all recorded in history books that are available at our local Library. No Nation in history EVER got away with their NONSENSE of secularism/humanism/paganism, predicated on the same premise – THE MATERIALISTIC/ANTI-RELIGIOUS CONCEPT OF LIFE, and Canada is NOT going to be the first.

Those pagans are now accrediting the CHRISTIANS: Actually,

this would not necessarily be a matter for full-scale ALARM, IF education in Canada was in the hands of the people...BUT IT IS NOT. For the most part, the GOVERNMENT is controlled by the CHURCH OF EDUCATION.

Specifically, the TEACHER COLLEGES INDOCTRINATE every school Teacher in Canada, in their latest "EDUCATIONAL THEORIES", based on the SECULARISM, HUMANISM, and PAGANISM, developed by the CHURCH OF EDUCATION "ELITE", gleaned from fallen, long gone PAGAN EMPIRES. And to add INSULT to INJURY, the educational church passes this nonsense off as "NEW" AGE THINKING...THE "NEW FREE THOUGHT"... "NEW" WISDOM...ETC., when in ACTUAL FACT, it is nothing more than the GROSS THEOSOPHY; SPURIOUS SPECULATION; and PAGANISM, of ATHEISTS; AGNOSTICS; ANTI-RELIGIOUS; ANTI-NATION STATE, instruments of Lucifer, the father of DECEIT and DECEPTION.

Consciously or unconsciously, they are being preached and taught in our SECULAR/HUMANISTIC SCHOOLS and UNIVERSITIES, and who will dare deny that these EVIL influences are not felt even in the SUPPOSEDLY guarded environs of our CHRISTIAN institutions of higher learning. Most terrible of all, secular/ humanism/ paganism is APOTHEOSIZED in the lives of the Canadian people.

Educational Associations are thoroughly committed to ANTI – CHRISTIAN PRINCIPLES, and CONTROL Provincial Legislatures. University Faculties are more influenced by FEMINISTS and "NEW" AGERS than CHRISTIANITY; and "NEW" FREE THINKERS, and an EDUCATIONAL PHILOSOPHY GONE AWRY, than CHRISTIANITY. In practice, and under the GUISE of "RELIGIOUS NEUTRALITY". Public school and University Students are INDOCTRINATED in the pet beliefs of the uneducated "ELITE" philosophers of the "NEW

AGE", and the so-called "ENLIGHTENED NEW FREE THINKERS" of the EDUCATIONAL CHURCH "ELITE".

Thanks to these UNEDUCATED "ELITE" PHILOSOPHERS OF EDUCATION, Canadian children are participating in HUMANISTIC – WORSHIP RITES, under the GUISE of TOLERANCE and COMPROMISE; learning to call up DEMONS, through "STRESS MANAGEMENT" (actually EASTERN MEDITATION); And FINDING THE wise person inside themselves; learning about CASUAL / SAME SEX; Learning about CONDOMS / THE PILL; Learning about SAME SEX FAMILIES; Learning how to PARTY and USE DRUGS/ALCOHOL; and more ABUSES than I have time to mention.

The Educational Church "ELITE" realize that if they are allowed to continue, the number of "NEW AGERS" will be swelled by litterly millions of young adults, who have been indoctrinated to unquestionable belief in their "NEW AGE" thinking, via BRAIN-WASHING THEM, (Trestrail syndrome), and they will have accomplished their goal..."RELIGIO DELANDA EST". (Religion Must Be Destroyed).

JOHN DEWEY the famous EDUCATIONAL PHILOSOPHER, was the ORIGINATOR of the "DEDICATED BELIEVER PHILOSOPHY", and who also wrote the HUMANIST MANIFESTO, followed EXACTLY that strategy, and took over the ENTIRE American Educational System.

And what affect did this have on the Canadian Educational system??? Canada now has the largest UNACKNOWLEDGED EDUCATIONAL CHURCH, (one of the many churches in Lucifer's realm), in our history. And the majority of Christians SEND their children to it. And the Christians are FORBIDDEN by Supreme Court Law to teach Christian teachings. Whereas the "new agers" of the pagan educational church, are NOT forbidden to teach THEIR doctrine. Now you know WHY **Canada** is in the mess it is.

What is the Answer ??? Are Canadians doomed to see the "new age" pagan educational church "elite" take over the reins of POWER, while parents are FORBIDDEN to lift a finger??? LET'S SEE! ... LET'S SEE!

PRE – HERMENEUTIC

1. EDWARD HOLYOKE 1689 – 1769 (pseudonym ICONOCLAST)
2. VOLTAIRE 1694 – 1778 (pseudonym for FRANÇOISE – MARIE AROUET)
3. IMMANUEL KANT 1724 – 1804
4. GEORG HEGEL 1770 – 1831
5. HORACE MANN 1796 – 1859
6. SOREN KIERKEGAARD 1813 – 1855
7. HELENA BLAVATSKY 1831 – 1891
8. CHARLES BRADLAUGH 1833 – 1891 (INFLUENCED BY HOLYOKE)
9. ANNIE BESANT 1847 – 1933
10. JOHN DEWEY 1859 – 1952 (INFLUENCED BY MANN)
11. JIDDU KRISHNAMURTI 1895 – 1986
    RENAISSANCE: 14TH CENTURY TO 17TH CENTURY
    REFORMATION: 16TH CENTURY

1. EDWARD HOLYOKE: 1689 – 1769 (pseudonym ICONOCLAST) 10th President of Harvard University. Strengthened liberalized Academia. He liberalized the educational curriculum, granting aid to 'deserving' students. He graduated at Harvard with high honours in 1705. He remained at Harvard for 7 years in the dual capacity of tutor and librarian, and then as a FELLOW of the Harvard Corporation. 1737 – 1769. Though not considered a commanding intellect by his peers, he strengthened Harvard's academic programme in mathematics and science, and established the first laboratory for experimental Physics in North America.

Then embarked on theological studies, and was ordained a Pastor of the Congregational Church 1716 – 1737.

2. VOLTAIRE: (pseudonym for FRANÇOISE-MARIE AROUET) 1694-1778. Noted for his wit; satire; and critical capacity. Radical and atheist.

3. IMMANUEL KANT: 1724- 1804 (Kahnt) German philosopher of the educational "elite". Developed the KANTYIAN PHILOSOPHY, which began to influence the educational intellectual "elite" of the age, developing a classical philosophy that taught, THEIR **VALUES** WERE ABSOLUTE. Kant triggered the ideas, which resulted in the philosophy introduced by Georg HEGEL.

4. GEORG HEGEL: 1770-1831 (WILHELM FRIEDRICH) A German philosopher of the educational "elite". Hegel took the Kantian Philosophy and began to press it forward, and Hegel left a heritage of brutal and violent fallout. He was called the philosopher Dictator of Germany.

The convicting evidence that Hegel was a saint of Lucifer's realm, is the fact that via the help and grace of Lucifer, Hegel took the dialectic thinking process of God's Realm, and perverted that truth into the empirical thinking of Lucifer's realm…(Lucifer ALWAYS starts with a truth, then perverts that truth into a lie).

Hegel's resulting philosophy was the basis of the communistic political and economic ideas of Karl Marx, and the National (so called) socialism of Adolph Hitler. (It was Burdick Trestrial who would, years later, brain-wash the people via Edward Bernays's "ENGINEERING OF CONSENT", designed to CONTROL and REGIMENT the masses (of people), via PROPAGANDA (PR FLAK), into thinking that Socialism and communism were the same…i.e. "Socialism" was simply another name for "Communism", 1945. Hegel glorified the State. He taught that the State did not have to obey moral law, nor did Governments have to keep agreements. Hitler followed this philosophy of Hegel to perfection.

Hegel introduced RELATIVE THINKING and REFLECTED ABSOLUTES; he literally altered, (via Lucifer's help, power and might), the future course of the world. (IN KEEPING WITH LUCIFER'S PLAN TO TAKE THE 'WORLD' INTO HIS REALM). As Hegel did away with CAUSE AND EFFECT logic, there was no need for ULTIMATE TRUTH; no necessity TO BELIEVE IN A CREATOR-GOD. Hegel's philosophy soon influenced Europe and North America.

The educational "elite" of Europe and North America were now working as a team. (The more 'educated' people became, via the "NEW" thought or thinking, the educational "elite", and the Theosophical Society "Elite"; the more they rejected the absolutes of God, truth and morals). Even those who HAD a true Faith in Jesus Christ, found their faith weakened in College, but they could not discover WHY... (PR FLAKS). (That Lucifer is one smooth cookie).

Today, the College student is not educated; he simply receives job training, and is graduated uneducated.

Relative ("NEW AGE") thinking is now in the earliest levels of elementary education. It is a "Trojan Horse" few Christian parents understand, much less actively FIGHT.

5. HORACE MANN 1796- 1859 The first use of the term "SECULARISM" (about 1846), coincides with the endeavours of Horace Mann, (PR FLAK), known as "THE FATHER OF AMERICAN PUBLIC SCHOOLS". As Secretary of the first STATE BOARD OF EDUCATION, MASSACHUSETTS, in 1837, he worked per-severingly to establish Public Schools "WITHOUT RELIGIOUS INFLUENCE".

That Horace Mann's EXTREME programme for Public Schools made RAPID and CONSIDERABLE progress may be gathered from Abraham Lincoln's PROCLAMATION re Divorce of education from religion, issued in March 1863.

This should remind us in Canada, of the CONSTANT INCLINATION of this Country to turn away from God, and be immersed in material pursuits. In OUR day, widespread yielding to this TEMPTATION (from whom??? LUCIFER) has given rise to an even GREATER danger – the way of life we call "SECULARISM".

6. SOREN AABEY KIERKEGAARD 1813 – 1855 Danish Philosopher of the educational "elite", another theologian and saint of Lucifer's realm. He rejected Lutheranism and established his own church of Denmark. (A product of the Reformation). The father of EXISTENTIALISM. His writings are a denial of the basic tenets of the Christian faith, and a show of disdain for those who do not agree with him.

He introduced the tenets of KANT and HEGEL, into the theology of the Christian Faith. When KARL BARTH, (a disciple of Kierkegaard), came along, in the early twentieth century, Karl developed a "NEW" system of theology which he called "NEO – ORTHODOXY" (which was neither "new" nor orthodox). This EXISTENTIAL, RELATIVE thinking became thoroughly spread throughout Christianity, laying the foundation for the polluted pulpits, sanctuaries, tabernacles and Scriptures; and the gross theosophies and spurious speculations; the cowardice, tolerance, and compromise; and the nominal Christianity of the wayward bride of Christ, (His Church) of our present day.

7. HELENA BLAVATSKY 1831 – 1891 A saint of Lucifer's in the field of OCCULTISM, MYSTISM, AND SPIRITISM. A co-founder, with ANNIE BESANT, of the THEOSOPHICAL SOCIETY. Her victims were all of the SOCIAL "ELITE" Society of Europe and North America. The English Psychic Association proved her a fraud, in spite of her grandiose performances and claims. Through her, God mocked the Social Elite Societies of Europe and North America to their faces.

8. CHARLES BRADLAUGH 1833 – 1891 An anti-religious lecturer, who lectured and published under the pseudonym of ICONOCLAST. A RADICAL and an ATHEIST, in the tradition of VOLTAIRE and THOMAS PINE. Between 1868 –1869 he was prosecuted for blasphemy and sedition. In 1876 he distributed a birth-control pamphlet by Dr. CHARLES KNOWLTON, an American phy-

sician, and received a light sentence for selling an indecent book, which he circulated aggressively, incurring severe penalties.

In 1885 he became associated with ANNIE BESANT, (co-founder with HELENE BLAVATSKY), of the THEOSOPHICAL SOCIETY. Bradlaugh and Besant were VERY active within the Society, promoting and selling their gross theosophies and spurious speculations, dealing mainly with the high society of both Europe and North America, duping them royally.

In 1880, Bradlaugh, campaigning as a RADICAL, was elected to the House of Commons (in England). However, for more than 5 years he was denied his seat because he would not swear the necessary Religious Oath on the Bible.

During that time, he was re-elected 3 times (via the power and might of Lucifer). Bradlaugh later offered to take the oath, but was forbidden to do so. Finally, in 1886 permission was granted, he made the oath and was "seated". By that time, public opinion swung in his favour, and Bradlaugh himself, who opposed socialism, became increasingly conservative.

9. ANNIE BESANT 1847 – 1933 She was converted to the pagan doctrines of HELENE BLAVATSKY. Besant plunged vigorously into theosophical work. She was promoted to be the leader of the Society in 1889.

Besant supported and promoted JIDDU KRISHNAMURTI, a Hindu religious philosopher, claiming Jiddu was actually BUDDHA reincarnate. Jiddu worked vigorously with the Theosophical Society, until he renounced Besant in 1929.

10. JOHN DEWEY 1859 –1952 Accepted for over 50 years as the philosopher of American Education. He was founder of the Dewey Decimal Classification system of classifying books.

In Dewey's teachings, man is no more than a biological organism; man has no separate soul or mind; man's natural inclination, instinct, and impulses grow and develop under controlled and directed experience. Traditional religious (Scriptural) and cultural values, according to Dewey, CANNOT, therefore, be material for the School Curriculum. There are no absolutes in Dewey's philosophy. "Man MUST grow and develop INDIVIDUALLY and SOCIALLY, SOLELY by meeting or adopting himself to his present problems and environment". (John Dewey, 1888).

Dewey was DEEPLY IMPREGNATED with DARWINISM. His teaching is MONIST (Single...empirical). He has no place for God, or a separate soul. His teachings are sheer, rampant SECULARISM and PAGANISM. God is banned.

11. JIDDU KRISHNAMURTI 1895 – 1986 Hindu religious philosopher, linked with the THEOSOPHICAL SOCIETY. After a stint in Europe and North America, he returned to India.

"MODERN" thinkers or philosophers plagiarized crushed ancient pagan civilizations, passing such "WISDOM" off as their OWN "modern" or "new age" thinking. They were, in FACT, saints, instruments and servants of Lucifer, and they served their master well.

And all this further compounded and complicated by the "ANGELS OF LIGHT" (2 Cor 11: 14-15) such as Dr. Benjamin Spock, that Lucifer has snared and entangled, and used as his saints, instruments and servants, to promote the Parental Incompetence Syndrome, that has bound, and is binding tighter and tighter, our Nation, Canada, producing the IMMATURE, IRRATIONAL, ARROGANT, and REBELLIOUS CITIZENS God has said He will destroy, and condemn to the fires of hell for ETERNITY, requiring the blood of the children, at the hands of their fathers, because the children were not trained up within the confines of the Precepts, Oracles, and commandments of God, and were not trained how to train THEIR children.

And all this is ours, thanks to the "ELITE" of the Church of Education of Lucifer's realm.

During the Renaissance...(14th to 17th Century) THEOLOGIANS, SCHOLARS, PHILOSOPHERS and ANTIQUARIANS became interested in uncovering new proof of the glories of Greece and Rome. These so-called "SCHOLARS" were Christians interested in "SPOILING THE EGYPTIANS". In other words, they wanted to

glean whatever wisdom, knowledge, and insights they could, from the "ACHIEVEMENTS" of the ancients, "WITHOUT BECOMING ENSNARED BY PAGAN PHILOSOPHY OR EVIL."
1. They opened their hearts to pagan gods and evils THEMSELVES;
2. Then they mourned the demise of the pagans;
3. They then SECRETLY decided the gods were no longer to be mocked, and were to reign BESIDE Christ, but not to REPLACE Christ.

Lucifer hit "PAY DIRT", RICH, FERTILE, SOIL. Want to know what the end result was??? Read on...

Via malicious cunning, Lucifer led these "SCHOLARS" to his pagan gods, goddesses, women whose great charm and beauty induced swoon or trance, somnolent, sophisticated, arousers/inducers to adoration. Lucifer gave them the grace to be cunning, delusional, pseudo, fallacious, sham, vanity, false belief regarding themselves, made them schizophrenic, and gave them demiurge, hallucinations, retroversion, and they thought themselves to be 'ADMIRABLE'. And this became the source of polluted scriptures, sanctuaries, tabernacles and pulpits. ISA 3:16 etc.

The PRECEPTS, ORACLES and COMMANDMENTS are TOTALLY NON-NEGOTIABLE re TRADITIONS, PRINCIPLES, CEREMONIES, RITUALS, and CUSTOMS. ISA 1:11-20 ISA 5:20-25 EZEK 18:25 etc. Argue with GOD??? HOW DARE YOU... FORGET IT.

The so-called "NEW AGE" is nothing but microwave PAGANISM. It is nothing more, or LESS, than a conglomeration of WORN-OUT pagan doctrines of FAILED ANCIENT EMPIRES.

We will begin with a brief recap of a few favourite "NEW AGE" beliefs... (we must be SURE to recognize them.)
ROLL-YOUR-OWN RELIGION: Western paganism preaches that each person must "do what is right for HIMSELF". People tend

to select bits and pieces of various practices, (i. e. crystals and witchcraft), then glom them together as their FANCY suits them. This is the way "POPULAR" religion, (opposed to the OFFICIAL Religion of God), has been practiced in ancient cultures, and the culture of OUR Nation, these days. They are NOT loyal to any one type of teaching, preaching, or practice. Most pagan practices fit into several different categories at once. For instance, much of what a shaman does falls under SPIRITISM; magic is tied closely with ANIMISM...you roll-your-own Religion.

DIVINATION: Astrology, (ASTROLABE) the teaching that the stars in the sky guide our lives, is the most popular form of DIVINATION in the west. It is the "GATEWAY" to paganism (pagan religion) for MANY people.

Like ALL other techniques for predicting the future, (Horoscope), astrology puts NATURE in control, and dispenses with the Sovereignty of God. DIVINATION is completely amoral. The stars NEVER guide us to make RIGHTEOUS choices, or even hint that RIGHTEOUSNESS exists. The PERVERT, REPROBATE, and the UPRIGHT all receive their readings on an equal basis. The BIBLE PROHIBITS (FORBIDS) astrology etc...ABSOLUTELY and COMPLETELY. In fact, part of the reason for God's JUDGEMENT OF BABEL was the towers built "UNTO THE HEAVENS". GEN 11:4.

In ancient times, the future was divined by sheep livers and chicken entrails. The BABYLONIANS devoted THOUSANDS of volumes to the "SCIENCE" of liver DIVINATION. To THEM, those COPIOUS 'observations' constituted the PINNACLE of "SCIENCE".

TEA-LEAF diviners; PALM READERS; the "CURIOUS"; and the "SERIOUS"; mostly favour TAROT CARDS and I CHING in our day and age.

SPIRITISM: The "ancient" "SCIENCES" and "CHANNELLING"

have taken the WESTERN world 'BY STORM'. The DARK ROOM, TRUMPETS, FLOATING TABLES, ECTOPLASM, and "DEAD 'UNCLE HARRY'S VOICE", have been replaced by BRIGHT LIGHTS and "VOICES" that speak in Near East accents with a dash of King James English.

Today, one of the most- used forms of SPIRITISM, is contact with a "SPIRIT GUIDE". You empty your mind and BINGO! Something is speaking to you, or even appearing before you (THIS IS QUITE DIFFERENT FROM CHRISTIAN PRAYER, WHERE YOUR MIND STAYS ACTIVE AND FOCUSED ON GOD'S WORD).

Exactly WHAT are those "SPIRIT GUIDES" ??? CHRISTIANS recognize so-called "SPIRIT GUIDES" as old fashioned DEMONS, and the process of emptying one's mind to receive a DEMON; is an INVITATION to DEMON POSSESSION. However, "DEMON POSSESSION" does not sell, so the DEMONS are being 'billed' as WONDERFUL HELPERS who will lead you to godhood, as long as you are WILLING to "TOTALLY SURRENDER" to THEIR LEADERSHIP.

Mystic "NEW AGERS" see their 'GUIDE' as one of the gods; an angel; a dead person; or an ascended master like Buddha. A HUMANIST will see it as HIMSELF TALKING TO HIMSELF -a hidden part of his OWN mind. Under the PRETENCE that "SPIRIT GUIDES" are simply "IMAGINARY FRIENDS", PUBLIC SCHOOL TEACHERS are leading little children to invite such 'guides' INTO THEIR LIVES.

Most adult "new age" types view the 'GUIDE' "the god within". For some, this allows them to skip the gurus and swamis, and go directly to the "SOURCE" (the demons), and become "SELF-GUIDED". One writer explains: I KNOW THIS SOUNDS FAR-FETCHED... PART OF THE FADDISH TREND TOWARD SELF-ACTUALIZATION WORKSHOPS; PSYCHICS; CHANNELS;

and SPIRIT MEDIUMS LIKE RAMTHA; SETH; (and BOAPSIE'S "HUNK-RA" in DOONESBURY). ALL THESE THINGS CAN BE EXPENSIVE AND ADDICTIVE BUT THE GUIDE MEDITATION IS FREE AND DONE IN SOLITUDE, MAKING THE DEPENDENCE ON NO ONE BUT MYSELF, AND SOLELY RESPONSIBLE FOR MY OWN "MOVIE", (as the jargon has it). The PHRASE "WE CREATE OUR OWN REALITY" IS DEMONSTRATED BY, AND THROUGH THIS MEDITATION" MURRAY HOPE, NEW YORK 1984.

The Bible PROHIBITS seeking contact with spirits other than God's Realm -be they billed as dead people; demons; ascended masters; spirit guides; or aliens. These contacts, whether made by Ouija Boards, automatic writing; channelling; meditation; or centring; are ALL DANGEROUS: opening the 'door' to EVIL SPIRITS.

"NEW AGERS" fail to take into account that they have no way to check the accuracy of the 'spirits' claims. Generally, they ASSUME the 'spirit' is a GOOD SPIRIT. In fact, they assume ALL spirits are good. The BIBLE, on the other hand, FLATLY STATES THAT ALL such contacts are EVIL.

Over and over, CHANNELLED SPIRITS offer the same basic teachings. The first is 'thou art god'. THIS familiar LIE, dating back to the Garden of Eden, is then linked with the teaching that "ALL YOU NEED FOR SALVATION (enlightenment, or whatever), is within YOU.

Oddly enough, the ground rules then state that you have to TOTALLY surrender to the control of the spirit in order to experience this "WONDERFUL GODHOOD" and FREEDOM. All you need, to become free, is to MAKE YOURSELF THE SPIRIT'S SLAVE.

SHAMANISM: A SHAMAN is a person who serves as a spiritual leader because of his ALLEGED ABILITY to contact and control spiritual forces, often within the use of "POWER ANIMALS" or TOTEMS (i.e. your basic black cat). This is also the textbook definition of a SORCERER but "SHAMAN" still sounds better than "SORCERER" to the man in the street. The visual image of the SHAMAN is that of a WITCH DOCTOR with feathered headdress and bone ornaments. Most 'modern' SHAMANS skip the feathers.

Like the channelled entities (and, as we will see, like certain popular psychologists), shamans often refer the "seeker" to his OWN inner guidance as "the way to truth". Acting on IMPULSE in this manner, just like you did when you were a baby crying in dirty diapers, is called "INTUITIVE" by "New Age" pagans. They make MUCH of the difference between the "FREEDOM OF INTUITIVE LIVING, as opposed to the STRICTNESS of "1iving by rigid rules", (although, oddly enough, no "new ager" so far, has come out against toilet training).

The shaman himself attempts his "CURES" and other "SPIRITUAL" processes by "INTUITIVE" ceremonies and spells. Classes are offered in shamanistic dancing and drumming; the making of "medicine" bags; peyote beading; and power animal contacts, coming SOON to a University near you.

ANIMISM: Here is the good old-fashioned all-African paganism, with which we are so familiar. ANIMISM is the belief that SPIRITS or POWERS inhabit objects and "ANIMATES" them. PANTHEISM, the belief that ALL NATURE IS GOD, falls under this category, as does the belief that INDIVIDUAL SPIRIT BEINGS INHABIT THE TREES, ROCKS, WIND, ETC. A deeper look at most of these teachings reveals a belief in "MANA", a nameless, faceless power, not dissimilar to "THE FORCE" as portrayed in the "STAR WARS" series.

The use of AMULETS, TALISMANS, CRYSTALS, or SYMBOLS TO BRING POWER, LUCK, or "ENERGIES" TO BEAR, is an extension of this belief. This, of course, is UNBIBLICAL AND DENIES

THE SOVEREIGNTY OF GOD. If "powers" reside in objects to be used at will by ANY individual, then God is unnecessary.

MYSTERY RELIGIONS: Mystery religions do not necessarily focus on a particular god or goddess, but they THRIVE ON CLAIMS; that they hold "SECRET KNOWLEDGE" that leads to GOD, HAPPINESS, NIRVANA, or WHATEVER.

Most of these CULTS APPEAL TO the "WISDOM OF THE ANCIENTS". ROSICRUCIAN'S claim to possess the wisdom of Egypt and Babylon. Mainline "New Agers" are fond of ASSERTING THEY HAVE THE GOOD WORD FROM ATLANTIS. (A NEAT TRICK SINCE THEY HAVE NOT EVEN FOUND ATLANTIS YET). MORMONS VIGOROUSLY maintain that they and they alone, have the records of otherwise unknown ancient Athenian civilizations.

Secret INITIATION RITES and SPECIAL KNOWLEDGE are the earmarks of these CULTS. Often, Christianity is accused of being just another of the mystery religions that sprang up around the time of Christ.

Those who SAY this, CLAIM that Baptism and Communion were the INITIATION RITES. But there is NOTHING HIDDEN or SECRET about BAPTISM or COMMUNION. In fact, outsiders are URGED TO ATTEND CHRISTIAN WORSHIP.

The Apostle PAUL speaks ELOQUENTLY about the "MYSTERIES OF THE FAITH" but ONLY in the context of being "revealed by grace mysteries". Most of this "mystery" was hidden until Christ. Unlike the MYSTERY CULTS, though, the mysteries were even hid from the Prophets who proclaimed them...hidden FROM the chief initiates.

The MYSTERY CULTS are designed to EXCLUDE PEOPLE

FROM GOD, HAPPINESS, NIRVANA, or WHATEVER, unless they qualify in INTELLIGENCE, WISDOM, or SOME OTHER ABILITY. JESUS CHRIST was sent to INCLUDE PEOPLE.

IDOLATRY: When people think of PAGANISM, they usually think first of IDOLATRY. They picture wood or stone figures surrounded by dancing and bowing people; a fat smiling Buddha with clouds of incense or smoke rising before him; or the superheated arms of a brass Molech awaiting the tiny, squirming infant sacrifice.

But idolatry, by GOD'S definition, is when ANYTHING is placed ahead of GOD. For this reason Scripture condemns COVETOUSNESS as idolatry. CAREER, WEALTH, CONVENIENCE, POSSESSIONS, and POPULARITY can ALL fill the bill of IDOLATRY. The common element of them all is SELF. In ALL of these, (and MANY others), man vaunts HIS WILL before GOD'S WILL.

The most common idol worshipped in the WEST today, lives in the MIRROR. Even the ATHEIST does his homage at the silvered glass alter. People say there is NO GOD because they think THEY are God. Both Scripture and experience WILL bear out this simple truth.
Now being layered over this CULTURAL SELFISHNESS is the "THOU ART GOD" teaching of the 'NEW AGE' PAGANS.

"TO FIND GOD" intones THOMAS E. MAILS (1988), "BE YOURSELF". Another says I'VE FOUND HUMILITY IN ACKNOWLEDGING THE POWER I HAVE IN CREATING ALL THAT COMES TO ME. THE 'BEING' AND 'DOING' OF MY LIFE AS WRETCHED AND WONDERFUL AS IT IS, IS THE PERFECT UNFOLDING OF ME". KAY RIES, 1988. (Lord, preserve us from such "HUMILITY").

Have you fallen down and worshipped 'NEW AGER' CHRIS PRINGER today? He thinks you should. He says, "MY PART OF THE PLAN FOR EARTH IS BEING RESTORED, I AM THAT I AM, (through me) THE POWER OF ALL LIFE IS MANIFESTED". 1989.

TRADITIONAL (EASTERN) IDOLATRY IS being practiced in the WEST today. MANY 'NEW AGE' writers and speakers now recommend resurrecting the 'ancient' PANTHEONS, and ESPECIALLY THE WORSHIP OF THE MOTHER GODDESS. But so far, it's easier to tease people into mooning into their mirrors, than into investing in bulky statues that clutter up their busy living rooms.

SYMPATHETIC MAGIC: Often called "EARTH MAGIC", claims that natural laws as seen in the visible sphere, affect the spiritual realm, as well. i.e. since dirt (earth) brings about growth in seeds, then dirt may be selected for any SPELL or MEDICINE BAG related to growth. So if you want to grow tall, eat some dirt, roll in the dirt, or rub dirt in your hair.For REAL power, use the dirt off a tall basketball player's sneakers. YUM! It is a practice associated with SHAMANISM.

"THE LAW OF SIMILARITY' is the basis of all "SYMPATHETIC MAGIC" i.e. VOODOO DOLLS etc. Actions done to an OBJECT also affects the OBJECT or ENTITY that is LIKE IT. The ASSOCIATION may only exist in the mind of the MAGICIAN". JAMES FAUBEL 1989.

Unhappily, the more hard-core 'NEW AGERS' have discovered that in ancient OCCULT THINKING, BLOOD is the most POWERFUL substance one can use.
"BLOOD HAS THE MOST POTENT VIBRATION OF ANY SUBSTANCE ON THE PLANET, AND IS USED IN MOST MAGIC WORK. TIBETAN LAMAS STILL USE IT TODAY. WHEN YOU

RELEASE BLOOD FROM YOUR BODY, YOU GET POWER; MANY THEN WHO WERE IN VIET-NAM CAN ATTEST TO THIS "MAGICAL" POTENCY OF THE SPILLING OF "the DARK FORCES". THE PLANET NEEDS BLOOD TO BE RELEASED, IT NEEDS IT IN SOME WAY TO FEED THE PLANET (THE GODDESS, MOTHER EARTH), AND MAINTAIN NATURAL BALANCE". EILEEN SHAVELSON, 1988.

Interesting ecology, this. Our planet wants BLOOD. It is a big planet and must have a big appetite. Releasing blood from YOUR body (we're NOT talking chicken blood here) gives POWER; Human blood = power. Mother Earth wants to eat YOU. Watch out where this bloodthirsty trend leads. IT COULD GET NASTY!

HINDUISM: We will have more on Hinduism later, but we must mention it quickly here because the two most basic "NEW AGE" DOCTRINES ARE REINCARNATION (the notion that you will be REBORN into many future lives), and KARMA (the notion that the good and ill in your present life comes as a DIRECT result of your actions in a PREVIOUS life). These two doctrines are at the root of a whole series of ABUSES.

The cycle of REINCARNATION and KARMA presupposes a "WORKS" Salvation, and an UNLIMITED NUMBER of 'TRIES' for the goal. Unfortunately, the "GOAL" is not worth having, since Hindu heaven is to ESCAPE THE CYCLE OF REINCARNATION AND BECOME "GOBBLED UP" INTO THE god BRAHMIN, avoiding the endless misery of suffering and dying in LIFE AFTER LIFE. Hindu's have not yet realized that REINCARNATION is NOT really a 'cute' way to avoid the Hebrew/Christian doctrine of HELL, it IS hell.

Within Hinduism, this life isn't the greatest either, since everything bad that happens to you is YOUR OWN FAULT AND DESERVES NO SYMPATHY FROM OTHERS. If you are in POVERTY; SICK; or AFFLICTED, YOU DONE IT TO YOURSELF.

(a result of your response and behaviour patterns (good or bad) in your PREVIOUS life on earth. On the other hand, if you are rich and healthy, you have no obligation to spread the "BLESSINGS" around. ANY suffering you inflict on your social inferiors is THEIR OWN FAULT for having BAD KARMA. Such is the compassionate "NEW AGE" TEACHING. (hence the CASTE SYSTEM of India).

SYNCRETISM: The attempt to blend MANY religions into an AMORPHOUS MASS. It's the teaching that, since ALL 'roads' lead to God, you might as well try them all out.
The MYSTIC RELIGIONS; PHILOSOPHERS; GNOSTICS; AND OTHERS, ALL TRIED TO ABSORB Christianity into their happy little SYNCRETISM...BUT WITHOUT SUCCESS.

Pagans today try to imply that BIBLICAL JUDAISM and CHRISTIANITY are actually SYNCRETISTIC RELIGIONS. They point to the SIMILARITIES between CREATION and FLOOD LEGENDS of BABYLON, and the BIBLICAL ACCOUNTS, then IMPLY THAT the BIBLICAL ACCOUNTS WERE BORROWED FROM THE PAGAN NATIONS......it ACTUALLY HAPPENED the OTHER WAY AROUND. The pagan versions are DISTORTED, with their totally impossible adventures of emotional gods and mystical beasts, IN CONTRAST TO THE RESTRAINED SENSIBLENESS OF THE BIBLICAL ACCOUNT.

SYNCRETISM demands TOLERANCE OF DIFFERENCES in pagan teachings via the teaching that each person HAS HIS OWN PATH...it makes little difference since ALL paths lead to the same place.

Western pagans can simply select ANYTHING from a smorgasbord of religious ideas, and concoct their OWN private religion. They can even toss out old pieces, and add new ones with abandon, and it is viewed as part of their OWN EVOLUTION... their OWN path. The only way you can come up with anything these pagans will look upon with contempt, is to CLAIM to know the "ONE AND ONLY RIGHT WAY" (It's O.K. to know the "ONE BEST WAY", as long as it's only best for YOU). Once you claim to KNOW the "ONE RIGHT WAY FOR ALL", the gloves come off; you will be LABELLED:

"UNENLIGHTENED"; (Maharishi Mahesh Yogi 1975)
"FUNDAMENTALIST FASCIST"; (Psychic Guide Sept- Nov 1986)
"A DARK POCKET OF RESISTANCE" (John Price 1984)
"AN IDOLATER" (Mathew Fox 1981)
"NEGATIVE" (Moira Timms 1980)
"INFERIOR" (Richard M. Bucke 1901)
"UNFIT" (Maharishi Mahesh Yogi 1975)
"ANTICHRIST" (JOHN R. PRICE 1984)

All in the name of universal LOVE and PEACE and BROTHERHOOD, of course.

NEW THOUGHT: "NEW THOUGHT" teaches what has come to be called "THE POWER OF POSITIVE THINKING" -that man may shape his OWN reality with his THOUGHTS. This is ALSO a perfect example of how satan perverts GOD'S NATURAL LAW.

Is "NEW THOUGHT" a "NEW AGE" teaching? NEW AGERS themselves think so. "FROM AN OCCULT POINT OF VIEW, the POWER OF POSITIVE THINKING, WHICH UNDERLIES MANY SELF-HELP PHILOSOPHIES, IS SIMPLY WHITE MAGIC" (Nevill Drury 1989).

"TRADITIONAL" appearing religious figures have prepared the religious public for this OCCULT belief. Like KARMA, this belief tends to STIFLE COMPASSION. "AFTER ALL", a "NEW THINKER" will argue, "I CAN'T REALLY HELP HIM UNTIL HIS THINKING CHANGES".

Some 'extras' have been added to the practice, such as USING SPEECH to "AFFIRM" the truth of the SELF-CREATED; SELF-DESIRED reality. "THE LAW OF REPETITION INVOKE OFTEN!

THE SUBCONSCIOUS MIND IS IMPRESSED BY REPETITION" (James E. Faubel, 1989, ("LAWS OF MAGIC")).

The ALEISTER CROWLEY we are urged to follow, was a notorious SEXUAL PERVERT and WITCH of the EARLY TWENTIETH CENTURY. (just to give you an idea of the "ROOTS" of "NEW" THOUGHT).

ANOTHER way to turn your cloudy thoughts into real hard cash or health, or WHATEVER, is 'the technique of VISUALIZATION. SHAKTI GAWAIN, a PROMINENT 'New Ager', explains how it works: WHEN WE CREATE SOMETHING, WE ALWAYS CREATE IT FIRST IN A THOUGHT FORM. THE IDEA IS LIKE A BLUEPRINT; IT CREATES AN IMAGE OF THE FORM, WHICH THEN MAGNETIZES AND GUIDES the PHYSICAL ENERGY FLOW INTO THAT FORM, AND EVENTUALLY MANIFESTS IT ON A PHYSICAL PLANE". (Shakti Gawain's book "BASICS OF CREATIVE VISUALISATION").

Shakti says: "THE MORE CLEARLY YOU CAN PICTURE WHAT YOU WANT, IN YOUR MIND, THE MORE POWERFUL THE FORCE TO BRING IT INTO REALITY". Supposedly, THIS is the driving force behind the "VISUALIZE WORLD PEACE" bumper stickers seen across Canada and the United States. (You will note that we do NOT yet have world peace).

I COR I :28 must be taken into consideration and juxtaposed within this pagan scenario.

HUMANISM: Most people have difficulty recognizing HUMANISM as a pagan practice. This is due to the MISCONCEPTION that HUMANISM is merely a FORM OF ATHEISM, with no particular teachings of it's own. In reality, HUMANISM is a sophisticated form of IDOLATRY.

HUMANISTS can be religious or non-religious; it amounts to the same thing in practice. In HUMANISM, man collectively OR individually, is the centre of all things. The HUMANISTS get to tell the rest of us what we want, and FORCE it on us. (ANOTHER distortion of God's Natural Law). i.e. in a relationship with God, there is no democracy...it is an emphatic dictatorship (in a sense)... it's HIS way or the highway...PERIOD. The PRECEPTS, ORACLES, COMMANDMENTS AND GOD'S NATURAL LAW ARE TOTALLY NON-NEGOTIABLE. There is NO ROOM FOR WHEELING, DEALING, BARGAINING or TRADE-OFFS...To reiterate, they are TOTALLY NON-NEGOTIABLE. The non-religious humanists tell us that "IF God exists, He has left us to our own devices".

1. COLLECTIVE HUMANISTS: Tend toward POLITICAL and/or TOTALITARIANISM. MOSTLY as MARXIST COMMUNISTS. They seek the long-range evolution and betterment of society - UNDER THEIR CONTROL, of course. CHRISTIAN Socialists ARE, in spirit and truth, saints, instruments and/or servants of God, indwelt by the Holy Spirit, TRULY walking the path God created them to walk for HIM.

"Religious Humanism considers complete realization of human personality to be the end of man's life, and seeks it's development and fulfilment in the here and now. This is the explanation of the HUMANIST'S Social passion" (The Humanist Manifesto 1, eighth affirmation).

2. INDIVIDUALIST HUMANISTS: Tend to seek SELF-FULFILMENT, whether SPIRITUAL or MATERIAL. They seek the improvement of their OWN LIVES, and PERHAPS the lives of a few close friends. PERSONAL FULFILMENT, however, can mean anything from being a RUTHLESS businessman, to a SERIAL KILLER. HUMANISM offers no particular moral concepts.

"Believing that Religion must work increasingly for joy in living, religious humanists aim to foster the CREATIVE in man, and encourage ACHIEVEMENTS THAT ADD TO the SATISFACTION OF LIFE". (The Humanists Manifesto 1, Twelfth affirmation).

The above two quotes emphasize subjective things like "REALIZATION OF THE PERSONALITY" and "SATISFACTION OF LIFE" leaving EVERYONE to define what this means TO HIM/HER. What if someone feels "CREATIVE" and finds "SATISFACTION" in being a BUM or a RAPIST ???

3. FEMINISM: Is humanism with "WOMAN" replacing "MAN" as the 'CENTRE'. This form of HUMANISM holds all the same political and social goals, but emphasizes that a MATRIARCHAL society is more likely to achieve those IDEALS than the PATERNALISTIC society.

4. SCIENTISM HUMANISM: Humanism also includes the subheading of SCIENTISM - the INORDINATE workshop of 'science'. This is only true, however, when 'science' agrees with Its presupposition. Any AMOUNT OF EVIDENCE FOR BIBLICAL CREATION, FOR EXAMPLE, IT TOTALLY IGNORED AND REJECTED. If the FACTS do not support the hypothesis, the FACTS are set aside, allowing the hypothesis to reign supreme. (DUMB EMPIRICAL THINKING).
  * "Religious Humanist regard the universe as self-existing and not created"
  * "Humanism believes that man is part of nature and that he has emerged as a result of a continuous process"
  * "Humanism asserts that the nature of the universe depicted by modern science, makes unacceptable any supernatural or cosmic guarantees of human values"
  * HUMANIST MANIFESTO, AFFIRMATIONS 1,2, and 5.

Quite old-fashioned, these humanists quotes. They could have come straight out of ancient Greece or Rome. In brief, humanism is simply upper class PAGANISM. If you are rich enough and/or arrogant enough, you can do whatever you want, without even consulting the gods. Morality is irrelevant- or at least subject to change without notice. For more on this subject, see RELIGIO DELANDA EST by R. A. Pratt.

THE REFORMATION - 16th Century

The Reformation led to the establishment of a number of Protestant churches in England, Germany, Scandinavia, Scotland and Switzerland. But Europe paid a great price for the Protestant victory. Civil and international wars took many lives. Religious cowardice, compromise, tolerance, and individualism grew via disunity.

    The Christian Church at Rome held a supreme position. It was the centre of all culture; the defender of Christianity, and the mainstay of the people. It was also the framework that united the various States of Western Europe. At the height of the Church's power, under Pope Innocent III, who reigned from 1198- 1216, all European Rulers accepted the Pope's Spiritual and temporal Sovereignty.

    In the course of the 1300's and 1400's, the Church began to fall from this position of universal power. * Satan was about his work; setting his angels, spirits, saints, instruments and servants into place, preparing for the battle to take the world out of God's Realm, and bring it into his realm, knowing that the first phase would be to fragment the Church people; the second phase to fragment the Bride of Christ itself...the Church.*HERMENEUTICS.
    Struggles with Rulers;
    Religious schisms;
    Corruptions among the Church people.

    Demands for reform of the Church's people, came from many sources, even from among their friends. The public became indignant with the abuses that had crept into the administration and organization of the Church, and with the decline in the morals of the clergy.

The growth of heretical sects further weakened the Church. The number of Church people, (especially theologians), that began to reject Official Church Doctrines, grew alarmingly.

At the same time, a new force gradually spread through the world. Rulers were trying to build strong national Governments, and gain absolute sovereignty for themselves. They began to look jealously at the power and vast material wealth of the Church. The aims of the Rulers came into conflict with those of the Popes. In the struggles that followed, the Rulers lost much power to their Princes. In Luther's youth, English and German towns led relentless attacks on both the Pope and the Ruler.

Concurrent with the "new force", another factor, the RENAISSANCE supported and prompted the Reformation. The renaissance began in Italy about 1300, and spread throughout Europe during the 1400's and 1500's.

These two new developments swept away customs and institutions that had dominated Europe for almost 1000 years. The "new" ideas and attitudes that grew up then, STILL influence our lives today, and was the conception time of the pagan church of education, that would bring into birth, the "elite" of the pagan church of education, after the necessary gestation period.

This whole scenario was further compounded and complicated by another new scenario....peasants suffered bitter poverty, and grew discontented and rebellious. The growth of commerce, and the rise of the "middle class", led to FURTHER discontentment. The "new", "middle class", made up of businessmen and merchants, many guilty of greed and chicanery, did not fit into the traditional division. Most of the "middle class "members tended to ally themselves with the Princes and Rulers. This "middle class" opposed the Church, because the church represented the mainstay of an order that had blocked their rise to power, in their opinion.

The Reformation began with an Augustinian monk, Martin Luther. Luther's thinking led him to believe that only faith in the sacrifice of Jesus Christ, rather than priests, sacraments, or good works, could ensure salvation. Luther also concluded that only the Bible, not the Pope, was INFALLIBLE, or free from error. The Bible Luther referred to, was the Vulgate version, the Bible of the Roman Catholic Church.

Luther's outrage at the way INDULGENCES, or SPIRITUAL PARDONS, were sold in Saxony by a Cardinal, (an instrument of satan), led him to speak out against the Catholic Church. On Oct. 31, 1517, Luther nailed his "Ninety Five Theses "to the door of his Catholic Church in Wittenberg.

Luther had no intention of starting a movement to destroy the authority of the Catholic Church. He meant only to reform satan's abuses within it. But, when the theses were circulated throughout Germany, they caused a major upheaval, playing into satan's hand.

In 1518, Pope Leo X declared Luther a heretic. But Luther had found many powerful protectors among the rebellious Princes of Germany. The Princes that sided with Luther, did so, to gain control of Church government, and church property in their lands. Many HUMANISTS flocked to Luther's side. In 1519, Johann Eck challenged Luther to a debate at Leipzig. He forced Luther to the position of denying the Pope's supremacy. Luther wrote 3 pamphlets in 1520. Through these writings, he hoped to make his Reformation a national movement. Luther wrote HIS version of the Scriptures in 1522 AD, in rebellion and defiance of REV 22: 18-19.

The Pope issued a * bull, *(a solemn official letter from the Pope) "Arise O Lord", condemning Luther's heresy. Luther responded by burning the Papal bull at Wittenberg. In 1521, the Pope excommunicated Luther. Then Emperor Charles 5th ordered Luther to appear before the Imperial *Diet At Worms. *(DIET: [more at DEITY] A formal deliberative assembly of Princes and Rulers; various national or provincial legislatures). Once there, Luther refused to retract any of his statements. The Emperors ruled against Luther and forbid him to preach. On the way back to Wittenberg, a group of Luther's followers kidnapped him, and hid him in a Wartburg Castle, to protect him from his foes. At the castle, Luther translated the New Testament from Greek into German. It is unlikely that Luther did not translate that New Testament, influenced by his OWN thinking or conclusions.

Luther defied the Pope and the Emperors, and began to organize his conservative Lutheran Church in 1522.   Lutheranism spread rapidly throughout Germany, the Netherlands, and parts of Switzerland. It might have united the entire German-speaking world. But during the bloody peasant's uprisings in 1524 and 1525, Luther sided with the Princes. Millions of disillusioned Germans then returned to the Roman Catholic Church.

In 1530, PHILIP MELANCHTHRON prepared a conciliatory statement of Luther's views called the AUGSBURG CONFESSION. When the Roman Catholics rejected it at an imperial Diet, the Protestants banded together in the SCHMALKALDIC LEAGUE, to fight the Roman Catholics. After fierce fighting, the two sides made peace at Augsburg in 1535.   Their treaty recognized the legality of Lutheranism in principalities where the Rulers wished it. But no other sects were to be tolerated in the Empire. This unsatisfactory settlement led to the 30 Years' War, which began in 1618.

In Switzerland, the 13 cantons, torn by internal strife, were receptive to Protestantism. HULDREICH ZWINGLI, a priest from Zurich, began preaching a reformed religion in 1519. HIS views spread to Bern, Bonel, Glarus, St. Gallen, and other Swiss cities.

The Zwinglian reform also triumphed in Strasbourg, Constance, Memmingen, and Lindau in South Germany. These towns submitted a Zwinglian confession to the Diet at Augsburg in 1530. But differences in doctrine blocked a union between the Lutheran and Zwinglian Churches.

JOHN CALVIN dominated the second part of the Swiss Reformation. His writings in 1536, was the most profound treatise of the Reformation. Aided by WILLIAM FAREL, Calvin established a powerful centre for his teachings in Geneva. Calvin's views on the worthlessness of man; predestination; the Bible; and Church governments; made Calvin famous. Calvinism spread to Germany, France, Scotland, England and the Netherlands. It's huge success split the Protestant world into 2 major camps.

In France, the Kings had already gained considerable control over the national church. As a result, FRANCIS 1st had no interest in supporting the Reformation. But Protestantism found many followers among the people.

The Protestants were severely persecuted after 1540. But the Calvinists, called HUGUENOTS, could not be wiped out. Instead, they gained political power. Many nobles and rich merchants joined them in protest against the Crown. Conflicts between the Huguenots and Roman Catholics caused 8 SAVAGE civil wars from 1562 to 1598. The BOURBONS of Navarre led the Protestants. The GUISES of Lorraine, backed by Spain, led the Roman Catholics. Thousands of Huguenots were massacred in Paris on St. Bartholomew's Day in 1572.

The Coronation of Henry of Navarre, as HENRY 4th of France, marked the end of the civil wars. Henry became a Roman Catholic in 1593. In 1598 Henry issued the EDICT OF NANTES, giving the Huguenots the right to worship. LOUIS 14th revoked the Edict in 1685.

In Scandinavia, King Frederick 1st of Denmark took the lead in introducing Lutheranism. A Danish translation of the Lutheran New Testament appeared in 1524. (twice removed from the Vulgate???) HAND TAUSEN published his "43 Articles", based on Melanchthon's Augsburg Confession in 1530. CHRISTIAN 3rd, an ardent Lutheran, influenced the national assembly at Odense to approve the new church in 1539, (approved by man), and to recognize him as it's head. He also forced Norway to accept Lutheranism.

Swedish Lutheranism began during the war for independence from Denmark. King GUSTAVUS favoured Protestantism. He confiscated Roman Catholic Church Property; ordered Church services held in Swedish; and had the Bible translated into Swedish. (3rd removed from the Vulgate). He also forced Lutheranism into Finland, a Swedish dependency.

In England, the Reformation began with HENRY 8th's quarrel with the Pope over his right to divorce his first wife, CATHERINE OF ARAGON. The Pope refused to allow the divorce, and Henry 8th broke with the Roman Catholic Church. The ACT OF SUPREMACY, of 1534, made the King, rather than the Pope, the head of the Church of England. The Roman Catholic Priests and Nuns in England were given two options: Join the Church of England, or be executed...Martyrdom.

Protestantism made deep inroads under EDWARD 6th. In 1549, THOMAS CRANMER, Archbishop of Canterbury, complied the masterly BOOK OF COMMON PRAYER. Mary 1st, a zealous Roman Catholic, succeeded EDWARD in 1553. She, and her husband PHILIP 2nd of Spain, tried to force Roman Catholicism back into England. ELIZABETH 1st reversed "BLOODY MARY'S" policy. She encouraged a mild Protestantism, "ANGLICANISM", and broke with Spain and the Pope. Her compromise "39 ARTICLES" of 1563 aimed at uniting as many Englishmen as possible. But England did not achieve religious peace until the 1600's. The "ACT OF TOLERATION" of 1689 granted almost complete freedom to Protestant dissenters. The Roman Catholic Minority obtained equality in 1829.

In Scotland, JOHN KNOX led the Reformation. He persuaded the Parliament to adopt a CALVINIST confession in 1560. Political considerations played a decisive role in the Protestant victory. The nobles and merchants, who controlled the country, wanted to break off the ancient alliance with France, in favour of England. When MARY STUART, the Roman Catholic Queen, tried to block them, they drove her from the throne.

In Ireland, the established Roman Catholic Church, via tolerance and compromise, followed all the changes that took place in England, during the reigns of HENRY VIII; EDWARD VI; MARY I; and ELIZABETH I. But the Irish people did not waver in their loyalty to the Roman Catholic faith. Protestants colonized the north, but most of Ireland remained Roman Catholic.

Religiously, the Reformation shattered the unified church of the Middle ages, and with it, the Spiritual unity of the Christian world. Protestantism became the chief religion of the countries of north-western Europe. Protestantism made their Bible the centre of a simpler church service, in the VERNACULAR (language of the people).

Economically, the Reformation greatly strengthened the position of the mercantile and industrial classes, but it dramatically lowered the position of the peasants.

Politically, Lutheranism promoted a belief in absolute Monarchy based on powers attained by Divine Right. But Calvinism encouraged self -determination and the right of revolution against tyranny. Protestantism in general led to the subordination of the church to the State, and strengthened the system of national territories, independent of each other.

To quote from my synthesis "RELIGIO DELENDA EST" (Religion must be destroyed) d/Nov. 2000, page 128, of the "CHRISTIANS MAKE SOME MISTAKES" chapter..

"All of this would only have historical interest, if it had not been for several other MAJOR CHANGES, that occurred around the same time. One was the PROTESTANT REFORMATION.

HAROLD LINDSELL, former Editor of CHRISTIANITY TODAY; himself a Protestant, plainly states. "The Reformation was a major factor in opening the door, WIDE, to "THE ENLIGHTENMENT" of the eighteenth century. Once the protestant Churches claimed THEIR freedom to DISSENT; and FREEDOM TO BELIEVE OTHER THAN WHAT WAS TAUGHT BY ROME, they opened the door to WIDER DISSENT; and to IRRELIGION as well.

The very notion of RELIGIOUS FREEDOM, of necessity, INCLUDED the right to DISSEMINATE, and PROPAGATE religious ideas of EVERY sort, whether they were in accord with the Commandments, Oracles, Precepts, and Spiritual Standards, or not. This DANGEROUS PRECEDENT had its roots in the REFORMATION, and was to bring forth its OWN FRUIT, in the years to come.

Since RELIGIOUS FREEDOM has implications in the fields ECONOMIES, POLITIC*, and SOCIAL LIFE, and RESPONSE and BEHAVIOUR PATTERNS, there was no church that could render COMPELLING DECISIONS, to determine what the CIVILIZATION of the people should be". (LINDSELL, "THE NEW PAGANISM", 1987, PAGES 40-43).

> **politic: "Characterized by Shrewdness in managing, contriving, or dealing; sagacious in promoting policy; shrewdly tactful; malicious cunning if necessary "Albert Einstein. (The chicanery of party politics).*

RENAISSANCE 14TH TO 17TH CENTURY

HERMENEUTICS: (her..:mi-nu'tiks) -GREEK hermeneutikos; from *hermeneus* -an interpreter; (from *Hermes,-* MERCURY- swift messenger of the gods in pagan Roman mythology). THE ART (?) OR SCIENCE (?) OF INTERPRETATION; ESPECIALLY APPLIED TO THE INTERPRETATION OF THE CHRISTIAN SCRIPTURES; HERMENEUTIC; HERMENEUTICAL; (her-mi- nu' ti-kal) ; EXEGESIS (ek-se-je-sis) INTERPRETING; EXPLAINING; EXEGETICAL; UNFOLDING THE SIGNIFICATION- GREEK *exegesis;* from *exegeomai* TO EXPLAIN *-ex,* and *hegeomai,* TO LEAD; TO GUIDE). THE EXPOSITION OR INTERPRETATION OF ANY LITERARY PRODUCTION, BUT MORE PARTICULARLY THE EXPOSITION OR INTERPRETATION OF CHRISTIAN SCRIPTURES; ALSO THE PRINCIPLES OF THE ART(?) OF SACRED INTERPRETATION; EXEGETICS; HERMENEUTICS -EXERGETIC (ek- se-jet'ik) - EXEGETICAL (ek-se-jet' -kal-li,) EXPLANATORY; TENDING TO ILLUSTRATE OR UNFOLD; EXPOSITORY. -EXEGETICALL Y (ek-se-jet' -kal- li), BY WAY OF EXEGESIS OR EXPLANATION. EXEGETICS (ek-se-jst'iks), THE SCIENCE (?) WHICH LAYS DOWN THE PRINCIPLES OF THE ART (?) OF CHRISTIAN SCRIPTURAL INTERPRETATION; EXEGESIS; HERMENEUTICS - EXEGETE (ek'se-jet) ONE SKILLED (?) IN EXEGESIS; AN EXPOUNDER OR INTERPRETER. HERMETIC (her-met'ik) FRENCH *hermetique*- from the ancient pagan *HERMES TRISMEGISTUS* WHO WAS REGARDED AS SKILLED IN OCCULT SCIENCE (?); APPELLATIVE; PERTAINING TO THE DOCTRINES OF OCCULTISM. ALCHEMY *(al-k -me) (French alquemie).* A MEDIEVAL SPECULATIVE PHILOSOPHY, CLAIMING THE POWER OR PROCESS OF TRANSFORMING SOMETHING COMMON INTO SOMETHING PRECIOUS ASSOCIATED WITH ALCMENE -THE MOTHER OF HERCULES BY ZEUS IN THE FORM OF HER HUSBAND AMPHITTYON.

THE ABOVE WAS TAKEN FROM THE NEW WEBSTER

ENCYCLOPEDIC DICTIONARY. THIS SHOULD TELL US WHERE THEY ARE COMING FROM. NO WONDER THE EDUCATIONAL 'ELITE' WERE FOULED UP. THIS IS THE GARBAGE THEY FEASTED ON. EDUCATIONAL CHURCH PR FLAKS (PROPAGANDISTS) THAT WERE CONNED BY THE HERMENEUTIC PR FLAKS (PROPAGANDISTS) OF THE RENAISSANCE.

DECONSTRUCTION: A form of PHILOSOPHICAL and LITERARY ANALYSIS, derived MAINLY from work begun in the 1960's by the French philosopher(?) JACQUES DERRIDA (q.v.), that questions the fundamental conceptual distinctions of WESTERN PHILOSOPHY through a close examination of the LANGUAGE and LOGIC of PHILOSOPHICAL and LITERARY TEXTS.

In discussions of INTELLECTUAL TRENDS of the late 20th century, the term DECONSTRUCTION was sometimes used PEJORATIVELY [(pi-jor-at-ivly) -to suggest NIHILISM (ni-(h)a-liz-am) (1 a) a viewpoint that traditional values and beliefs are unfounded, and THAT existence is SENSELESS and USELESS; [b] a doctrine that denies any objective ground of truth and especially of moral truths [2 a] a doctrine or belief that conditions in the social organization are so bad as to make DESTRUCTION desirable for its own sake, independent of any constructive program or possibility.[2 cap] : the program of a 19th century Russian Party advocating REVOLUTIONARY reform and using TERRORISM and ASSASSINATION]. (NIHILIST / NIHILISTIC; NIHILITY- absence of existence)] To suggest NIHILISM and FRIVOLOUS SKEPTICISM.

In popular usage, it came to mean A CRITICAL DISMANTLING OF TRADITIONAL MODES OF THOUGHT. (SPIRITUAL).

DECONSTRUCTION IN PHILOSOPHY: A MAJOR aim of DECONSTRUCTION is to examine the fundamental conceptual distinctions, or "BINARY OPPOSITIONS", that have been inherent in Western Philosophy since ANCIENT times -i.e., nature and culture; speech and writing; mind and body; presence and absence; and MANY others.

Each of these oppositions is "HIERARCHICAL", in the sense that one of its terms is assumed to be PRIMARY or FUNDAMENTAL, the other SECONDARY or DERIVATIVE.

To "DECONSTRUCT" an opposition is to explore the TENSIONS and CONTRADICTIONS between the HIERARCHICAL ORDERING ASSUMED (and sometimes EXPLICITLY ASSERTED) in the text, and other aspects of the TEXT'S MEANING, especially those that are INDIRECT or IMPLICIT or that rely on FIGURATIVE or PERFORMATIVE uses of LANGUAGE. Through THIS analysis, the OPPOSITION is shown to be a PRODUCT or "CONSTRUCTION", of the text, rather than something given INDEPENDENTLY of it.

For example, according to the SPEECH / WRITING OPPOSITION, SPEECH is a more AUTHENTIC form of language than WRITING, because in SPEECH the IDEAS and INTENTIONS of the speaker are immediately "PRESENT", whereas in writing they are more REMOTE or "ABSENT" from the author, and thus more liable to MISUNDERSTANDING.

As DERRIDA argues, however, spoken words function as LINGUISTIC SIGNS only to the extent that they can be repeated in DIFFERENT CONTEXTS, in the absence of the speaker who ORIGINALLY utters them.

Therefore, speech functions as language only to the extent that it has CHARACTERISTICS TRADITIONALLY ASSIGNED TO WRITING, such as "ABSENCE" "DIFFERENCE" and THE POSSIBILITY OF MISUNDERSTANDING.

One indication of this fact, according to DERRIDA, is that DESCRIPTIONS OF SPEECH IN WESTERN PHILOSOPHY OFTEN

RELY ON EXAMPLES AND METAPHORS RELATED TO WRITING. In effect, speech is described as a FORM of writing, even in cases where writing is EXPLICITLY claimed to be SECONDARY SPEECH.

For example, to show that writing is really PRIOR to speech. Neither does DERRIDA wish to show that there are no differences between SPEECH and WRITING. As with ANY Deconstructive analysis, the point is not to establish a new OPPOSITION, but to RESTRUCTURE, or "DISPLACE", the traditional one, so as to show that NEITHER term is PRIMARY.

DERRIDA contends that the SPEECH / WRITING OPPOSITION is a MANIFESTATION of the "LOGOCENTRISM" [[1] A STRUCTURALIST METHOD OF ANALYSIS, ESPECIALLY OF LITERARY WORKS, THAT FOCUSES UPON WORDS AND LANGUAGE TO THE EXCLUSION OF NON - LINGUISTIC MATTERS, SUCH AS AN AUTHOR'S INDIVIDUALITY OR HISTORICAL CONTEXT.[2] EXCESSIVE ATTENTION PAID TO THE MEANINGS OF WORDS OR DISTINCTIONS IN THEIR USAGE. (logocentric; logocentrist) [(LOGODAEDALY: word speech cunningly wrought; playing with words; passing from one meaning of words to another meaning. (DAIDALOS).

WALTER ONG claims that the RISE of literacy and the DECLINE of "ORALITY" in the middle ages were fundamental to the CULTURAL FLOWERING known as the RENAISSANCE, (14th to 17th Century). -(info only REFORMATION, 16th Century) of WESTERN CULTURE -i.e., the ASSUMPTION that there is a realm of objective truth existing PRIOR TO and INDEPENDENT OF the linguistic signs we use to conceive and describe it.

DECONSTRUCTION IN LITERATURE, THE SOCIAL SCIENCES, AND THE ARTS. In the United States, in the 1970's and 1980's, DECONSTRUCTION played a MAJOR role in the development of LITERARY THEORY, (often referred to simply as "theory"). Briefly stated, "theory" was concerned with questions about the NATURE OF LANGUAGE; the PRODUCTION OF MEANING; and the NUMEROUS DISCOURSES THAT STRUCTURE HUMAN EXPERIENCE AND ITS HISTORIES.

In PSYCHOANALYSIS, DECONSTRUCTIVE readings of texts by SIGMUND FREUD and others, (Jung also, no doubt), questioned the LOGOCENTRIC PRESUPPOSITIONS OF PSYCHOANALYTIC THEORY.
Some strands of FEMINIST THINKING engaged in a DECONSTRUCTION OF THE OPPOSITION BETWEEN "MAN" and "WOMAN" and CRITIQUED essential notions of GENDER and SEXUAL IDENTITY.

THIS work, in turn, influenced "QUEER THEORY", as the ACADEMIC avant- garde (an intelligentsia that develops new or experimental concepts) linked to movements of GAY LIBERATION styled itself. In ANTHROPOLOGY, DECONSTRUCTION contributed to an INCREASED AWARENESS of the role that anthropological field- workers play in SHAPING, rather than merely describing, THE SITUATIONS THEY REPORT ON.

DECONSTRUCTIVE THINKING also spread to the ARTS and ARCHITECTURE. Combining DECONSTRUCTION'S interests in TENSION and OPPOSITIONS, with the DESIGN VOCABULARY of RUSSIAN CONSTRUCTIVISM, DECONSTRUCTIVIST architects such as FRANK GERRY challenged the FUNCTIONALISTS AESTHETIC of' 'modern' architecture through designs using radical geometries, irregular forms, and complex, dynamic constructions.

CRITICISM OF DECONSTRUCTION: DECONSTRUCTION joined with OTHER currents of FRENCH PHILOSOPHY to inspire a suspicion of established INTELLECTUAL CATEGORIES and a SKEPTICISM about the possibilities of OBJECTIVITY.
Consequently, its diffusion was met with a sizeable

body of OPPOSITION. Some philosophers dismissed it as OBSCURANTISTS wordplay, whose MAJOR claims, when INTELLIGIBLE, were either TRIVIAL or FALSE.

Other critics accused it of being AHISTORICAL and APOLITICAL. Still others regarded it as a NIHILISTIC endorsement of RADICAL EPISTEMIC RELATIVISM.

DESPITE such attacks, DECONSTRUCTION CONTINUES TO HAVE AN ENORMOUS IMPACT ON A VARIETY OF INTELLECTUAL ENTERPRISES.

DECONSTRUCTIONISTS: CONSTRUCTIONISTS OF HERMENEUTICS. ONE WHO CONSTRUES A DOCUMENT IN A SPECIFIC WAY; (A STRICT DECONSTRUCTIONIST). DECLARED SUCH BY JUDICIAL CONSTRUCTION OR INTERPRETATION (-FRAUD); PROMOTING IMPROVEMENT (?) OR DEVELOPMENT (?) (-CRITICISM). CONSTRUE -TO ANALYZE THE ARRANGEMENT AND CONNECTION OF WORDS; TO UNDERSTAND OR EXPLAIN THE SENSE OR INTENTION OF THE USUAL (THEIR "USUAL"), IN A PARTICULAR WAY OR WITH RESPECT TO A GIVEN SET OF (THEIR) CIRCUMSTANCES. AN ACT OF CONSTRUING BY PIECEMEAL TRANSLATION; THE TRANSLATED (THEIR) VERSION; RESULTING FROM SUCH AN ACT. CONSTRUCTIONAL -DEDUCED FROM (THEIR) CONSTRUCTION OR INTERPRETATION.(PR FLACKS - PROPAGANDISTS).

ADDENDA (MACROPAEDIA) For both Jews and Christians, throughout their histories, the primary purpose of HERMENEUTICS, [(utilized by LUCIFER, (the practiced deceiver, and counterfeiter and copycat (Lucifer CANNOT be ORIGINAL), to produce his OWN methodology to weaken / destroy the SPIRITUALITY OF GOD'S REALM and GOD'S PEOPLE. And God's people HELPED Lucifer to do it, and to accomplish it)), and of the other exegetical methods (and their MANY ancillaries) employed in INTERPRETATION, has been to 'discover' the TRUTHS and VALUES of the Bible... [(to produce contention; dissention; animosity and quarrels, among themselves, within Christ's Church on earth, for Lucifer)].

In the history of Biblical interpretation, 4 major types of HERMENEUTICS have emerged: LITERAL; MORAL; ALLEGORICAL and ANAGOGICAL.

LITERAL INTERPRETATION asserts that a Biblical text is to be interpreted according to the "PLAIN MEANING" conveyed by its grammatical construction. The LITERAL meaning is held to correspond to the intention of the AUTHORS. [The "authors" did NOT write; The Holy Ghost wrote, THROUGH them]. JEROME, an influential 4th century Biblical Scholar, championed the LITERAL interpretation. JEROME was in opposition to what he regarded as the EXCESSES OF ALLEGORICAL INTERPRETATION. The PRIMACY of the LITERAL was later advocated by such figures as THOMAS AQUINAS (died 53 AD.), NICHOLAS OF LYRA (died 1349), JOHN COLET (died 1519), MARTIN LUTHER (died 1546), and JOHN CALVIN (died 1566).

The Christians made some mistakes too i.e. the RENAISSANCE (14th to 17th centuries) and the REFORMATION (16th century), as orchestrated by Lucifer. See RELIGIO DELENDA EST d/27 NOV 2000, page 127.   (Lucifer ALWAYS has HIS "elite" to work through as well) i.e. the "Religious" Philosophers ("elite") of the Christian Church, spending time and energy, concerning themselves with what was none of their darn business in the first place; they might have better spent their time keeping their PRAYER TIME, BIBLE READING, and SPIRITUAL MEDITATION in balance, on a regular DAILY basis. These are those who TEACH THEMSELVES, rather than ALLOWING the PARACLETE to teach them. They are usually SELF MADE men who worship their creator...THEMSELVES.

MORAL INTERPRETATION seeks to establish EXEGETICAL

principles by which ethical lessons may be drawn from the various parts of the Bible. (**B**ASIC **I**NSTRUCTIONS **B**EFORE **L**EAVING **E**ARTH). ALLEGORIZATION was often employed in this endeavour. The LETTER OF BARNABAS (100 AD.), for example, interprets the DIETARY Laws prescribed in the Book of LEVITICUS as forbidding not the flesh of certain animals, but rather the VICES IMAGINATIVELY associated with those animals.

ALLEGORICAL INTERPRETATION; interprets the Biblical narratives as having a second level of reference BEYOND those PERSONS; THINGS; and EVENTS explicitly mentioned in the text. A particular form of ALLEGORICAL interpretation is the TYPOLOGICAL, according to which the KEY FIGURES; MAIN EVENTS; and PRINCIPLE INSTITUTIONS of the Old Testaments are seen as "TYPES" or FORESHADOWING'S of PERSONS; EVENTS: and OBJECTS in the New Testaments. According to this THEORY, interpretations such as that of NOAH'S ARK, as a "TYPE" of the Christian Church, was intended by God from the beginning.

PHILO, a Jewish Philosopher, and contemporary of Jesus, employed PLATONIC and STOIC categories to interpret the Jewish Scriptures (Cannon). HIS general practices were adopted by the Christian Philosopher CLEMENT OF ALEXANDRIA, who sought the ALLEGORICAL sense of Biblical Texts. CLEMENT "discovered" deep NARRATIVES and PRECEPTS of the Bible. (self-taught ?). ORIGEN (Bishop), systemized those HERMENEUTICAL principles. ORIGEN distinguished the LITERAL, MORAL, and SPIRITUAL senses, but acknowledged the SPIRITUAL (i.e. ALLEGORICAL) to be the highest.

In the Middle Ages, ORIGEN'S threefold sense of Scripture was EXPANDED into a FOURFOLD sense, by a SUBDIVISION of the SPIRITUAL SENSE into the ALLEGORICAL and the ANAGOGICAL.

The 4th major type (all of the "TYPES" have MANY ANCILLARIES) of Biblical HERMENEUTICS is the :

ANAGOGICAL or MYSTICAL INTERPRETATION. This mode of interpretation seeks to explain Biblical events as they relate TO or PREFIGURE THE LIFE TO COME. Such An approach to the Bible is exemplified by the Jewish KABBALA, which sought to disclose the MYSTICAL significance of the NUMERICAL VALUES OF HEBREW LETTERS AND WORDS. A chief example of this MYSTICAL interpretation in JUDAISM, is the MEDIEVAL ZOHAR. In Christianity, many of the interpretations associated with MARICOLOGY falls into this ANAGOGICAL category.

In the MODERN, as in the OTHER periods, shifts in HERMENEUTICAL emphasis, reflected broader ACADEMIC and PHILOSOPHICAL trends; HISTORICAL -CRITICAL; EXISTENTIAL; and STRUCTURAL interpretation have figured PROMINENTLY during the 20th century.

On the NON-ACADEMIC level, the interpretation of PROPHETICAL and APOCALYPTIC biblical material in terms of PRESENT - DAY events remains a VIGOROUS pursuit in some circles. (see also EXEGESIS).

N.B. The "New Age" educational "elite" promoted EMPIRICAL THINKING, which in turn, knocked Educational Philosophy totally out of orbit, (into "left field"), PROMPTING and ALLOWING the "NEW AGE" of HERMENEUTICS, sown by LUCIFER, that, from THAT time onward, POLLUTED man's THINKING and IMAGININGS, and laid the FOUNDATION for DECONSTRUCTIONISM, that became LUCIFER'S ultimate weapon, to drag MANY SOULS OUT OF GOD'S REALM, VIA DECEIT AND DECEPTION, INTO his REALM, VIA THE STUPIDITY OF 'MODERN' MAN'S THINKING AND IMAGININGS. And THAT'S what happened to Educational Philosophy, and the "educational elite" are not even aware of that FACT!

Instead of allowing the PARACLETE to teach man about the "things" of God, MAN decided to TEACH HIMSELF, thereby having a FOOL for a teacher, making a fool of himself; a farce of his Christian experience; and a friend of Lucifer; whereby the BRIDE OF CHRIST, (CHRIST'S CHURCH) became a WAYWARD BRIDE, with POLLUTED Scriptures, Sanctuaries, Tabernacles, and Pulpits, INSULTING our Lord and Saviour, Jesus Christ, thereby arousing THE FATHER'S ANGER, prompting the END OF TIME. But we can take hope; Lucifer will NOT prevail against the Church of Christ, and the faithful few WILL enjoy ETERNITY WITH CHRIST, AS HE PROMISED.

PSALM 50 : 16 -23. "WHY do you recite My statutes and profess My covenant with your mouth, though you hate discipline and cast My Words behind you?

: 18 When you see a thief, you keep peace with him, and with adulterers you throw in your lot. :19 To your mouth you give free rein for evil, you harness your tongue to deceit. :20 You sit speaking against your brother *** you spread rumours. :21 When you do these things, shall I be deaf to it? Or think you that I am like yourself? I will correct you by drawing them up before your eyes. :22 Consider this, you who forget God, lest I rend you and there be no one to rescue you. :23 He that offers praise as a sacrifice glorifies Me; and to him that goes the right way I will show the salvation of God ". (see also verse :7)

(DISCIPLES ELIPHAZ, BILDAD, AND ZOPHAR) DEADLY ENEMIES OF THE DISCIPLES OF ELIHI).

2 of 6 THE CHURCH OF PSYCHOLOGY/ PSYCHIATRY/PR FLAKS:

Because the realm of present day politics has been further polluted by the Church of Psychology/Psychiatry/ Pr Flaks, lets take a look at THAT church: I refer to psychology/psychiatry as a "church" for the same reasons utilized for the educational Church.

As soon as Psychology/ Psychiatry is mentioned in connection with paganism, the battle flag goes up, and the battle is on. (For your information, Psychiatry is the illegitimate child of Psychology).

Psychology, promoted by **EDWARD BERNAYS**, (A nephew of Sigmund Freud), who was one of the most amazing and influential propagandist of the 20th century, popularized, via propaganda, Freudianism, and the Medical Model Theory. (For your information, Propagandists are now known as **PR FLAKS)**.

Bernays developed a 'scientific method of managing behaviour, to which he gave the name N. B. "PUBLIC RELATIONS". Bernays, believing that democracy needed wise and hidden manipulators, was PROUD to be a propagandist, and wrote in his book "Propaganda": quote: "if we understand the mechanisms and motives of the group mind, it is now possible to CONTROL and REGIMENT the masses, according to OUR will, without them knowing it". Bernays called this "ENGINEERING OF CONSENT", and proposed that, "those who manipulate this unseen mechanism of society, constitute an invisible government which is the TRUE ruling power of a country".

In almost every act of our daily lives, whether in the realm of politics or business; in our social conduct or our ethical thinking, we ARE dominated by the relatively small number of persons (Pr Flaks)... who pull the strings which control the public mind, WHEN THE PUBLIC MIND IS NOT GOVERNED BY THE SPIRITUAL STANDARDS OF GOD, ACCORDING TO GOD'S PRECEPTS, ORACLES AND COMMANDMENTS, WHICH IS THE ONLY DEFENCE A HUMAN BEING HAS AGAINST THE PROPAGANDA OF LUCIFER'S REALM. When ANYONE does NOT have that standard to measure against, they are easily duped, and to brainwash them is a very simple matter.

It appears not to have dawned on Bernays until the 1930's, that his 'science' of propaganda could also be used to subvert democracy and promote fascism. That was when journalist Karl Von Weigand told Bernays that Nazi propagandist, Joseph Goebbels had read all Bernays's books, and that Goebbels possessed an even better library of propaganda than Bernays did.

"The most successful, longest running and deadliest propaganda campaign in history...Re tailor made cigarettes, was one of Bernays's projects also". Quote from a book by John Stauber/ Derrick Jeson, "War on Truth" March 1999.
Psychology/ psychiatry enjoys the status of a 'science' thanks to Pr Flak Bernays, and is well-integrated into our culture.
Consider for a moment all of the departments of a school district that are BASED on one tentacle of Psychology/Psychiatry or another – behavioural training for teachers; IQ testing; Personality tests; counselling; and DOZENS more. And when we realize that SOCIOLOGY is simply Psychology applied to GROUPS OF PEOPLE, you can DOUBLE that number.

Now think of the people in the Police department, starting with the officers themselves, who are taught and expected to USE Psychological/ Psychiatric training.

Think of the Justice system; Employment and Unemployment Offices; Welfare Programs; Children's Services' Public Relations Depts; - and those are only Government applications of Psychological/ Psychiatric tentacles.

Psychology is fed to us daily via the Media, TV and Radio. There are even 'Counsellors' with phone – in advice shows.

Talk shows would be a WASTELAND without Psychologists/ Psychiatrists to air their latest pet theories.

First, however, we must look at the SOURCE of this so-called 'science'. The 2 great founders of Psychology/ Psychiatry were FREUD and JUNG – a drug addict and an occultist, respectively. Freud's addiction to cocaine is WELL known; less known is that Jung wrote many of his theories under the influence of a 'SPIRIT GUIDE', which he never recognized as a DEMON of lucifer's realm, but Jung labelled it as a "COLLECTIVE ARCHETYPE". (Jung was also much influenced by Edward Bernays).

The leaders of the psych world that followed were hardly any better. Maslow, Rogers, Fromm, ALL of them "made the trip east", and ended up in occultism. These three popularized, with the help of Pr Flaks (Propagandists), the now- dominant theory in both "new Age" and Psychological/Psychiatric thinking, that a high self-esteem is the solution to ALL Psychological Problems. They claim that people suffer from low self-esteem, and are driven to 'act out' bad behaviour to fulfill their unmet "needs".

Researcher David Meyers tested (and disproved) the theory that self-esteem tends to be low, and came to the following conclusions:

1. We are more likely to accept credit than to admit failure;
2. Almost all people see themselves as better than average;
3. Not only do we take credit for what we may not be entitled to (#1), We also deny responsibility for what we HAVE done wrong;
4. We consistently overestimate our beliefs and judgements;
5. We more readily perceive, remember, and communicate pleasant information than unpleasant information;
6. We overestimate how desirable we would act in certain situations; i.e. giving blood; helping the homeless; etc.

Quoted from the book "UNMASKING THE NEW AGE", by Douglas R. Groothuis, 1986. (The peace of a clear conscience; or the guilt of webs of deceit ???)

For the sake of comparison, see the following example. It shows the difference between Psychology and the "new Age" pagan teachings is often only one letter of the alphabet:

NEW AGE : THOU ART GOD.	PSYCHOLOGY: THOU ART GOOD.
YOU MUST REALIZE	YOU MUST REALIZE
THAT YOU ARE GOD.	THAT YOU ARE GOOD.
WHEN YOU KNOW YOU ARE GOD,	WHEN YOU KNOW YOU ARE GOOD,
THEN YOU WILL BE GOD.	THEN YOU WILL BE GOOD
IN THE PROPER ENVIRONMENT,	IN THE PROPER ENVIRONMENT,
YOUR INNER SELF, WILL NATURALLY LEAD YOU TO BE GOD.	YOUR INNER SELF, WILL NATURALLY LEAD YOU TO BE GOOD

Psychologists' hostility toward the doctrine of 'Fallen Man' and 'Sin' have resulted in pronouncements that such "MIS-BELIEFS" are the cause of Psychological problems; "A SICKNESS IN ITSELF". In Russia, pesky Christians get slammed into mental hospitals.

Here in the west, Psychologists/ Psychiatrists try to EDUCATE the client away from the very presupposition of right and wrong via non-directive, non-judgemental "treatments" a la Carl Rogers and others. I myself have researched and disproved the myths of the ALLOGENIC Modality via "lusdicere", 1975 and "Eklegete", 1982.

Postulates of Psychology/Psychiatry are DISTINCTLY anti-Christian. B.F. Skinner, for instance, says that man is so rigidly moulded by his environment, that he has no free will at all. "Man deserves neither praise nor punishment for any of his works." B. F. SKINNER, 1971.

Others, like the "new Thought" people, say that "everything

that happens to you is a matter of your CHOICE –Poverty, Illness, Death". This is like the Hindu Doctrine.

Thanks to Psychology/Psychiatry, the doctrines "fallen Man" have been replaced by the quest for "self-esteem"; "Creation" has been replaced by "GUIDED EVOLUTION"; "SALVATION" has been replaced by "SEARCH FOR PERSONAL FULFILLMENT". "SOLID GODLY COUNSEL" has been replaced by "FLIMSY" PSYCHOLOGY/PSYCHIATRY TREATMENTS.

TRUE SCIENCE looks at things you can weigh and measure, and depends on experiments that can be repeated. But mental phenomena are neither measurable nor repeatable; and no two cases are ever identical.

One of the best proofs that Psychology/Psychiatry is outside of the realm of science, and into the realm of religion, (and a pagan religion at that), is the FACT that people CONTINUE to believe in it, although study after study has shown "IT DOESN'T WORK". People who get advice and support from their friends CONSISTENTLY do better than people who spend $80.00 to $100.00 an hour, or even more, for the privilege of talking to a 'degreed' counsellor.

Many books, both secular and Christian, have CATEGORICALLY demonstrated the MONUMENTAL and CONTINUOUS FAILURE of Psychology/Psychiatry. Three of these are:
PSYCHO HERESY, 1987;
THE MYTH OF NEUROSIS, 1986;
PSYCHOLOGICAL SEDUCTION, 1983.
FAILURE, on the level that, if Psychology/Psychiatry were a drug seeking food or drug administration approval from the Government, it would be PERMANENTLY BANNED. Yet Psychology/Psychiatry STILL maintains the cloak of a 'science'. See what a good Pr Flak can accomplish via PROPAGANDA, with people that do not have the Spiritual Standards of God to mea-

sure against? (or not ALLOWED to measure against?) (Precepts; Oracles; and Commandments).

One former Psychologist and Psychology Professor told Paul De Parrie that:
"while there are over a hundred different 'modalities' for Psychological treatment, there were REALLY only two basic ideas:
1. Live with your Guilt, and /or
2. Blame it on somebody else.
3. A look through the multitude of books on the subject, will confirm this simple truth. The fundamental failure here is that both approaches DENY the AVAILABILITY of FORGIVENESS; MERCY; GRACE; STRENGTH; and HELP OF GOD THROUGH CHRIST. There is no hope; a fatal failure indeed. Psychology/Psychiatry has even displaced scripture as an authority in some churches. I have seen Christian leaders literally roll their eyes in DISGUST when a believer has, using Scripture, challenged faulty Psychological/Psychiatric concepts being touted by pagan Psychologists/ Psychiatrists. And it is through Psychology that hypnosis, guided imagery; self-esteem (pride) teaching; pagan visualization techniques; and even past-life regression; have entered the church. (WILFUL SIN OR IGNORANCE OF THE PEOPLE ???).

Christians today know very little about PAGANISM, or know only the SANITIZED VERSION OF PAGANISM recently adopted by the media, and public educators, duped by Pr Flaks. It is easy to persuade those who know NOTHING about the ancient pagan empires that the "NEW AGE" is "NEW", or that certain ancient pagan techniques are the LATEST "SCIENTIFIC" ADVANCES.

Those of lucifer's realm, DUPED our nation with the folly of "SELF - PRESERVATION", and we turned away from God's Realm which DEMANDS of us repentance; faith; self-discipline; believing, submission, obedience; faith and trust, in spite of the malicious cunning heaped on us by instruments and servants of LUCIFER'S REALM. How amazing is the general APATHY of our nation. It seems we have forgotten how to function as a nation. We seem to prefer the madness of LUCIFER'S REALM, rather than acting like rational beings of GOD'S REALM.

A Psychologist who has practiced for more than two decades in an impressive variety of settings, denounces her profession as a SHAM. She says Psychology is neither a science nor a profession, but an industry that turns healthy people into victims, to give itself a constant source of income.

She accuses Psychologists of warping people's understanding of themselves so as to funnel endless services, of dubious quality, into their lives.

She says Psychologists do this warping not only through RECOVERED MEMORY THERAPY, (The black eye of Psychology), but also by translating all of life into a series of ABUSES; ADDICTIONS; AND TRAUMAS. People come up with memories they never had before. Her name is Dr. Tana Dineen, her book, "MANUFACTURING VICTIMS" was published in 1996.

For my part, as a result of seeing my clients deteriorating before my eyes, session after session, I became alarmed; I cared about my clients, and wanted very much to help them. The question "Why, in spite of all that is being done, the clients were not getting any better ?", MUST be addressed.

It was decided I would research that question, to be addressed via a thesis. It was decided I would go onto skid road, to see what I could see.

Moving into the Brazil Hotel on the Vancouver skid road, the research project began. My project was not funded by anyone; all expenses I paid. Six months were allocated to the project.

The information gleaned from the Vancouver skid road had to be double checked and verified. Dr. Greenberg and Dr. Mendes were utilized to verify my experiments, and the results of those experiments, and the necessary research. I proceeded onto the Calgary skid road to accomplish these ends.

To make a long story short: Over a four-year period, I worked every skid road between Vancouver and Halifax…all of the large cities coast to coast. It was determined that Psychology simply doesn't work, and IS a pseudo science.

Which raised ANOTHER question: "If Psychology is not effective, what WOULD be ?" The end result was that I conducted two separate Research Projects, producing two Thesis, one published in 1975, the other in 1982. Both projects were worked concurrently; 1. "WHAT IS WRONG ?" 2. "HOW DO WE FIX IT ?".

How NAÏVE I was; I HONESTLY believed everyone was just as concerned as I was, and would WELCOME the NECESSARY course of action to clean the whole mess up, for CANADA and the CANADIAN PEOPLE. It broke my heart to see that I was wrong in that assumption.

The Case Histories and Experiments, and Research Projects Methodology, and Results, were GIVEN to the Alcohol and Drug Commission, in a spirit of SHARING and COOPERATION, for the purpose of cleaning up the MESS **WE** in the Field and Discipline of COUNSELLING and REHABILITATION **CREATED**, FOR THE CANADIAN PEOPLE.

RECEIPT OF THAT MATERIAL WAS ACKNOWLEDGED, VIA A LETTER FROM THE COMMISSION, SIGNED

BY Mr. J. H. SYMON, HIS FILE REFERENCE T2 – 1 PLANNING, d/ 13 JULY 1982.

54 copies of the Thesis "EKLEGETE" were distributed via double Registered mail, (CONFIRMING that they were DELIVERED and SIGNED FOR), to the Governments of EVERY Province and Territory in Canada, and to the FEDERAL GOVERNMENT of Canada, to the appropriate Ministry's, and to all main-line Church Denominations, and to the appropriate people that had a record of dealing in the subject.

Being the NAÏVE individual that I was, I FIRMLY believed that the recipients were just as concerned for the Canadian People as I was, and would be just as shocked, as I was, to learn that we simply did not have an INKLE (it takes forty inkle's to make a 'CLUE'), of what was ACTUALLY HAPPENING within the Counselling and Rehabilitation Field. (I was correct in THAT thinking at least).

ALL of the recipients were in a position to DO something about the Problems, and if they did NOT actually know what was happening at the time, they WOULD know NOW, and were in a position to DO something about it, with Canada once again re-gaining the LEAD in this field.

That material, along with the material that was given to the alcohol drug commission of B.C., was shared with the view of rallying those recipients to work as a collective group, to address the problems, AND RESOLVE THE PROBLEMS, for the good of Canada and the Canadian People. In retrospect, I can CATEGORICALLY state, that those recipients did not give a darn for Canada OR the Canadian people; OBVIOUSLY.

ALL TO NO AVAIL: there was no dialogue; no questions; no challenges; no rebuttal; verbally or in writing. The resulting attack upon myself by the Psychological/Psychiatric interests and the Alcohol and Drug Commission and the educational "ELITE", were vicious, scathing, reviling, persecutory, and insulting, indefatigable; not to myself, (I was not aware of this until about three years later), but AMONG THEMSELVES. What actually DID occur, is that they utilized an oracle of Lucifer's realm that says; "WHERE REALISTIC REBUTTAL IS NOT POSSIBLE, MUD SLINGING IS A GOOD SUBSTITUTE" ... "OPPRESS VIA DISCREDITING".

TO THIS DAY, the Freudian/Jung/Rogerian Skinner theories, that have been disproved, continue to usurp the role of the Priest/Minister, and are literally destroying Canadian society, in co-operation with the other pagan churches, (OF LUCIFER'S REALM), taking liberal, humanistic, tolerating, compromising, cowards, and unthinking theologians, and lay people down with them. And all this made possible via PAID pr flaks. However, I was elected to the rank of "FELLOW" as a result of those research projects and thesis.

And to this day, those in the counselling and rehabilitation field, via their paid pr flaks, STILL refuse to address the question; "WHAT STANDARDS DO WE USE?" When we attempt to ascertain whether or not something is right or wrong, good or bad within a client's response and (or) behaviour patterns; What STANDARD can we use to measure against? (That is because they feel they have already addressed the question, and the answer was; "Why OUR OWN PERSONAL STANDARDS, of course").

And the answer to THAT question will CLEARLY pinpoint the problems that are simply further compounding and complicating the problems within the counselling and rehabilitation field, to this day. And their paid pr flaks will STILL cover their butts, by duping the public at large, who they KNOW, will ALLOW the pr flaks to do just that, via their lack of God's Spiritual standards to measure against.

Whose or what standards can we use to measure against, to determine whether or not something is good or bad; right or wrong??? We certainly cannot use the Therapists standards, OR the client's standards.

(TEA / COFFEE BREAK TIME)

In order to address this question, it is necessary to juxtapose the presuppositional underlying philosophies of both alternatives, in attempt to identify a true synthesis. (the sequences were reversed about 50 years ago).

ALLOGENIC (formerly Anti-thesis) NOW THESIS	AUTOGENIC (formerly thesis) NOW ANTI-THESIS
Each person is their own standard. The thinking and reasoning process is through the head, and totally Empirical, without any though being given to the structuring of the subconscious mind. The subconscious mind simply develops 'naturally'. However, this scenario is seriously compounded and complicated by the PARENTAL INCOMPETENCE SYNDROME. (usually accompanied by immaturity; impaired rationale; arrogance; rebellion; ego and/or power trips, and may be further compounded and complicated via developing megalomania). (this syndrome is literally destroying our Society). This is further compounded and complicated by an Educational philosophy gone awry, further compounded and complicated by the empirical thinking process.	The standards utilized are outside of the person. (precepts, Oracles and Commandments). We utilize the Dialectic thinking process, prompted by a realistic Educational Philosophy, true to God's Natural Law. The thinking and reasoning process, is through the HEART, not the head when re-structuring the subconscious mind. Harmful syndromes are easily recognized and identified, allowing intervention to be accomplished where necessary.

3 of 6 THE CHURCH OF LABOUR/PR FLAKS (SEE ALSO THE CHURCH OF POLITICS/PR FLACKS).

Where does the Labour Movement fit in the scheme of things???

Historically, labour had operated within the confines of democracy, truth, and justice, and did a superb job of it. However, in June 1945, democracy was MURDERED in Canada, (and has not been resurrected to this day), by paid pr flaks, imported from the U.S.A. paid out of a fund that was raised between the Liberals, Conservatives, Communist Party, and the industrialists of the day. The occasion was the destruction of the C.C. F. Party. (more on this when we deal with the Church of Pr Flaks.).

During my research project in 1975, I worked on labour arbitration cases for National and International Unions, in the lower mainland of B.C. Working on these cases, it became crystal clear, that the vast majority of those cases came about, by one union member, trying to make himself look like a hero, by making another union member look like a fool. I brought this matter to the attention of Art Kube, who was at that time, President of the B.C. Federation of Labour / Western Educational Representative for The Canadian Congress of Labour.

It was mentioned to Art, "the Labour Movement is fast crumbling, because FRATERNALISM is leaving the Labour Movement". Art disagreed totally. Further, I mentioned to Art that the "strong Labour Movement BC was famous for is fast becoming a paper tiger". Again Art disagreed.
In my opinion, that scenario was a direct result of the destruction of the C.C.F. party, because in that process, the pillars that labour built on, were left cracked and leaning, as a result of the attacks by pr flaks, on labour, to discredit the C.C.F. Party, i.e. Gangsters running Labour", "The Labour Goons", "Communism

Runs Labour", "Socialists are communists in Disguise", etc. The pr flaks told the public. In the process of brain-washing the people of Canada, those hired pr flaks also brain-washed union members, via virtue of their being part of the Canadian population. When the Labour Movement abandoned the C.C.F. Party, they unwittingly abandoned the Labour Movement as it existed at that time.

And from that day to this, the Labour Movement regressed via the "high prices are the fault of Labour" propaganda, by brain-washed people, that were simply passing on gossip they heard, but knew nothing about, to the point where today, the greatest enemies the Labour unions face, is their OWN members. These 'Grumblings' first came from the fathers and grandfathers of 1945, as a result of THEM being brain-washed, or rather ALLOWED themselves to be brain-washed, by paid pr flaks. And those 'Grumblings' have been passed down from generation to generation, (with each generation adding a little more) ever since. Those pr flaks were paid from a fund set up by the Liberals, conservatives, communist Party, and the industrialists, set up to crush the C.C.F. Party and Labour.

The end result was, (Via FRATERNALISM leaving the Labour Movement), that today, the Labour Movement has crumbled, and is so badly fragmented, it is no longer a force to be reckoned with, and management KNOWS that.

The old vanguard (those who KNOW what the Labour Movement should be; or could be) are either dead or out of the mainstream, and what labour was in the 1930's and '40's, is long forgotten.
By 1975, The "Employee Assistance Program" concept, as provided by management, was up and running. The "Broadbrush" technique, supported by the Hazeldon Foundation, was generally utilized. It was a good technique, and was designed to identify

any employee that was a "troubled" employee, and it was done in an impartial, impersonal and fair manner.

During my 1975 research project, working, as mentioned, with labour unions, it was noticed that some unscrupulous managements, were using their "employee" program as a witch hunt tool, and their modus Operendi became "terminate rather than rehabilitate" to save money. In fact, with one employer, their industrial nurse resigned over this issue.

Another scenario that I noticed, was that after 3-4 years, the company "employee" program existed on paper only, and was not realistically utilized any longer.

My research indicated that with the former scenario, those managements were simply out to bust the unions.

With the later scenario, the problem was that the 'employee' program was functioning too well... it identified ALL troubled employees, in all levels of management, and Labour, from the employee in the plant, to the upper management people, and it became a problem for THEM. Their response was to scuttle the program, in order to keep their own 'skeletons' in the closet.

The end result was that the employees resented being identified, because the middle and upper management people, were worse off than any employee referred to treatment. That scenario rendered the program a sham, and the program became nothing more that a joke to the workers in the plant. Thus the program was effectively scuttled, and existed only on paper.

Because of the way management was treating their union members, and because the program was in fact truly needed, I suggested to Art Kube, that the unions should take over the 'employee' program for troubled employees, and provide care for these members, and their families, themselves.

The Amalgamated Transit Union, Vancouver, was the first union to provide their members with a 'member Assistance Program' which I operated.

Ann Harley, Program co-ordinator, continuing Studies, Simon Fraser University, Burnaby, B.C., knowing that I was very active, and interested in this field, asked myself, to address a workshop that was called by Art Kube, to address the question of 'Member Assistance Programs" for unions and their members.

The following is the presentation I made to the workshop, (to which every union in B.C. sent a delegation), 1 Oct. 1977.

Quote: "Brothers and Sisters, I bring you greetings and best wishes from our A.T.U. President, Brother Len Doyle.

It is a pleasure for me to be here, and take part in a workshop as important as this one. My topic will be "alternate solutions & the A.T.U. MODEL". The alternatives, as I see them are: To HAVE a member assistance program within your union; or NOT TO HAVE a member assistance program within your union.

Your decision can only be as sound as the facts on which you base that decision.

"EMPLOYEE ASSISTANCE PROGRAM" is the term I will use when discussing assistance programs originated by management, for their employees; and I will use the term "MEMBER ASSISTANCE PROGRAM", when discussing assistance programs originated by unions for their members.

Management became involved in employee assistance programs, originally for one reason...dollars and cents...Employees with problems COST management money, due to absenteeism, mistakes in their work, accidents, etc.

In the lower echelons of management there were, and still are, those who REALLY care...but in the upper echelons of management, it's mainly a matter of money.

Problems for 'employee' programs began to develop with MIDDLE management. (some of THEM were being 'flagged' as troubled employees, and they sure didn't like that). There is no need to go into the frustrations and havoc these people cause... I'm sure we all are aware of that. This same scenario also applies to many upper echelon management people.

It is however, these middle and upper echelons of management that sour 'employee' programs, and eventually render the program quite ineffective, within 3-5 years, the program lives on paper alone, then falls by the wayside. 'Employee' Assistance Programs have not been, up to now, and probably will NEVER be, a permanent solution to the problem of the "Troubled Brother or Sister".

On the other hand, labour unions have had their very beginnings in FRATERNAL CONCERN...The concern for Brothers and Sisters and their families, within the union, is a GENUINE concern. "LABOUR" is MY concern for you and your family, and YOUR concern for me and my family.

In August of this year, I had the pleasure of being part of the Canadian Delegation to the World Federation for Mental Health congress... We would do well, I think to adopt the motto of that congress... "TODAY'S PRIORITIES...KNOWING AND DOING".

May I share some facts with you... The percentage of

"Troubled" Employee within the labour force is estimated to be 13%. (about 15 years ago it was 1%).

The percentage of "troubled" employees within the Labour force for 1978 is projected as being 16%;
1980 is projected as being 20%;
1982 is projected as being 25%;
1984 is projected as being 30%.

These projected percentages may be a little high in my opinion... Nevertheless, the TREND is a certainty. The percentage is going to get higher each year.

In order to cope with these projected percentage increases, and in order to avoid many "Egg on the face" situations...We better get started...and establish union member assistance programs NOW.

But before you decide whether or not to establish a union member assistance program, PLEASE...ask yourself these 5 questions:
1. Are you willing to end the cruel hoax of the "cover-up"?
2. Are you willing to have "troubled" Brothers and Sisters confronted about their problems by competent counsellors, before serious job difficulties or terminations arise?
3. Are you willing to assist in identifying and motivating "troubled" brothers and Sisters to seek the necessary help from the Union Member assistance Program?
4. Are you willing to give Fraternal "tough love" to your Union Members?
5. Are you willing to establish a criteria for referral to your Union Member assistance Program?

And may I add here that you are not "ratting" on anyone you refer to your program... Would you hesitate to call the Fire Dept. about a fire in your house, because you felt you were "ratting" on the fire?

Each of the union executive board members must answer these questions for THEMSELVES...If each cannot answer "yes"... Then please do not start a Member Assistance Program within your union, because if you do, you will make fools of yourselves; a farce of support for the Union Member Assistance Program; and a friend of those in management that love to see bickering or division within a union.

(At this point, I did a "tied-up" exercise with volunteers from the workshop, to illustrate the situation).

To resume the quote: "The aloneness" is very real and terrible for the troubled Brother or Sister in that kind of a mess, and the Union Officer caught in that kind of a mess feels the same thing... But the Union Officer or Member dealing with human beings; and dealing within the areas of:
Alleviation of suffering;
Restoration of individual physical health;
Restoration of individual mental health;
Restoration of self-respect;
Preservation of families; and
Gainful employment;
Above all, must never be 'tied-up" as we have just observed, either by himself, his union executive board members, or his fellow Brothers and Sisters...back and support your Member Assistance Program...All the way...or not at all.

THE A. T. U. MODEL:
We of the Member Assistance Program Staff are responsible to the President, directly, but to each and every member, indirectly. Our program was 8 months in the development or engineering stage ('on the drawing board').

We are pioneering the all inclusive, self-sufficient Member

Assistance Program Field... The areas where assistance is available to our members are: Alcohol/Drug abuse... Family Problems... Financial Problems... Homecare... Childcare... Health Problems... Youth Guidance... Rehabilitation... Big buddies for Children of single Parent Families... Nursing Service... and Mental Health Problems.

The Executive Board of the A. T. U. is certainly to be thanked and congratulated for their foresight and courage, to embark on a project of this sort and magnitude... We have the first all-inclusive, self-sufficient Member Assistance Program on this continent... we are not a referral group, we handle our own members and their families ourselves, within our program. The credibility and competence of the program has been established by Riverview Mental Hospital, to the extent that one of our members has been picked up by the R.C.M.P., and committed to Riverview by a court, for a minimum of three months, was released from Riverview, to his own Union Member Assistance Program, and was back on the job within 3 weeks.

The technique utilized within our program is one developed by myself, after 5 years of research, and is called the "NOUTHETIC TECHNIQUE". The Technique has been described as "RADICAL SURGERY" IN THAT WE CAN ACCOMPLISH WITHIN A MATTER OF WEEKS, WHAT IN MANY CASES, IS NOT ACCOMPLISHED IN MONTHS, utilizing the present "ALLOGENIC" technique that exists today...We utilize the "AUTOGENIC" Technique. We hold the member responsible for his response and behaviour patterns, to the full extent of his responsibility, however small his responsibility level is at that moment.

We are on call 24 hours a day, 7 days a week... A "duty" counsellor on call each day. We have, at the moment, a staff of 6 counsellors (all volunteers I might add), Trained and licensed by myself, and in order to prepare for the projected Percentage increase of 'troubled' Brothers and Sisters within our union, we will begin another team counsellor training course, for 10 more counsellors, within the next month. The course is a 30 week course, and again, volunteers from within our membership that have been selected because of their established aptitude for the art of counselling. A total of 35 volunteers were interviewed, 10 were selected, of which 6 finished the last course.

It has not been a 'bed of roses' for either THE A. T. U. Executive Board Members, or the Counselling Staff. We HAVE had our differences...But each time, proper rationale prevailed, in the main, I feel, because of the rationale of our President, Brother Len Doyle and Chief Job Steward, Brother Jim Daley. Our President and Brother Jim Daley have brought us through some mighty rough waters, on a few occasions, thanks to their sound judgement and expertise.

There were many pitfalls that we experienced, that you need not experience, because we are willing to share our experiences with you. Any connections we have developed, we will also gladly share with you.

Any problems that did develop, developed because of a lack of communication between the A. T. U. Executive Board and the program Staff...Guard well against this pitfall.

No doubt you will be involved in a "Referral" situation, although this is a very rare occurrence, but if it happens, ensure you are referring to a competent agent... shop around, use only the very best agent available. There are, unfortunately, some very incompetent agents out there.

(explain intake procedure. Medical Tests Required. Family involved. Final Distribution of member's file).

Thank you, 1 OCT 1977. END OF QUOTE.

One year later, the program was scuttled by the A. T. U. Executive Board, who themselves, were "flagged" as "troubled" members, that became furious at being "found out", and would not participate in the necessary recovery program. Within 2 months they all had been terminated, by the company, for their behaviour. Six months later the membership revolted, and decertified the A. T. U., and the membership was taken over by I. C. T. U., which was also decertified by an angry membership. To the best of my knowledge, the Auto Workers Union now represent the Transit Operators.

The actual problem facing the Labour Movement in B.C., is the loss of Labour Fraternalism, and the true spirit that the Labour Movement was built on. There must be a Province wide revival of the labour movement, restoring democracy and the true spirit of Labour Fraternalism.

Today we have Social Assistance; A Medical Plan that was a 'Universal' Plan originally, (not the mess we have today); and U.I.C. or I.E. as we know it today.

Where do you think these came from? A Political Party? Advocate-Anti-Poverty Groups? NO! These were brought into being by the labour Movement via the C.C.F. Party.

When the Labour Movement of old existed, if a Union Member was not pulling his fair share of the work-load because of a lack of skills, his fellow Members helped him to acquire the needed expertise; they did not stand back and watch him make a fool of himself, to make themselves look better in the boss's eyes; they taught him what he needed to learn, in order to do a better job, to make the Union look good.

If a fellow member was messing up, the Union disciplined

him, not Management. THE UNION, and for HIS good... to help him... and his family.

In order to over-come the problems facing labour today; (The 'conflict') Labour must utilize FORCE and FERVOUR; DECISION and DEVOTION; VALOUR and VEHEMENCE, must be brought together, then brought on line, via FRATERNALISM, FOR THE GOOD OF THE MEMBER AND HIS/HER FAMILY, AND THE UNION.

4 of 6 CHURCH OF POLITICS/PR FLACKS (SEE ALSO LABOUR).

We will now address POLITICS and PR FLACKS : During the B. C. Provincial Election of 1941, the C. C. F. Election Slogan was "Victory Abroad, Security at Home", and the Election Platform included public ownership of the War Industries. This naturally, very much upset the Industrialists. The Industrialists were well aware of the fact, a war enables them to make multi-million dollar profits.

The C. C. F. was also saying what the labour Movement said during World War one...i.e. "conscription of wealth if manpower is conscripted, and an end to wartime profiteering". To this the Industrialists replied: "Industry and wealth are already conscripted, and that the C.C.F. was merely hitting at a straw man."

Just how misleading the Industrialist's statements were, was not made known until 8 Feb. 1945. On that date, the Bank of Canada reported the working capital of the 625 War industry Businesses increased by over $316 million each. (BIG Bucks in those days), from the fall of 1939 to the spring of 1942, and that the largest 129 companies made the largest gains, i.e. half the total money of all 625 companies. (to date, no one has determined which war made the most Canadian Millionaires, 1st or 2nd.)

The Industrialist were also aware of the fact that Canadian Labour was getting too strong; although they knew how to handle the problem at the moment, the Industrialists didn't want the problem to get any bigger. The Industrialists were thinking of the Oshawa, Ont. G. M. strike in 1937, when 4, 000 men went on strike for a first union agreement. The Liberal Premier of Ontario, Mitchel Hepburn, was VIOLENTLY opposed to the strike because, to quote him... "If unions were allowed to get into G.M., they would spread into the mining industry of Northern Ontario". Liberal Premier Hepburn started up a 'special' Police Force (Made up from the Ontario Provincial Police), known as "HEPBURN'S HUSSARS", and was prepared to use them to break the G. M. Oshawa strike.

But the Mayor of Oshawa threatened to counter with the Oshawa City Police Force if those "Sons of Mitches" so much as crossed the City Limits. The strike lasted 8 days, and was orderly and peaceful.

Up to 1937, the C. C. F. Party grew and became very strong. Something had to be done about them. Liberal Premier Hepburn, Industrialists, Businessmen, and the Mining companies, with the aid of the Newspapers, scared the wits out of the public about UNIONS and their "COMMUNISM", (which was not true at all). The Liberals swept to a landslide victory in the Ontario Provincial Election of 1937, crushing the C. C. F. Party.

The first important lesson had been learned by the Liberals, Conservatives, and the Communist Party; the Propagandists, (Now known as "Pr Flaks"), utilized their most effective weapon... "OPPRESS VIA DISCREDITING", and to add insult to injury, the hired U.S. Propagandists added to their report, quote: "The Canadian General Population can be conned via Propaganda; They're not overly bright".

However, the Labour Movement's fight against Liberal Premier

Hepburn's crude attempt at dictatorship, and the realization by the general Canadian population that they had been 'duped' caused a back-lash that helped the Labour Movement plant their banners throughout the Auto Industry; the Steel Mills; the Electric; Rubber; Mining; and other industries, where they'd never been before.

Starting in 1940, the pro - C. C. F. sentiments in the Labour Movement was rising rapidly, and the C. C. F. Party Membership was growing fast.

In the Ontario Provincial Election of 4 Aug. 1943, when we went to bed on election night, the C.C.F. was tied with the conservatives in seats won. When we woke 5 Aug. 1943, the Tories had 38 seats, the C.C.F 34 seats; the Liberals 12 seats; the Communist Party had 0 seats. The C. C. F. was the Official Opposition for the first time in history. The C. C. F. membership in Ontario rose to a record membership of 800,000.

In the Saskatchewan Provincial Election of 1944, the C. C. F. Party won 50 of the 55 seats. The C. C. F. in Nova Scotia had peaked.

This was enough for the Industrialists and Big Business... if they were going to continue to 'call the shots', the C. C. F. had to be eliminated... quote: "There would be no profiteering under a C. C. F. Government".

The C. C. F. Party in Ontario and across Canada, came under increasingly VIRULENT hammering from the Propagandists like Gladstone Murray, who headed a company called "Responsible Enterprises", and Montague Sanderson, (the "Bug Man") of "Reliable Exterminators". Very LARGE contributions were made by Big Business Interests. (A veritable 'Who's Who' of Canadian BIG Business), towards the anti- C.C.F. Campaign. And the

Newspapers cooperated like trained seals, but with much less intelligence.

The Anti- C. C. F. Campaign strategy was engineered and handled by paid propagandists, headed by the man from Missouri, U.S.A., BURDICK TRESTRAIL. (HE WAS PART OF THE TEAM THAT CRUSHED THE C. C. F. IN 1937, WHO, BY THIS TIME, HAD HIS OWN COMPANY).

The closer the Federal and Provincial Elections came, (4th & 11th of June 1945), the more money was poured into the barrage of Anti-C. C. F. Propaganda; Propaganda of the most contemptible kind. Charges that C.C.F. Government would meant 'Muscle Men and Gangsters' that "the C.C.F. was Nazi"; "The C.C.F. was Communist"; "The C. C. F. was Anti- British"; "The C. C. F. was revolutionary", etc. and so on. NOT just from the paid propagandists who published and distributed, nationwide, the poisonous pamphlet "STAND UP AND BE COUNTED" (Patently Anti-Semitic into the bargain, because the C.C.F. Federal Leader Mr. Lewis, was Jewish), but also from prominent politicians like Premier Drew of Ontario, and also from well-known Big Business Men coast to coast. The Liberal, conservative, and communist Parties also contributed mega bucks to the Anti-C.C.F. Campaign.

To show just how widespread and insidious the Anti - C. C. F. Campaign was, I'll quote from Weekend Magazine, 26 Feb. 1977, From an article about Lloyd Shaw. "Lloyd ran for Parliament in Halifax in the 1945 Federal Election. (A C. C. F. Candidate). He might even win. But when the Liberal Prime Minister King Government, and the Big Business Interests brought out the (Burdick Trestrail) pamphlet, (it went into every home in Canada, via mail); just the dirtiest literature imaginable". Speaking of the day after the pamphlet had been distributed..."Going down the street the next day - and it was not just imagination – The whole atmosphere changed; just that quick". "It was a shattering of the

C. C. F. Party". The Canadian Population had been duped AGAIN; ROYALLY this time...to the point where we have not recovered from that royal "DUPPING", from that day to this. June 1945 was the date that democracy was murdered in Canada, and to this day, it has not been revived. Remember what Edward Bernays, the Propagandist, and Freud's nephew said??? "If we understand the mechanisms and motives of the group mind, it is now possible to CONTROL and REGIMENT the masses, according to OUR will, without them knowing it". (But remember, this is ONLY possible, where the masses do NOT have the Spiritual Standards of God's Realm, to measure against).

Bernays also proposed that "Those who manipulate this unseen mechanism of society, constitute an invisible Government which is the TRUE ruling power of a nation". The ONLY power the propagandists have over us, is the power WE GIVE TO THEM...WE give them that power FREELY, when we do NOT have God's Spiritual Standards to measure against, then stand back and ask, "WHAT IS THE MATTER WITH THE KIDS AND OUR COUNTRY OF TODAY??? HELLO...

With meagre Election funds, both Provincially and Federally, and small staff, against that slanderous onslaught, the C. C. F. was virtually helpless; the Trade Unions were virtually speechless...in utter shock; and that was the beginning of the end for the labour Movement.

The communists were secretly lined up with the Conservatives to beat the C. C. F. Provincially, and with the Liberals Federally, for the same purpose.

Ted Jolliffe, Ontario Provincial C. C. F. Leader, on the 24th of May, 1945, over a Provincial Radio Network, charged Conservative Premier George Drew with maintaining a "Secret Police Force, out of public funds".

On 29th July 1945, the Trades and Labour congress demanded that Premier Drew stop spying on Ontario Labour.

The Ontario Government's Secret Police Force was in charge of Capt. Osborne – Dempster, of the Ontario Provincial Police, whose job it was to link all non-Conservatives with the Communist Party. He held ILLEGAL UNION CARDS so he could attend Union Meetings.

Union Offices were rifled; documents taken; spies were sent to Union Meetings; Blacklist of people of whom Premier Drew's Gestapo disapproved were prepared, and Businessmen were given the Blacklists to check against their employee name lists. The Blacklist of names was made available to the paid propagandists. (Pr Flaks).

All of this information, and more, was made available to Ted Jolliffe, Provincial C. C. F. Party Leader, by Ontario Provincial Police constable John Rowe, who was Capt. Osborne – Dempster's assistant since 1944, when the Secret Police Force was set up, at the recommendation of the paid propagandists.

Premier Drew, of course, denied the charge completely, and appointed a Royal commission to investigate the charges. The Royal Commission would, of course, meet after the Election. In the meantime, the lessons learned in the 1937 Provincial Election would be utilized to the fullest extent, with a view of scuttling the Royal commission when the time came.

But the Royal commission would not be scuttled, it functioned entirely within the confines of truth and justice. On the 28th of April 1949, a Front Page headline read "JOLLIFFE VINDICATED". There WAS a "GESTAPO". Jolliffe's charges that there was a Secret Police Force in Ontario where proven by findings of the Lebel Royal commission 4 YEARS LATER. The Chief of this

Special Branch of the Ontario Provincial Police was dismissed. The Deputy commissioner was relieved of his duties, and the spying was ordered to cease.

See what's possible when Global corps/ Multi-nationalists, and Politicians teams up??? Especially when their paid Pr Flaks know how to 'work the system' with a people that do not have the Spiritual Standards of God's realm to measure against???

5 OF 6 CHURCH OF MULTI-NATIONALS/GLOBAL CORPS/ PR. FLAKS

Trust ??? How can I trust even my own Government??? Trust the Global Corporations that can, and do, more to HARM a Country, than the Government can do to HELP the Country???

Canadian against Canadian? How about the Global corps against the Canadian problem???
It is NOT unusual, or beyond possibility, for Politicians to shaft ROYALLY the population they pretend to serve; it is NOT unusual for Global corps to rape and ravage a population, then grin at the people for allowing them to do it.

Because Multi-national/Global corps are new, bold, and powerful, they cross the frontiers of academic disciplines as easily as they cross National frontiers. The men who run the Global Corps today, are the first in history with the organization, technology, money, and ideology to make an attempt at managing the world as an integrated unit.

George Ball, former Under Secretary of State for the U. S. A., and Chairman of Lehman Bros International, said: "We are able for the first time, to utilize World Resources with an efficiency dictated by the objective logic of profit".

Jacques Maisonrouge, of I. B. M. fame, said "Simply by doing it's thing; by doing what comes naturally in the pursuit of it's business objectives, Global corps are ushering in a Global Shopping Centre, in such a way as to maximize Global Profit". He also adds, "The boundaries that separate one nation from another are no more real than the equator line".

Success or failure of Global Corps is measured on Global profit; on fundamental efficiency in creating profits; NOT on social impact in any country... THE GROWTH OF GLOBAL PROFITS.
The rise of the Global Corp has produced an Organizational Revolution as profound in it's impact and implications for man, as the Industrial Revolution, and the Rise of the Nation-State.

In 1973, the annual sales of Global Corps, compared with gross National Products of Nations, showed that G.M. was bigger than Switzerland, Pakistan, and South Africa; the Royal Dutch shell is bigger than Iran, Venezuela, and Turkey; that Goodyear Tire is bigger than Saudi Arabia.

By their EXTRAORDINARY power, Multi-nationals transform the world political economy, thereby transforming the historic role of the Nation-state. This power does not come from the barrel of a gun; it comes from the means of creating wealth on a worldwide scale, engineered by paid Pr. Flaks.

In the process of developing a new world, managers of Global Corps like G. M., I. B. M., PEPSICO, G. E., SHELL, VOLKSWAGON, EXXON, and a few hundred others, are making daily business decisions that have more social impact than those of most Sovereign Governments, on where people will live; what work (if any), they will do; what they will eat, drink, and wear; what sort of knowledge schools and universities will encourage; as well as dictating what society will be like.

The whole thought of such diabolical unconcern for a nation or it's people, especially when the nation is the home and country of themselves and their families, might be thought of as a pill that is simply "too big to swallow", i.e. not believable. May I point out... Their total unconcern, greed, selfishness, not giving a damn for the people, duping the people by what ever means is necessary, even to the point of outright lies and con-shots, is nothing new...We experience this every day of the week in these times; the metric conversion program is a prime example.

These distorted, disgusting, loathsome, deceitful, cheating, devious, pregnant with destruction and subversive tactics; in an out rightly bold, callous, openly blatant fashion, first dared to be openly displayed in Canada, in 1945. The big Businessmen of that epoch were the forerunners of today's Multi-national/ Global Corps.

What Global corps are demanding, in essence, is the right to transcend the Nation-state, and in the process, transform the Nation-state. Carl A. Gerstacker, of the Dow Chemical Co. says: "I have long dreamed of buying an island, owned by no nation, and of establishing the World Headquarters of the Dow Company on the truly neutral ground of such an island, beholden to no nation or society".

A company spokesman for a principal competitor of Dow Chemical, Union Carbide, agrees: "It is not proper for an International Corp to put the welfare of ANY country in which it does business, above that of any other". Even if that country is the home of the Multi-national Corp.

Christopher Tugendhat points out "The Global interests of the world company are separate and distinct from the interests of every government, including it's own government of origin".

In terms of management and ownership, all Global Corps are either American, British, Canadian, Dutch, French, German, Italian, Japanese, Swedish, or Swiss, (Most are American). In outlook and loyalty, they are becoming (or became), companies without a country.

Extraordinarily high profits on low over-seas investments is the norm. for example, in 1972 United Brands reported 72. 1% return; Parker Pen 51. 2%; Exxon 52. 5%; by 1973 America's 7 largest Banks were obtaining 40% of their profits from abroad, up from 23% in 1971. Was the money being loaned at a higher or lower interest rate than we Canadian consumers could get at home? How about the Royal Bank of Canada? The American Government secretly paid the loans off for Poland, so that the Multi-national Bank that loaned the money to Poland would not be forced into bankruptcy. These same countries, however, have no qualms about forcing a small independent Canadian Businessman into bankruptcy... Public tax dollars are not available to small Independent Businesses in competition with Global Corps.

Business International warns it's corporate clients... "The Nation-State is becoming obsolete; tomorrow, it will, in any meaningful sense, be dead – and so will the corporation that remains (loyal) essentially National. A new breed of Globalists have launched an attack on the Nation-state more radical than anything proposed by World Federalists.

The men who run global corps, (aware that ideologies, like soda crackers, travel well, only if skilfully packaged), are putting great energy into marketing a new gospel that has more potential to change the face of the earth, than even the marketing miracles that have brought Pepsi Bottling Plants to Moscow, and coca-Cola to China.

Roy Ash, former head of Litton Industries, and President

Nixon's Director and Chief consultant in Managerial matters, feels "Nothing can stop an idea whose time has come". Men like Ash know that their vision of a world without borders, is the most important product they have to market (or sell). The extraordinary role they intend to play, in human affairs, challenges what Arnold Toynbee calls "Mankind's Major Religion, the CULT of National Sovereignty". They intend to END National Sovereignty.

Manhattan Bank, calls for a massive "Public Relations", (Bernays Brain Child), campaign to dispel the dangerous "Suspicions" about the Global Giants, that lurk in the minds not yet able, (not willing), to grasp an idea whose time has come. Remember the slogan (con-shot) of the Global corps yesteryear??? "Investment abroad is investment in Canada", and they ACTUALLY expect us to 'buy it'. If THIS is coupled with the lessons learned in Canada in 1937, can there be any doubt as to the success of that "Public relations" Campaign, if we, the Canadian people, do not get a grip on ourselves, and STOP IT ???

David Rockefeller calls for a public relations campaign... A "Crusade of Understanding" to explain why the Global Corps SHOULD have freer rein to move goods, capitol, and technology, around the world, without the INTERFERENCE of the nation-states, realizing THAT SUCH A CRUSADE CALLS FOR THE public relations (Bernays) campaign of the century. The "CAMPAIGN" will be of the Burdick Trestrail Syndrome Variety, (The campaign used by Trestrail in Canada, when the Industrialist and big Business teamed up with the Liberals, Conservatives, and the Communists to 'do a number' on the C.C. F. Party and Labour 1944/45). Their campaign may be quite successful, because what happened then, has been forgotten generations ago, and the Canadian people are even further way from the Spiritual Standard's of God's Realm, (Precepts, Oracles, and Commandments) with which to measure against, to protect them.

The new Multi-nationals are well aware of the problem Rockefeller is trying to address. George Ball says "Corporations

DO have the power to affect the lives of people AND Nations, in a manner that necessarily challenges the prerogatives and responsibilities of the Nation-state Political Authority. How can a National Government make an economic plan with any confidence, if a board of directors, meeting 5,000 miles away can, by altering it's pattern of purchasing and /or production, affects, in a major way, the Nation's Economic Life?"

The Multi-national's answer to the charge of being a Nation-state usurper, is not to deny the extraordinary power they seek to exercise in human affairs; but to RATIONALIZE it.

The continuing struggle for national identity is the unifying political theme of our day. The Chairman of Unilever, one of the earliest and largest Multi-national Corps, warns his colleagues... "The Nation-state may not wither away, a role may have to be found for it".

In Canada and the United States, the most seriously damaged members of society will be the bread-winner and the family. Singer Sewing Machine reduced it's main U.S. plant from 10,000 employees to 2,000 employees; General Instruments cut it's labour force by 3,000 in the U.S., and increased it's labour force in Taiwan by 5,000. this process shows no sign of stopping. The Multi-nationals claim the net effect is a net increase in jobs. This is how the laying off of 3,000 in the U.S., and hiring 5, 000 in Taiwan is being Rationalized.

Thousands of Canadians are losing jobs because of plant relocations; that other workers, in other places may be getting jobs in the process, is small comfort to the unemployed bread-winner, that is faced with a home mortgage foreclosure.

Most of us have heard that Multi-nationals employ cheap

labour, under 'sweat-shop' conditions. Is this what Multi-nationals are asking Canadians to do??? To settle for???

Multi-nationals must work on a profit margin of between 700 and 1000% in order to pay their executives, and their Pr. Flaks, the exorbitant wages they receive. For example... Go to the sheets... Then they rob the Nation-state of the revenue the Nation-state rightfully is entitled to...go to the sheets.......They defer these taxes, giving themselves room and time to dispose of taxes, for their OWN benefit, producing receipts for the expenditures, then all of a sudden, they don't owe those taxes, forcing the Nation-state into a financial dilemma, then criticize the Nation-state for being in a financial dilemma, thereby setting the stage for their highly paid Pr. Flak to 'do a number' on the Government.

Herein we see the solution to the 'problem'. Let's take a look....

W.P. Gullander, in my opinion, was the first to realize the havoc the Multi-nationals will cause the Nation-state. He said "Profound changes will take place in the kinds of jobs available...Some jobs will disappear and some new jobs will be created. Jobs calling for new skills, and the willingness to learn them, and adapt, requiring workers to change jobs.

It will become the "NORM" for some workers to have 3 or 4 DIFFERENT careers in their lifetime, perhaps requiring them to move with their families to a number of different localities. There will be a RESULTING sense of ROOTLESSNESS and superficial relationships, to others in the new community, when one doesn't expect to stay very long. The effects of rapid, frequent changes are discomforting to a person or family.

This quiet revolution is "RATTLING OUR CAGE". THERE WILL BE ACCIDENTS, ABSENTEEISM, AND ALCOHOLISM. We must remember that friction in the work place can damage or destroy a sensitive human mechanism".

People with problems show it in many different ways; i.e. Belligerent employees; the employee with the 'blues'; The exaggerated worrier; The suspicious; The selfish and Greedy; The leaner; the person who has poor emotional control. They have no "SAFETY VALVE"; Human Beings persist in acting like Human Beings.

And to add insult to injury, because of the fact that when Poverty comes in the door, Love goes out the window, and family separation becomes the "NORM" in this situation, and the very backbone of our Nation, THE FAMILY, goes down the tube, taking Canadian Society with it.

We could stabilize the Canadian Economy over-night, and there would be jobs galore, if we had the courage and the sense to enact a 33 AND 1/3 profit margin, with all that goes with that scenario. This would cause one heck of a commotion within the Canadian Population, (especially from the selfish and greedy), and the Multi-nationals Corps.. But it would save Canada and our Canadian society, by throwing the multi-nationals out of Canada.

The disclosure of the C.I.A.'s efforts to bring down the Allende Government in Chile, became a major concern after the Chilean Government Nationalized Anacondas's and Kennecott's Copper Mines, have confirmed wide-spread fears that Multi-nationals not only have too much power, but that they also abuse that power.

According to a former U.S. Ambassador to Chile, the C.I.A. spent $20 Million dollars to defeat Allende; The line of Bank Credit shrank from $220 Million to $35 Million in the first year of Allende's Government. I wonder who paid the Cold hard cash dollars to generate unrest and subversive activities in Chile, and hollered "C O M M U N I S T S" for all the world to hear, and condemn Chile?

The Global Corps are in a position to dominate large Governments (like Canada & the U.S.A.), dislocate National Economies, and upset world currency flows. Corporate Managers have the power to shift capital, develop or suppress technology, and mould public moods and appetites; to the extent that even the most powerful Governments, doubt their ability to control Global Corps., so they go along with them.

Whether Global Corps should be welcomed, barred, or fitted with a legal straight jacket is shaping up as a prime political issue in most countries. But there is hope; the attitude of young people around the world, toward Global Corps is a cause for particular concern; it will be fuel for Revolutionary fires.
The developing confrontation between Global corps and it's enemies, promises to influence the shape of Human Society, more than any other Political drama of our time. The Global Corps are winning in that fight as of this date.

6 of 6 THE CHURCH OF CANADA'S CITIZENS /PR. FLAK

THE CHOICE IS OURS: Oh boy; Oh Joy; Where do we go from here???

There are 3 necessary components to effect change:
1. The URGE to change;
2. The belief that we CAN change;
3. The realization that we MUST change.
If we will not ACCEPT the pain of SELF-DISCIPLINE, we will be GIVEN the pain of REMORSE and REGRET.

Canadian's have forgotten how to function as a Nation. Clarification of our Canadian National thinking is overdue.

Applying doctrines of Philosophic indifference, isolation, and "wait and see" tactics, injustice, deceit, and hate, destructive strategy and intrigue, have brought us a heavy harvest of agony, and has wrung the hearts and hopes of many un-offending Canadian Men and Women.

We Canadians must come to a sudden discovery of ourselves. We have not consciously appraised our Nation, according to the measure of our capacity as a Nation.

The unhappy continuance of a Political life that still anchors itself in our colonial history, in spite of what the Politicians tell us.

The efforts of opportunist Politicians, to capitalize on Racial and Religious differences, and the failure of government to teach immigrants to get in step with Canadian people, rather than encouraging them to get the Canadian people to get in step with them, have caused a lot of damage. WE must find new solutions to old problems.

The Politicians have, for the most part, left only blurred impressions, on the superficial levels of our existence.

"Canada and Canadians are easy to scam" according to Burdrick Trestrail 1945, and Diane Francis, in her article in McLean's Magazine 31 May 1999.

Our Nation is dying; perishing for lack of patriotism's vital oxygen; cut off from the very source of her life; slowly dying the death of the asphyxiated – laboured breathing; - uneven, strenuous, spasmodic.

No one even recognized her peril. What chance does our dying Nation have, when her citizens are groggy in slumber??? She languishes in bleak despair; her citizens unaware of the digression of Canada as a Nation, instead of experiencing a spectacular demonstration of growth in productivity capacity and power, in any other like period of time.

Canada's Political Leadership has been more absorbed with the exigencies of Party Politics, rather than the concept of National Unity and purpose. We must learn to discriminate between true statesmanship and chicanery of Party politics. In recent years, there has been a too obvious tendency on the part of Canadian Politicians, to adopt some of the less desirable tactics that have been observed elsewhere.

A critical examination of Political life in Canada, especially as exemplified in some of the Provincial administrations, would find many illustrations of how things should NOT be done. AND considerable evidence of irresponsible, haphazard, and even venial Political Leadership.

The deeply perturbed National conscience of the present day; the multiplying of Political Party groups; the abortive efforts of Minority Governments; the carping of one locality against other localities; are 'things' the people of Canada must address.

Canadians must re-establish a TRUE democracy and fraternalism. There is much yet to be learned by Canadians everywhere, as to what a full application of true democracy and Fraternalism can mean. We will find, that the much vaunted Political party system of this day, is a very incomplete expression of the true democratic, Fraternalistic ideal, i.e. paid Lobbyist and Pr. Flaks dictating policies and regulations, and duping Politicians, for the benefit of their multi-national Corps, (who pay their exorbitant fees), thwarting Canadian sovereignty, forcing Canada into their own WORLD sovereignty Government, i.e. they don't give a damn about Canada or the Canadian people. Thereby thwarting the silent, purposeful human stream of Canadians, by which Canadian values are determined, and all National attainment is made possible, robbing the Canadians of their capacity to direct their growth and destiny.

Unless we turn our Nation around, taking Canada out of the grip of the Educational, and Multi-national, Church 'elite', and the paganism of the "New Age", our children will remain in the warp and woof of the old dying Canada, and will remain there, until THEIR children rise up, and bring the old Canada down. If WE don't turn this nation around, there are two alternatives;

1. Our grandchildren will be forced to fight a revolution, to rebuild Canada, as a judgement against the Parental Incompetence Syndrome the grandparents caused, by not teaching their children, how to teach THEIR children, to function within the confines of God's Precepts, Oracles, and Commandments. Or
2. Canada will disappear as a Nation.

It is NOT, therefore, to the textbooks of our Educational Church 'elite' that we can turn to, for an understanding of what has come to pass, in the land we call Canada.

We must AVOW ourselves to a ceaseless effort on behalf of our dying Nation; to cease from the business of merely superficial activities, and give ourselves to the true business of going to the aid of our Nation.

There is no indication over the past 50 years, that Canadians have worked together, to go to Canada's aid, to help Canada via serious, sustained, concentrated effort.

Many people, who begin with a serious concern about mortally wounded Canada, are soon switched off the main issue by unscrupulous paid Pr. Flaks, working for the Multi-national/global corps. Deceiving and deluding Canadians into imaging that we are doing just fine.

With undisguised suspicion, based on a crude and childish conception of Canada's Political parties, we see Canadians resolving themselves into little more than opportunities for 'fleeting' emotional display, at best, i.e. Canada Day; Remembrance Day, etc. Now you know HOW Canada was dealt the mortal blow, that has her mortally wounded.

Patriotism, in the final analysis, is worth EXACTLY as much –or as little, as the individual person behind it. If the person has an obstinate, prejudiced, undisciplined mind, the Patriotism will suffer from the same defects. If the patriotism is limited, gross, and ill-guided, so will be the attitude toward Patriotism.

This does not mean that we can afford to wait, before reviving Canadian Patriotism and Democracy, until we have secured the ideal presuppositions. We must begin at once, ready or not; we CAN learn from each other as we go along. But remember, no one can safely lead, until he has first learned how to follow, via self-disciplined exercise. And one of the first things he must learn is how to think, reason, see, hear, and speak from the HEART, not the head, to be in tune with his soul, and to master the dialectic thinking process.

Before we can revive Patriotism, Fraternalism and Democracy in Canada, for Canada, there are THREE necessary components to effect change; you know what they are.

Learning, undigested by THOUGHT, is labour lost; thought, undigested by LEARNING is PERILOUS.

We are quite ready to admit the fact that a person's home life and friendships, have more to do with his work for his country, than a whole lifetime of public activity. This is a truism that we wouldn't dream of questioning. But we seem curiously reluctant to measure our Politicians by the same truism; we seem to think that morality is not required of Politicians. "AMONG US THE WICKED STRUT, AND IN HIGH PLACES, ARE THE BASEST OF MEN". How do we topple the Multi-national/ Global Corps. in and for Canada??? NOUTHETIC FRATERNITY CLUB COALITION SOCIETY.

THIS MILLENNIUM: THE BEGINNING OF THE END

SOCIAL JUSTICE NOW 'OUT'! The attitude and concern for the weak; the lost and confused; the poor; the widows and orphans; the sinners; the simpletons; and for those who have fallen through the 'nets' and' cracks' are gone and out; "they must now reap what they have sown" is how this is rationalized by 'modern' thinkers.

The 'NEW' or 'MODERN' thinking regarding Social Justice developed via the paganism of the CASTE SYSTEM Lucifer has slid by us via his PR FLACKS, in direct opposition to the Christian doctrine of caring for the widow, the orphan, the sick, the poor, the destitute, and the sinner/reprobate. Lucifer is a VERY smooth operator.

Being as we have abandoned Almighty God, as a Nation, in favour of MULTI-NATIONALISM (GREED), also SLID BY US VIA Lucifer's PR FLACKS, via the PARENTAL INCOMPETENCE SYNDROME, with its ancillary's of IMMATURITY, IMPAIRED

RATIONALE, ARROGANCE and REBELLION, and VERY SUBTLE PAGANISMS, the end result is completely chartable and predicable. At whose hands the blood will be required of, is perfectly obvious.

They rob the afflicted, and the needy sigh; while about us the wicked STRUT, and in high places are the BASEST of men, generating profit margins between 700 and 1000 percent, providing EXORBITANT salaries and benefits for the chosen few, not giving a damn for ANY Nation or it's people. Their ONLY CONCERN IS PROFIT for themselves

We will now be led by PR FLAKS serving evil, uncaring and cruel, pseudo 'scientists', and the HARD and the PERVERSE, which have been falsidically educated via an educational philosophy gone awry, who will, from now on, focus on only technology and the DNA fields, cloning and creating via engineered reproduction, in defiance of God's Natural Law, Precepts, Oracles and Commandments, in arrogance and rebellion, resulting from IMMATURITY and an IMPAIRED RATIONALE. All of them INSTRUMENTS and SERVANTS of LUCIFER.

The only response or action possible now, is for Canada, as a Nation via Canadian Pastors and Evangelists, to turn (repent) and return to Almighty God. This COULD, conceivably, also prompt Almighty God to change His mind, and delay the end of time, allowing more souls to be saved from Lucifer's realm.

Lucifer now comes into his own world, in defiance, arrogance and rebellion, to claim it. The evil, defiance, arrogance and rebellion of Lucifer will come into it's own age, to reign supreme, and will attempt to 'steam-roller' over the world, claiming the world as his own.

Immaturity and impaired rationale, formally ANTI- THESIS,

is now reversed and has become THESIS, VIA PRACTICE and EXPERIENCE; a DIRECT result of the PARENTAL INCOMPETENCE SYNDROME, THAT HAS DESTROYED OUR SOCIETY.

We will be left alone, to reap what we have sown in our hearts; and what we HAVE and/or HAVE NOT learned from the Book, Basic Instructions Before Leaving Earth, being prepared or set-up for 1 COR 3: 13 -15.

Time is now running out...we are 'THERE'. God will allow the' chips' to fall where they may.

David SHOULD have been engaged in fighting The Lord's battles. Instead, he lingered in Jerusalem and rested in luxury; i.e. "for he arose from his bed in the evening". Idleness and luxury are Lucifer's jackals, and provide him with ABUNDANT PREY. (2 SAM 11:2 (2 Kings)).

When God rises from His Throne and says "THAT' S ENOUGH", AND BRINGS ABOUT THE LAST DAY OF TIME, Jesus Christ will return to establish HIS KINGDOM that will last for ever and ever, WORLD WITHOUT END...FOR ETERNITY...AMEN.

Which ever realm we die within, GOD'S Realm or Lucifer's realm, will be our realm for ETERNITY. And we are either, working toward, or actually in, that realm RIGHT NOW! And we WILL live it for ETERNITY. That is OUR choice. The outcome of our life is in OUR hands. Since we CAN re-shape ourselves, WE are responsible for the shape we are in. God is no respecter of persons.

Choose your realm NOW...we are 'THERE' and out of time, for all intentions and purposes. DO IT NOW.

Do NOT be numbered among the people that "KEEP A COMING, BUT THE TRAIN IS GONE".

Whether you believe it or not; like it or not, does not matter a WHIT to God.

My prayer is that you will choose God's Realm...if you do, get in; sit down; hang on; and shut up; DO your work in God's Realm and pray that GOD'S will be done. This is our last chance to live it out, and it WILL be as GOD Wills... good or bad.
The battle lines have been drawn; the die is cast...the gloves are off. Only God knows how much time is left. God stands aloof... His will WILL be done.

NOMINAL CHRISTIANITY : PAGANISM: THE MYTH OF THE NEUTRALITY OF OUR NATION.

WHERE IT'S AT: Those in God's realm are standing out there faithfully, but alone, in a world of cowardice, tolerance and compromise, which is Lucifer's realm.

A TIME FOR ANGER: Frank Schaeffer, author of A TIME FOR ANGER, writes of his personal experience within a family that functions as a family is SUPPOSED to function, within God's Realm, "I would like to thank Genie, my wife, and my three children, Jessica, Francis, and John. By their very presence and love, they allow me to exercise my creative powers; such as they are, in an environment that turns my energies toward, the causes of love, compassion, and beauty. Life would be bankrupt without them."
We need Christians of strong principle and faith; solid, standing, mature, saints, instruments, and servants of God, who REFUSE to be. manipulated by the MYTHS and MISNOMERS, of the RELIGIOUS and SECULAR HUMANISTIC "ELITE" of Lucifer's realm.

The NOMINAL CHRISTIANS have NAIVELY accepted the

role assigned to them by an anti-Christian consensus, within our Canadian Society, that functions within Lucifer's realm. They have been relegated to a cultural backwater, and told to take their 'Christianity' with them, where they are meant to paddle around, content in the knowledge that they are only allowed to exist in that backwater area.

We must learn WHY and HOW we can challenge the superficial, superfluous, glib, and anti-Christian stance of the pagan and humanistic culture around us. We do NOT have to apologize for the Christian FAITH and TRADITIONS, or SCRIPTURES...or GOD...or be ASHAMED of them.

Our world is deeply deceitful. The 'liberal', 'humanistic' elements of society of Lucifer's realm do NOT play by the rules THEY espouse; the rules of open-mindedness, fair play, and equality under the law. Deceit and evil ALWAYS go hand in hand, and our own era, in Canada, finds them wedded once more.

"LIBERAL" has come to mean an indefinite tolerance of EVERYONE and ANYTHING EXCEPT for those who disagree with them on SPIRITUAL issues, and/or on the basis of MORAL PRINCIPLES.

Some 'labels' are used to neutralize the actions of certain groups; other 'labels' denote being "one of us", or "acceptable". The words RIGHT WING... FUNDAMENTALIST... PRO-LIFE... ABSOLUTIST... DEEPLY RELIGIOUS...ETC... are PUT-DOWNS, not CATEGORIES. Conversely, think of the UNSPOKEN PAT ON THE BACK and BLESSINGS the following words convey: - MODERATE... PLURALISTIC... LIBERAL... CIVIL LIBERTARIAN... PRAGMATIC... ENLIGHTENED... of the 'NEW AGE'.

Life, people, politics, social action, etc., CANNOT be reduced to one-word categories; when they ARE reduced to one-word categories, FALSEHOOD, and POLITICAL MANIPULATION becomes the NORM. The DELIBERATE abuse of 'labelling' HAS conditioned the Canadian population to respond negatively to any mention of Religious concern in the public sphere. DECEIT always deals in STEREOTYPES; and stereotypes PERPETUATE BIGOTRY.

Hitler wrote only of the "Jewish race" in broad, general, and paranoid terms. Today, as TRUE Christians have DECLINED in influence, they have become subject to MIS-REPRESENTATION in similar ways.

The secular humanist would never dream of committing the social FAUX PAS of calling a coloured person a 'NIGGER', yet, he feels perfectly free to castigate Christians, and their leaders in ANYWAY HE LIKES. How totally FALSE the liberal, secular humanists of Lucifer's can be to their OWN SUPPOSED PRINCIPLES in this regard.

By far, the VAST MAJORITY of those who work in the mass media, with their secular humanist PRECONCEPTIONS, DENY THEIR true ROLE; they CONSIDER themselves OBJECTIVE REPORTERS who do NOT make value judgments...this is TOTAL FICTION...THE MYTH OF NEUTRALITY. Their PRETENCE of OBJECTIVITY, contributes MIGHTILY to this MYTH of COLLECTIVE ILLUSION. The MASS MEDIA, STATISTICS, and COMPUTERS, have one thing in common... THEY CAN BE MADE TO SAY ANYTHING ONE WANTS THEM TO SAY. (PR FLAKS).

The articles re "ABORTION" 6 Apr. 1981, and re, "CRADLE TO GRAVE" 7 Sept 1981, in TIME magazine, are PRIME examples of how stories are carefully SLANTED to influence PRECONCEPTIONS, and also shows CLEARLY THEIR DUPLICITY, and the IMPOSSIBILITY of a consistent ETHIC, without appealing to an OBJECTIVE STANDARD.

And yet, hardly anyone challenges TIME or OTHER medias

regarding their OPINION MAKING institutions, or about their incredible DOUBLE STANDARD... THEIR, ON AGAIN, OFF AGAIN "MORALITY", They, THEMSELVES, never examine and/or state PUBLICLY their OWN moral criteria, OR LACK OF THEM. Most coverage is not a matter of PRINCIPLE...not even of rigorous THINKING.

Besides, the way in which arbitrary value judgments INSINUATE themselves into the news, the "MYTH OF NEUTRALITY" includes widespread (OFTEN DELIBERATE) misunderstandings and/or propaganda from PR FLACKS. (propagandists).

The INSTITUTION of the Church is separated from the State, but not a religious understanding of TRUTH from the State. Legislation is supposed to provide freedom FOR GOD'S RELIGION, not freedom FROM RELIGION.

The American Revolution was justified on religious grounds... they formed a new Union that, by design, was to be in accord with "LAWS OF NATURE AND NATURE'S GOD". The basic legal framework of Canada was, until recently, based on 'COMMON LAW', WHICH LOOKED TO THE Ten Commandments and Biblical absolutes as it's basis. RELIGIOUS TRUTH, specifically the JUDEO -CHRISTIAN TRADITIONS, was the ground on which Canada stood.

In accordance with our Canadian SECULARIST views, we have DELIBERATELY ignored these facts... our THINKING and TEACHINGS have produced uneducated generations that FIRMLY believe in MIS-GOTTEN NOTIONS.

This MISINFORMED secularist group then uses this LIE to keep Christians and those with Religious principles out of "THE PROCESS", with the same immature logic of a two-year old refusing to share his toys. i.e. By branding (labelling) ABORTION as a "CATHOLIC" or "RELIGIOUS" issue; they try to preclude a FULL discussion of the PRO -LIFE stance in the media... and then they refer to abortion as a "SECULAR QUESTION", so that it will be handled exclusively by the Courts (Courts controlled by secularist thinkers)... they circumvent the Democratic process and successfully ELIMINATE any chance for Christian traditions to take a stand. Then, to add insult to injury, proceed to employ CASUAL SLURS, and their SECULARIST BIGOTRY to OPPRESS VIA DISCREDITING (an oracle of Lucifer's realm), Christian Traditions and Principles.

The NEXT step in the process of these BIGOTS, (in order to SECURE their SECULAR HUMANISTIC POSITION), is to bring up that emphatic "RED HERRING" of division of Church and State (originally Church and Education)... a convenient EXCUSE for MUZZLING, UNDESIRABLE OPINION, rather than a REAL concern, on the part of the LIBERAL, HUMANISTIC CONSENSUS.

This sort of 'WHEELING AND DEALING' within their POLITICS is not only well known, it is READILY ACCEPTED (everyone smiles and chuckles about it) as the "NORM".

The GREAT DANGER of this, like ALL PR FLAK PROPAGANDA is that IT IS EFFECTIVE, NOT ONLY WITH THOSE WHO OTHERWISE WOULD BE NEUTRAL, BUT ALSO WITH THOSE ON THE. OTHER SIDE... People with "NOMINAL CHRISTIANITY" religious convictions OFTEN have an INFERIORITY COMPLEX; they are HESITANT to express serious political concerns or opinions, let alone take action. Sin ALWAYS begets STUPIDITY.

Again, take the issue of ABORTION... we have an array of supposedly Christian political figures who say publicly that, although they hold an anti- abortion view themselves, they would not DREAM of IMPOSING THEIR VIEW ON SOCIETY. We Canadians have been CONDITIONED to view such PR FLACK PROPAGANDA as SENSIBLE AND BROAD –MINDED.

STRICTURES OF THIS KIND ARE NEVER RECIPROCAL. The FEMINISTS, GAYS, LESBIANS, or ANY OTHER LOBBYIST for one branch of secularism or another, may FREELY use his or her position or station to influence the PUBLIC or GOVERNMENTAL body, while the Christian that might do so, is considered to have made a MAJOR FAUX PAS...this is a PRIME EXAMPLE of THE MYTH OF NEUTRALITY... only ONE point of view is given CONSISTENT EXPOSURE...THE SECULAR HUMANISTIC PAGAN VIEW.

The greatest danger Canada faces in this epoch is from CHRISTIANS, NOT FROM THE OPPOSITION... from Christians failing Christianity via the GROSS THEOSOPHIES and SPURIOUS SPECULATIONS, that produce NOMINAL CHRISTIANITY, that is UNACCEPTABLE to God. They make fools of themselves; a farce of their Christianity; and a friend of Lucifer.

If we accept THE MYTH OF NEUTRALITY, and it's DOCTRINE of, 'our own one –sidedness', we will have ABANDONED our Constitutional RIGHTS and, BY DEFAULT, lose our ability, or rather, ABDICATE OUR COMMANDED DUTY to be the "SALT OF THE EARTH"...i.e. the PRESERVERS of our Canadian Christian culture.

Had we APPLIED, in the past, the principles of CHRISTIAN NON-INVOLVEMENT, NOW being THRUST upon us, we would have a FLOURISHING slave trade today. Our Christian forebears DELIBERATELY acted upon their CONVICTIONS to right the wrongs they perceived, through public action, ON THE BASIS OF RELIGIOUS FAITH. Many charitable endeavours, worldwide, were started by Christians who were deliberately acting on their Christian principles and traditions.

FAITH: EVERY human being has a FAITH... he/she holds certain values, and these values imply a certain rationale.. it makes no difference whether someone has accepted the values of an organized Religion, or has chosen his OWN beliefs...EVERYONE believes in SOMETHING...even if that SOMETHING is his/her REJECTION of ALL organized Religion. There is no such thing as a non-religious view of TRUTH...the value of one thing as opposed to another IS to make a declaration of FAITH...all life is Religious, whether it is the Religion of God's Realm or of Lucifer's realm; and all life is SECULAR...there is no REAL division between the two.

"SECULAR HUMANISM / PAGANISM" is a DANGEROUS ideological system because it seeks to IMPOSE it's ideology through the organs of the State. Because SECULAR HUMANISM PAGANISM has no tolerance, and is opposed to other Religions, it ACTIVELY REJECTS, EXCLUDES, and attempts to ELIMINATE traditional Christian Theism -from MEANINGFUL participation in our Culture"...so says Professor Harvey Cox and Frank Shaeffer, and so say I. When Professor Cox uses the term "SECULAR HUMANISM", he does NOT refer to HUMANITARIAN ENDEAVOURS, or WORKS OF CHARITY. HUMANITARIANISM and the study of HUMANITIES are OBVIOUSLY part of the CHURCH'S mission.

The term "SECULAR HUMANISM" as Professor Cox uses it, is a PHILOSOPHY which holds that God is NON -EXISTENT or IRRELEVANT to human affairs, and that man must CHOOSE or INVENT his OWN ethics; SECULAR HUMANISM makes man the measure of ALL things. This philosophy ALWAYS seeks to EXCLUDE God from the discussion of MORAL ISSUES, and to do so, COX argues, puts it at loggerheads with Christianity traditions.

EVERYONE has some moral base, even if his/her "MORALITY" is expressed in IMMORALITY; or his/her FAITH is faith in not having ANY faith at all... to suppose that those who do not hold traditional Religious or moral positions are somehow operating from a more "NEUTRAL "and "OPEN -MINDED stance is ILLOGICAL and preposterous, ESPECIALLY when seen in the light of the Religious fervour with which they PROPAGATE their "SECULARIST" position.

Persons of Religious convictions are no more biased than anyone else... They have the RIGHT to worship as they choose, AND they have the RIGHT, as does every other citizen, to engage in POLITICS and OTHER HUMAN ACTIVITIES like everyone else, on the basis of, and because of, their PRINCIPLES and MORAL CONVICTIONS. They have the RIGHT to SPEAK OUT, VOTE, and AGITATE FOR CHANGE, AS A CHRISTIAN, just as the secular humanist pagans have the right to speak out as HUMANIST.

All law IS in fact, some form of legislated morality...the question is WHOSE MORALITY WILL DOMINATE. Laws against racial discrimination are LEGISLATED MORALITY... so are the common laws against THEFT and MURDER. All of these laws 'RESTRICT' SOMEONE'S CHOICE, but are accepted as NECESSARY to the common good.

It IS, therefore, a LIE and a DECEPTION to PRETEND that moral Religious views CANNOT BE ALLOWED TO EFFECT CHANGE.

In FACT, those who would silence the Christian political voice, (the secular humanistic pagan "ELITE"), are attempting to IMPOSE THEIR VICIOUS VERSION OF MORALITY ON OUR CANADIAN SOCIETY... in DIRECT contradiction to THEIR ARGUMENT AGAINST POLITICAL INVOLVEMENT BY CHRISTIANS. Worst of all, THEY ARE TRYING TO PREVENT THE ISSUES FROM EVEN BEING DISCUSSED. To the chagrin of the 'CHRISTIANS', they have been very successful.

THIS MUST CHANGE! CHRISTIANS MUST FIGHT FOR THE

SAME RIGHTS OF FREE SPEECH AND ACTION AS SUPPOSEDLY ACCORDED ALL CANADIAN CITIZENS.

THE MYTH OF NEUTRALITY IN THE MEDIA: One group, more than any other FORMS PUBLIC OPINION: THE MEDIA; THE FILM INDUSTRY; THE TELEVISION NETWORKS; RADIO; NEWSPAPERS; PERIODICALS; AND THE PEOPLE WHO RUN THESE ENTERPRISES HAVE AN IMMENSE AMOUNT OF POWER, WHICH IS TOTALLY DISPROPORTIONATE TO THEIR NUMBERS, AND, UNHAPPILY, TO THEIR MORAL PERCEPTION AND COMPASSION.THEY HAVE SET ATTITUDES, (ETCHED IN CONCRETE), THAT CAN ONLY BE CHARACTERIZED AS "LIBERAL" AND "HUMANISTIC", IN SUCH OVERWHELMING NUMBERS, THAT OUR SOURCES OF INFORMATION HAVE BECOME. UTTERLY BIASED.

In 1982 S. Robert Lichter and Stanley Rothman conducted hour-long interviews with 240 Journalists and Broadcasters of the most influential media outlets, including the NEW YORK TIMES, WASHINGTON POST, WALL STREET JOURNAL, TIME MAGAZINE, U.S. NEWS & WORLD REPORT, C.B.S., N.B.C., P.B.S., and major public Broadcasting stations. The results of this survey are STARTLING and CONFIRM, even BEYOND one's worst suspicions, the religious commitment of the MEDIA to SECULAR / HUMANISTIC PAGANISM.

Material quoted is from "PUBLIC OPINION', and was reprinted in the "INDIANAPOLIS STAR" 25 JAN 1982, page 7, by FRANK SCHEAFFER... "in their attitude toward SEX and SEX RULES, members of the media 'ELITE" are virtually UNANIMOUS in opposing the constraints of both Governmental and Tradition: 90% agree that a woman has the right to decide for herself, whether to have an abortion (they agreed strongly with the pro-choice position. 54% do not regard ADULTERY as wrong; and only 15% agree that EXTRAMARITAL AFFAIRS are immoral". "When asked who ought to have the most influence re PUBLIC OPINION,

Black Leaders; Feminists; Consumer Groups; Intellectuals; Labour Unions; Business Leaders; or The News Media; THEY PUT THEMSELVES FIRST.

With such widespread agreement about basic issues, WHICH CAN ONLY STEM FROM THE SAME PHILOSOPHICAL OUTLOOK, it hardly takes a CONSPIRACY for the media machine to speak with one smothering voice. And these are those to whom we must look for UNBIASED "REPORTING".

TOM JONES, publisher of the L. A. TIMES, reflecting on the RESPONSIBILITY of the press, said, "In more than 1,500 cities in the U.S.A. with daily newspaper, fewer than 50 have 2 or more under COMPETING OWNERSHIP. And the influence of the major networks may be even more pervasive".

Given the concentration of the media's POWER in relatively few hands, and their SHARED values, we CANNOT avoid the conclusion that the MEDIA and PR FLAKS REPRESENT AN UN-ELECTED FORCE IN PUBLIC LIFE. A SELF-ASSURED; SELF-PERPETUATING "ELITE" THAT RELISHES ITS POWER AND WOULD HAVE MORE.

50% had no Religious affiliation. 86% SELDOM or NEVER attend Religious Services. LITTLE WONDER that ALL things Christian in origin are ROUTINELY DENIGRATED. In effect, the MEDIA have become the ENEMY of Religious Principles, and, because of their VAST, UN-ELECTED POWER, they RIVAL the DEMOCRATIC process and of ELECTED OFFICIALS.

Let a CHRISTIAN stand up and begin to CHALLENGE the DOMINANT, HUMANISTIC PAGAN FORCES, and the media will make every attempt to either IGNORE or RAVAGE that individual. Try to introduce BIBLICAL morality into politics and see what happens. The one thing the media ABHORS, without exception, is ANYONE WHO DARES TO TAKE A FIRM stand on ANY issue, out of RELIGIOUS principles, UNLESS that STAND happens to coincide with their expressed views.

Such as it is, the media has become the GREATEST POWER within the Western Countries. MORE powerful than the LEGISLATURE; THE EXECUTIVE; and the JUDICIARY... one would then like to ask; BY WHAT LAW HAS IT BEEN ELECTED, AND TO WHOM IS IT RESPONSIBLE??? ENORMOUS, FREEDOM EXISTS FOR THE PRESS... but NOT FOR THE READERSHIP, because the media mostly gives and stresses emphasis to those opinions that do not too sharply contradict their OWN, or the GENERAL TREND. Fashionable trends of THOUGHT and IDEAS in the West are CAREFULLY SEPARATED FROM THOSE THAT ARE NOT FASHIONABLE. Nothing is forbidden, but what is not FASHIONABLE, will hardly EVER find it's way into the MEDIA.

Remember 'the number' the NEW YORKER did on ALEXANDER SOLZHENITSYN in 1978 ??? In the 21 AUG 78 issue, they summarized the media's reaction in their "NOTES AND COMMENTS" section, without any attempt at so-called LIBERAL-MINDED FAIRNESS: "While Alexander Solzhenitsyn remained in the Soviet Union, it was possible for us to regard him as a marvellous steadfast believer in political freedom,' but now that we have him in our midst, airing his views on politics and society, we have had to review our impressions. We find that primarily he is the champion not of freedom, but of spiritual well being. The two causes are- by no means the same".
We must not call a CANNIBAL a BARBARIAN...but we can say anything we like about a Christian, RIGHT OR WRONG MATTERS NOT...just make SURE it's a "PUT DOWN', and it will be ACCEPTABLE. We must prefer the IDLE RAVINGS of the "ENLIGHTENED" HANS J. MORGENTHOU, to the merciful actions of the "UN-ENLIGHTENED" Mother Theresa.

A free press REQUIRES the presence of Organizations, which

compete not merely to see whether CBS, NBC, or ABC can predict the outcome of an election 30 seconds ahead of it's sister station, but Organizations which represent DISTINCTLY and SUBSTANTIALLY DIFFERENT POINTS OF VIEW... instead, they CONTROL the free flow of ideas to THEIR OWN ENDS, AND TO THE DETRIMENT of the public or audience...by 'LABELLING' people "FUNDAMENTALISTS"; "PRO- LIFE"; "DEVOUTLY CATHOLIC"; and "RIGHT WING" ETC.

This is NOT to suggest the media should be censored; on the CONTRARY, by DEMANDING the Christian voice be FAIRLY heard, we are saying that the "PHILOSOPHICAL CENSORSHIP" of TODA Y'S MEDIA, must be LIFTED in order to RESCUE the institution OF the media itself FROM itself.

The MASSIVE power of the secular media must NOT, be UNDERESTIMATED...The media analyst understands VERY WELL that 'REALITY' is often a state of mind inasmuch as the WAY something is reported determines WHAT is reported.
By the SELECTION it makes as to WHAT to report, and it's decision about HOW to report it, MANIPULATES the news, pushing it's OWN version of 'REALITY'. This is WHY they ROUTINELY play down traditional religious PEOPLE and IDEAS, and play UP SECULARIST HUMANISTIC PAGANISM THINKING and IDEAS, GLOSSING OVER IT'S GLARING INADEQUACIES AND MASSIVE FAILURES.

As LEOPOLD TYRMAND pointed out in his essay "THE MEDIA AS PRESENT DANGER", on a book called "OPEN MARRIAGE". The book received ECSTATIC publicity in the NEW YORK TIMES, and the TIMES contributed MIGHTILY to it's SUCCESS". The book recommended INFIDELITY, as a REMEDY to personal and SOCIAL PROBLEMS, in support of Freud's theory, that sexual gratification solves All PERSONAL PROBLEMS. Several years after it's publication, the Authors "admitted that their recipe- for easy happiness had FAILED, and that THOSE WHO TRIED IT, RUINED THEIR LIVES. There was no call, however, on ANYONE'S part, for a return to TRADITIONAL MORALITY". The authors' conclude, "in their perception, it was not the rottenness of their theorizing, but their victims lack of sophistication which was at fault".

The NEW YORK TIMES illustrates how the media will NOT admit to their mistakes, and WILL perpetuate those mistakes, in order not to undercut their credibility... "The Times once again advertised the book in an interview filled with catchy platitudes and phrased with sympathy and quasi- objectivity, thereby compounding the original offence".

An even MORE flagrant abuse of the media's power occurs when an organization moves from being a new REPORTER to a news MAKER. An example of this occurred during the "WHAT EVER HAPPENED TO THE HUMAN RACE?" seminar at Madison Square Gardens in New York City.

Inside the Hall were 1,000 people who were spending two days watching a serious film, and hearing lectures and discussions on the subjects of ABORTION and INFANTICIDE, and EUTHANASIA. These were concerned people from ALL walks of life...a TRUE cross-section, who were DIFFICULT to STEREOTYPE or LABEL, and therefore to put in the appropriate media pigeonhole of "PROFILE ACTIVISTS", (who the media prefer to characterize as senile retired Nuns).

Outside on the sidewalk, there was a group of 12 people (Frank Schaeffer counted them), who arrived to piquet the seminar within as being "ANTI- CHOICE" and therefore DANGEROUS.

"Coincidentally", they arrived and unpacked their four or five well-known "PRO-CHOICE" placards AT THE SAME TIME as a television truck arrived from the local news, and a photographer arrived from the VILLAGE VOICE newspaper, as well as some other media persons. Their piquetting lasted for the EXACT amount of time it took the television crew to unpack it's cameras, film them for a minute or so, and for the anchor person to do her "WRAP-UP" (twenty seconds) on the story.

The television cameras and the "REPORTER" never ventured into the auditorium, much less ask any of those who organized the Seminar, what they were doing and saying, or why 1,000 people- were inside talking and watching movies for two days.

The THREE MINUTE "PROTEST" WAS THE STORY; the SEMINAR itself was merely a footnote- to be added to the framework for the PRE-DETERMINED story itself, which was, in essence, an event showing the onward march of the FASHIONABLE, FEMINIST -LED PRO - ABORTION MOVEMENT.

The MYTH of the MEDIA'S NEUTRALITY can hardly be maintained when the media transforms the "NEWS "to be what the media PRODUCES.

The media's growing MANIA (prompted by PR FLAKS OF THE MEDIA ITSELF, and PR FLAKS OF THE EDUCATIONAL CHURCH "ELITE") for POWER AND THEIR DISCRIMINATION AGAINST CHRISTIANS and TRADITIONAL CHRISTIAN ETHICS, only represents ONE portion of their current DECEPTION. Since the ideology of the media is generally to the left of centre politically, "POLITICAL ACTIVISTS" and "TRADITIONALISTS" also come in for THEIR routine share of ABUSE.

While those within the media like to PORTRAY themselves as being, 'public servants' whose only interests in life is the GOOD OF THE PUBLIC...a description nearer the TRUTH would be a people GREEDY FOR POWER; resentful of ALL those who stand in their way; and DEDICATED to their OWN philosophical point of view. WE must REALIZE that "SENSATIONALISM"; and

"DISPROPORTION", is the base from which they draw large audiences, AND THEIR OWN EARNINGS (disproportionate to their labour) would be in JEOPARDY, if CAREFUL and REASONED ANALYSIS was their approach.

Therefore, in considering the media's POWER and their routine DENiGRATION (not very good or important; is the media attitude toward Christians) OF CHRISTIANS, it is well to remember, that this part of an even WIDER problem of THEIR IRRESPONSIBILITY, (the rejection by the media at large, of moral absolutes and fixed standards) by which to judge THEIR OWN BEHAVIOUR not to mention the behaviour of others they SUPPOSEDLY are reporting on. With the CLEVER MANIPULATION of QUESTIONS, even the most "OBJECTIVE FACTS" (from opinion polls, which the television network's are so fond of), can turn out to be NOT objective AT ALL.

Consider, for instance, this question; "DO YOU OPPOSE ABORTION ON ALL GROUNDS AT ANY TIME?" Not even a majority of the PRO- LIFE MOVEMENT would answer this question with a "YES", because if the life of the mother were TRULY threatened (an instance that is VERY rare indeed), they would NOT oppose the abortion.

Therefore, a news organization COULD issue the following statement..."according to a recent poll, 88% of the public polled do not oppose abortion".

But if THIS question were asked... "DO YOU OPPOSE PERMISSIVE ABORTION -ON -DEMAND BY ANYONE, FOR ANY REASON, OF ANY AGE, WITH OR WITHOUT THE CONSENT OF PARENTS FOR TEENAGERS, AND IN MOST CASES FOR MERE REASONS OF CONVENIENCE, UP TO THE 24th WEEK OF PREGNANCY AND OFTEN BEYOND?" Then the statistics would show the public being AGAINST abortion. (The- second: question ACCURATELY reflects what abortion, in fact, has become).

It's time to shed the NAIVE idea that modern media exists only to perpetuate the free flow of information and the right of free speech. These multinational corporate news machines, along with their LIBERAL ESTABLISHMENT "ELITE" COLLABORATORS, EXIST TO PERPETUATE THEMSELVES and THEIR view of the world at all costs... (PERIOD).

As Mr. TYRMAND asks: "DOES THE MEDIA REALLY CARE ABOUT WHAT PEOPLE ARE ENTITLED TO KNOW? OR DOES IT WANT MERELY TO LET PEOPLE KNOW WHAT THE MEDIA HAVE SAID?" And remember that it was the media who said it.

How long can we Canadian Christians, afford to underwrite, with our subscription dollars and viewing, HABITS of these vast media multinational Empires? How long will we Canadian Christians tolerate the bigotry and discrimination against ourselves???

It's time for Journalism to become a Christian Mission Field in Canada... time for Canadian Christian writers to transform this MONOLITHIC SYSTEM from WITHIN, and restore TRUTH to the machinery of the press.

Time for more Canadian Christians to be in Journalism schools, (and maybe fewer in Bible Schools???) Time for those Canadian Christians in the media to STAND UP and push their OWN AGENDA WITH CONVICTION. It's time for us to OVERWHELM news organizations with CALLS, MAIL, and CANCELLED SUBSCRIPTIONS, AT EVERY FRESH MANIFESTATION OF ANTI -CHRISTIAN BIGOTRY and INTOLERANCE.

Time for Canadians to DEMAND that the CHRISTIAN TRADITIONS be presented as an ALTERNATIVE whenever MORAL ISSUES ARE RAISED. It's time for Canadian Christian money to be used to acquire news organizations, and use them to EDITORIALISE for JUSTICE and LIFE. And it is time to buy up every new technology; CABLE SYSTEMS; UHF; SATELLITE NETWORKS; INTERNET; WEB SITES; ETC., and FIGHT FOR TRUTH THROUGH ALL THE MEDIA.

It is time Canadian Christians begin to MAKE OUR STAND... While there are STILL battles that CAN be won, via the POWER and MIGHT of THE HOLY SPIRIT that WILL be with us, up to the moment Almighty God rises from His throne and says THAT'S ENOUGH, and shuts this old world down, BECAUSE THE WAYWARD BRIDE OF CHRIST WAS NOT EQUAL TO THE TASK.

GOD THE CREATOR'S REALM

God has Angels, Spirits, Saints, Followers, Instruments and Servants, i.e. SOULS. God says of Himself, "Before Me there was no other God, and there shall never be any other God. I am The Lord, and I am God".

God gives those in His Realm: Grace, Blessings, Urgings, Counsels, Discernments, Guidance and Direction.

God IS, and can be, from Eternity, Original; Loving; Forgives sins; has Compassion, Mercy, Pity, and can Relent, and Rend. God is Omniscient, Omnipresent, Omnipotent, and Omni-directional.

God can make Decisions, Decree, Commands, Judgements, and consequence cycles.
God's Love is Steel- Centered and Unyielding. He is no respecter of persons.

God Requires/Demands of those in His realm that they MUST believe all that He has said, and that they MUST Submit to Him, and Obey Him, and His Precepts, Oracles and Commandments, and

His Urgings, Counsels, Discernments, Guidance and Direction, and these are TOTALLY NON -NEGOTIABLE. It's up to us... we must make a free decision/choice to DO this, or to REJECT this. We will either reap the benefits, or suffer the consequences of our decisions/choices. The outcome of our lives is not in God's Hands, it is in OUR hands... the outcome of our lives is not a matter of 'chance', it is a matter of decisions/ choices WE make, as we go through our life.

GAL 6: 7-8: A WARNING: -*don't be deceived;* A LAW: -*God is not mocked;* A PROMISE: -*what a man sows, that he will also reap.* (sevenfold).

Before Creation, a conflict developed between God and Lucifer. Through vanity, pride and stupidity, Lucifer came to the conclusion that, since he can do anything God can do, he should be equal to God, and not subservient to God. Unfortunately, some of God's angels agreed with Lucifer, and sided with Lucifer. Lucifer decided to take by force, what he thought he was entitled to, and the war was on. Lucifer and his angels were defeated and cast/exiled out of Heaven. God created Hell to accommodate them, and cast/exiled Lucifer and his angels into hell.

The battle STILL rages to this day. The battle is for SOULS, for their respective Realms. Via God's Holiness, He will fight fair, and He does. However, Lucifer DOES NOT/CANNOT fight fair; Lucifer fights on in revolution; in arrogance, defiance, rebellion, and stupidity.

God will reward/provide Peace, Joy, Happiness, Blessings, etc to all His Angels, Spirits, Saints, Followers, Instruments and Servants; the souls that will be with God in Heaven, for Eternity...(for ever and ever; world without end, Amen). Some souls will be required to spend some time in Purgatory, to 'balance the scales'. Those are the souls that will be awarded an 'edge' or 'corner' in God's Heaven; that just made it into Heaven by the 'skin of their teeth'.

LUCIFER'S REALM

Lucifer has angels, spirits, saints, followers, instruments and servants i.e. souls. Lucifer says of himself 'I can do anything God can do', in deceit, deception, and stupidity.

Lucifer gives those in his realm: grace, blessings, urgings, counsels, discernments, guidance and direction.

Lucifer CANNOT be original; forgive sins; is not capable of love, compassion, mercy, pity; and cannot relent or rend.

Lucifer is a master at copying, duplicating, counterfeiting things of God's Realm, for his use in his realm. Lucifer is a master of deceit, deception and malicious cunning, and the father of all lies.

Lucifer has precepts, oracles and commandments within which he functions. He is also a master of sowing discord, contention, dissention and animosity; the greatest con artist / PR FLAK that ever walked the face of the earth.

For example, the main weapons (oracles) Lucifer utilizes, where realistic rebuttal is not possible, is to 'sling mud' as a good substitute for rebuttal. And Lucifer ALWAYS oppresses via discrediting and tale-bearing. Lucifer's instruments and servants are BRANDED or MARKED by God, with the characteristics of tale-bearers and impaired rationale types, for identification purposes, by HIS (GOD'S) instruments and servants.

Lucifer knows most people will believe ANYTHING that is

'whispered', Hence, Lucifer's 'whisper campaigns', to oppress via discrediting.

Lucifer knows that most people do not have the common decency/sense to discuss the 'whisper' with the person that is being 'whispered' about, personally, (the person that is being whispered about, is usually not even aware of the 'whisper', and does not know this is going on), and they simply discuss the 'whisper' with anyone that will listen, proving themselves to be the talebearers Lucifer counts on so very much.

Lucifer has no regard whatsoever for the souls in his realm. It is said that one of the greatest torments of hell will be via Lucifer and his angels and spirits, constantly reminding the souls in his realm of ALL the times they failed to heed or respond to the chances they had to become part of God's Realm, and refused or neglected to do so. And this torment will be on-going for eternity. This is the 'thanks' Lucifer will give to ALL his, the souls in hell...for ever and ever; world without end. *Barren gain,. bitter loss.*

THE MYTHS / HOOKS OF LUCIFER

PARABLE OF THE SOWER
MATT 13: 3 – 51   :3 And He spoke to them many things in parables, saying, "Behold, the sower went out to sow. :4 and as he sowed, some seeds fell by the wayside, and the birds came and ate them up. :5 And other seeds fell upon rocky ground, where they had not much earth; and they sprang up at once, because they had no depth of earth; :6 but when the sun rose they were scorched, and because they had no root they withered away. :7 And other seeds fell among thorns; and the thorns grew up and choked them. :8 And other seeds fell upon good ground, and

yielded fruit, some a hundredfold, some sixty-fold, and some thirty-fold. :9 He who has ears to hear, let him hear!"

:10 And the disciples came up and said to Him, "Why dost Thou speak to them in parables?" :11 And He answered and said, "To you it is given to know the mysteries of the Kingdom of Heaven, but to them it is not given. :12 For to him who has shall be given, and he shall have abundance; *(:12 *one Grace prepares for another; one who fails to correspond with / to Grace will lose what he has.*) but from him who does not have, even that which he has shall be taken away. :13 This is why I speak to them in parables, because seeing they do not see, and hearing they do not hear, neither do they understand. :14 In them is being fulfilled the prophecy of Isaias, who says, (*ISA 6:9; John 12:40; ACTS 28:26; ROM 11:8*) Hearing you will hear, but not understand; and seeing you will see, but not perceive. :15 For the heart of this people has been hardened, and with their ears they have been hard of hearing, and their eyes they have closed; lest at any time they see with their eyes, and hear with their ears, and understand with their mind, and be converted, and I heal them.

:16 "But blessed are your eyes, for they see; (*LUKE 10:23*) and your ears, for they hear. :17 For amen I say to you, many prophets and just men have longed to see what you see, and they have not seen it; and to hear what you hear, and they have not heard it.

:18 "Hear, therefore, the parable of the sower. (*MATT 18:23, MARK 4:13-20, LUKE 8:11-15*) :19 When anyone hears the Word of the Kingdom, but does not understand it, the wicked one comes and snatches away what has been sown in his heart. This is he who was sown by the wayside. :20 And the one sown on rocky ground, that is he who hears the Word and receives it immediately with joy; :21 yet he has no root in himself, but continues only for a time, and when trouble and persecution come because of the Word, he at once falls away. :22 And the one sown among the thorns, that is he who listens to the Word: but the care of this world and the deceitfulness of riches choke the Word, and it is made fruitless. :23 And the one sown upon good ground, that is he who hears the Word and understands it; he bears fruit and yields in one case a hundredfold, in another sixty-fold, and in another thirty-fold."

THE WEEDS

:24 Another parable (*MARK 4:26*) He set before them, saying, "The Kingdom of Heaven is like a man who sowed good seed in his field; :25 but while men were asleep, his enemy came and sowed weeds among the wheat, and went away. :26 And when the blade sprang up and brought forth fruit, the weeds appeared as well. :27 And the servants of the householder came and said to him, 'Sir, didst thou not sow good seed in thy field? How then does it have weeds?' :28 He said to them, 'An enemy has done this.' And the servants said to him, 'Wilt thou have us go and gather them up?' :29 'No,' he said, 'lest in gathering the weeds you root up the wheat along with them. :30 Let both grow together until the harvest; and at harvest time I will say to the reapers: Gather up the weeds first and bind them in bundles to burn; but gather the wheat into my barn."

THE MUSTARD SEED AND THE LEAVEN

:31 Another parable (*MARK 4:30-32; LUKE 13:18*) He set before them, saying, "The kingdom of Heaven is like a grain of mustard seed, which a man took and sowed in his field. :32 This indeed is the smallest of all the seeds; but when it grows up it is larger than any herb and becomes a tree, so that the birds of the air come and dwell in its branches."
:33 He told them another parable: (*LUKE 13:20*) "The Kingdom of Heaven is like leaven, which a woman took and buried in three measures of flour, until all of it was leavened."

:34 All these things Jesus spoke to the crowds in parables, and without parables He did not speak to them; :35 that what was spoken through the prophets might be fulfilled, (*PSALM 77:2*) *I will open my mouth in Parables, I will utter things hidden since the foundation of the world.*

EXPLANATION OF THE PARABLE OF THE WEEDS

:36 Then He left the crowds and went into the house. (*MARK 4:34*) And His disciples came to Him, saying, "Explain to us the parable of the weeds in the field." :37 So answering them He said, :He who sows the good seed is the Son of Man. :38 The field is the world; the good seed, the sons of the Kingdom; the weeds, the sons of the wicked one; :39 and the enemy who sowed them is the devil. (*REV 14:15*). But the harvest is the end of the world, and the reapers are the Angels. :40 Therefore, just as the weeds are gathered up and burnt with fire, so will it be at the end of the world. :41 The Son of Man will send forth His Angels, and they will gather out of His Kingdom all scandals and those who work iniquity, :42 and cast them into the furnace of fire, where there will be the weeping, and the gnashing of teeth. :43 Then (*WIS 3:7; DAN 12:3*) the just will shine forth like the sun in the Kingdom of their Father. He who has ears to hear, let him hear.

THE TREASURE AND THE PEARL

:44 "The Kingdom of Heaven is like a treasure hidden in a field; he who finds it hides it, and in his joy goes and sells all that he has and buys that field.

:45 Again, the Kingdom of Heaven is like a merchant in search of fine pearls. :46 When he finds a single pearl of great price, he goes and sells all that he has and buys it.

PARABLE OF THE NET

:47 "Again, the Kingdom of Heaven is like a net cast into the sea that gathered in fish of every kind. :48 When it was filled, they hauled it out, and sitting down on the beach, they gathered the good fish into the vessels, but threw away the bad. :49 So it will be at the end of the world. The Angels will go out and separate the wicked from among the just, :50 and will cast them into the furnace of fire, where there will be weeping, and the gnashing of teeth.

CONCLUSION

:51 "have you understood all these things?" They said to Him "yes."
:52 And He said to them, "So then, every Scribe instructed in the Kingdom of Heaven is like a householder who brings forth from his storeroom things new and old."

TAKE HEED OF YOUR STEPS AS TO THE PATH YOU WILL WALK. BREAK THE COMMANDMENTS AND YOU WILL PERISH; KEEP THEM AND YOU WILL LIVE.

THE LAW WAS A DISPENSATION OF TERROR THAT DROVE MEN BEFORE IT LIKE A WHIP. (MYTH; re Precepts, Oracles and Commandments; the Law repels; the Law shows the difference between God's and man's response and behaviour patterns; the Precepts, Oracles and Commandments are still as valid as LAW now, as they were then, and are TOTALLY NON-NEGOTIABLE).

THE GOSPEL DRAWS WITH BANDS OF LOVE (Gospels not didactic Books; the Gospels do NOT render the LAW null and void, except for the sacrificial Laws of Atonement for sins. The

Gospels reinforce the Precepts, Oracles and Commandments, that are STILL TOTALLY NON-NEGOTIABLE).

Jesus Christ bridges that awful chasm, and brings SAVED, BORN AGAIN Christians across it, but NOT lost sinners; Christ calls to us "COME UNTO ME". Christ will always be ahead of us, bidding us to follow Him as the soldier follows his Captain, i.e. we must SUBMIT to His AUTHORITY, and FOLLOW HIS LEADING, as HIS instruments and servants, IMITATING HIM. (MATT 11:28).

"YEA, THOU HEARDEST NOT; YEA, THOU KNEWEST NOT; YEA, FROM THAT TIME THINE EAR WAS NOT OPENED" (ISA 48:8). This accusation may be made against "believers" who are SPIRITUALLY INSENSITIVE. We KNOW we do NOT hear the GENTLE Voice of God in our hearts and in our souls, as we should. There are GENTLE urgings, counsels, and discernments of The Holy Spirit of Christ and the Holy Ghost in our hearts and our souls, that we have IGNORED or MISSED; on matters that we should have understood, and were NECESSARY for us, but we IGNORED or MISSED them.

There were whisperings and Divine Instructions and Heavenly LOVE, UNOBSERVED by our INTELLECT. We have been CARELESSLY IGNORANT. There Are CORRUPTIONS that have made headway into our lives via pagan cowardice, tolerance and compromise, UNNOTICED. Sweet affections are blighted like flowers in the cruel frost. Glimpses of Divine Fellowship would be perceived if we did not wall up the windows of our HEARTS and SOULS, and we do not know of these things.

ALL of our folly, and ignorance; our unbelieving; backsliding; cold of heart; indifference; our careless lax in Prayer and Bible Reading and Meditation; our rebellion and arrogance; our stiff necked defiance, etc was ALL SEEN, and LAMENTED by Christ as he hung on the Cross; when He was on the Cross, YOU were on His mind. And how do WE respond to Jesus Christ, KNOWING THAT ALL THIS AND MORE WAS FOREKNOWN ?... NOT VERY WELL. And to add INSULT to INJURY, we repay Him via the game of HIDE and SEEK!!! SCOURGING JESUS ANEW, over and over. And NEVER forget...our station or position in Heaven will be decided by the assessment of our works via the TRIAL BY FIRE of 1 COR 3:13-15, AND NEVER FORGET THAT.

The outcome of our life is not in **GOD'S** Hands; it is in **OUR** hands. Since we **CAN** reshape our lives, via the HELP, GRACE, BLESSINGS, POWER and MIGHT of Christ, **WE** are responsible for the shape we are in.

Conduct yourself as though you always see Me. GEN 17:1 Garment-rending and outward signs of religious emotions are easily manifested, and are frequently hypocritical. True faith is too humbling; too heart-searching; and too thorough for the tastes of carnal man. They prefer something more flimsy and worldly; where ear and eye are pleased, and self-conceit is fed; and self-righteousness is puffed up.

Apart from VITAL GODLINESS, all religion is utterly vain. Offered without a sincere heart, every form of worship is a sham and an impudent mockery.

HEART-RENDING IS FELT; IT IS A SECRET GRIEF THAT IS PERSONALLY EXPERIENCED, not in mere form. Our heart is naturally hard as marble. Let us hear the death-cries of Jesus, and our hearts will be rent.

Every wise Christian will periodically update his accounts, examine his inventory, and discover whether his Christianity is prospering or declining. He will frequently set apart time for self-examination, to discover whether 'things' are right between God and his soul. The God we serve is a great heart-searcher. PSALM

139:23. Make a diligent investigation of your spiritual condition. Grey heads may cover wicked hearts. Do not let young Christians despise the word of warning for the greenness of youth may be joined to the rottenness of hypocrisy. The enemy continues to sow the tares among the wheat. The Blood of Christ was not shed to make you a hypocrite.

IF YOU ARE NOT AS CLOSE TO GOD AS YOU ONCE WERE, MAKE NO MISTAKE ABOUT WHICH ONE OF YOU MOVED. DID GOD SLIDE AWAY FROM YOU ??? OR DID YOU SLIDE AWAY FROM GOD ???

Heart not steadfast; Spirit not faithful; Mere lip service; flattered and lied to God with the tongue. If your God is God, serve Him. If your god is Lucifer, serve him. But whatever you do, don't be a hypocrite. Declare it... Who is your God?

TO PROMOTE UNITY

A heart of mercy, kindness, humility, meekness and patience. Bear with one another, forgive one another. If you have a grievance, forgive it. Charity, the bond of perfection. Col. 3:12-14.

Love is: Patient; kind; not jealous; is not snobbish; never rude; not self-seeking; not prone to anger; does not brood over injuries; does not rejoice in what is wrong; rejoices with truth; no limit to forbearance; trust; hope; power to endure; never fails. 1 COR 13:4-8

HOW DO WE HANDLE BEING WRONGED BY ANOTHER ?

Very often, certain persons pose conclusions and/or opinions, that they have ALREADY dealt with, and are passing on THEIR ALREADY FORMED conclusions and/or opinions on the matter. If their conclusions and/or opinions are ERRONEOUS or FALSE, How do we handle it?

IF their conclusions and/or opinions ARE false or erroneous, and damaging to our reputation, WE must realize that their conclusions and/or opinions are gleaned as a result of their OWN EMPIRICAL THINKING, rather than a result of DIALECTIC THINKING, (which is the thinking process taught within the Scriptures).

Empirical thinking ALWAYS leaves the door ajar, subjecting the thinker to possible urgings, counsels and discernments from Satan's realm, via Satan's spirits, instruments, and servants. It is an oracle, within satan's realm, "WHERE REALISTIC, HONEST REBUTTAL IS NOT POSSIBLE, MUD SLINGING IS A GOOD SUBSTITUTE. OPPRESS VIA DISCREDITING.

IF empirical thinking was utilized, that very process calls into question the competence, rationale, and investigative skills utilized by the empirical thinker. "Attempted distortion is a far greater weapon than attempted destruction". EDWARD BACH, 1936.

TAKE HEED OF YOURSELF, IF THY BROTHER SIN, REBUKE HIM, AND IF HE REPENT, FORGIVE HIM. LUKE 17;3 and EZEK 3:18-21. YOU SHALL NOT BEAR HATRED FOR YOUR BROTHER IN YOUR HEART. THOUGH YOU MAY HAVE TO REPROVE YOUR FELLOW MAN, DO NOT INCUR SIN BECAUSE OF HIM. LEV 19:17. BUT IF THY BROTHER SINS AGAINST YOU, GO AND SHOW HIM HIS FAULT, BETWEEN YOU AND HIM ALONE. IF HE LISTENS TO YOU, YOU HAVE WON THY BROTHER, BUT IF HE DOES NOT LISTEN TO YOU, TAKE WITH YOU ONE OR TWO MORE SO THAT BY THE WORD OF TWO OR THREE WITNESSES, EVERY WORD MAY BE CONFIRMED. AND IF HE REFUSES TO

HEAR THEM, APPEAL TO THE CHURCH, BUT IF HE REFUSES TO HEAR EVEN THE CHURCH, LET HIM BE TO YOU AS THE HEATHEN AND THE PUBLICAN. MATT 18:15-17.

HE WHO GLOATS OVER EVIL WILL MEET WITH EVIL, AND HE THAT REPEATS AN EVIL HAS NO SENSE. NEVER REPEAT GOSSIP, AND YOU WILL NOT BE REVILED. WHEN A FOOL HEARS SOMETHING, HE IS IN LABOUR, LIKE A WOMAN GIVING BIRTH TO A CHILD. LIKE AN ARROW LODGED IN A MAN'S THIGH IS GOSSIP IN THE BREAST OF A FOOL. ADMONISH YOUR FRIEND -HE MAY NOT HAVE DONE IT; AND IF HE DID, THAT HE MAY NOT DO IT AGAIN. ADMONISH YOUR NEIGHBOUR - HE MAY NOT HAVE SAID IT; AND IF HE DID, THAT HE MAY NOT SAY IT AGAIN. ADMONISH YOUR FRIEND - OFTEN IT MAY BE SLANDER; EVERY STORY YOU MUST NOT BELIEVE. THEN, TOO, A MAN CAN SLIP AND NOT MEAN IT; WHO HAS NOT SINNED WITH HIS TONGUE? ADMONISH YOUR NEIGHBOUR BEFORE YOU BREAK WITH HIM; THUS YOU WILL FULFIL THE LAW OF THE MOST HIGH. SIR 19:5-16.

FOR WHAT WILL YOU DO LATER WHEN YOUR NEIGHBOUR PUTS YOU TO SHAME? PROV 25:8 DISCUSS YOUR CASE WITH YOUR NEIGHBOUR LEST YOU ARE REPROACHED, AND YOUR ILL REPUTE CEASE NOT.
PROV 25:9-10.
HAPPY THE MAN WHOSE MOUTH BRINGS HIM NO GRIEF; WHO IS NOT STUNG BY REMORSE FOR SIN 1 SIR 14:1 FOR IN MANY THINGS WE ALL OFFEND. IF ONE DOES NOT OFFEND IN WORDS, HE IS A PERFECT MAN, ABLE ALSO TO LEAD AROUND BY A BRIDLE THE WHOLE BODY. JAS 3: 2.

To quote from a Synthesis dated 26 AUG 1998, pages 207/208: "9. YOU SHALL NOT BEAR FALSE WITNESS AGAINST YOUR NEIGHBOUR. The last 5 Commandments express that the respect for the rights of others is implicit in true love. To break these

Commandments is to rob a man of the things most precious to him, his LIFE (YOU SHALL NOT KILL) his HOME and HONOUR (YOU SHALL NOT COMMIT ADULTERY), his PROPERTY(YOU SHALL NOT STEAL), and now, his REPUTATION (YOU SHALL NOT BEAR FALSE WITNESS AGAINST YOUR NEIGHBOUR)".

"This Commandment is not only applicable to the LAWCOURT. It DOES include PERJURY. But it also includes all FORMS OF SCANDAL, SLANDER, IDLE TALK, and TITTLETATTLE, all LIES and DELIBERATE EXAGGERATIONS or DISTORTIONS of the truth. We can bear false witness by LISTENING TO UNKIND RUMOURS, as well as by PASSING THEM ON, by MAKING JOKES AT SOMEBODY ELSE'S EXPENSE, by CREATING FALSE IMPRESSIONS, BY NOT CORRECTING UNTRUE STATEMENTS, and by SILENCE as well as by our SPEECH". (end of quote).

ANYONE claiming to be a Christian that does not follow the teachings of the Scriptures, functioning within the DIALECTIC thinking process, but rather functions within their own EMPIRICAL thinking, (with all it's connotations regarding questions, conclusions, or opinions), violates the RUDIMENTS OF THE NECESSARY DIALECTIC APPROACH and I must conclude that we are in FACT dealing with one that is not even familiar with the RUDIMENTS of the Faith, (Precepts, Oracles, and Commandments), busying themselves with questions, conclusions or opinions that are beyond their competence, usurping with ignorance and arrogance, thereby, in FACT, incurring Guilt.

IF we ARE the Imitator's of Jesus Christ that we believe ourselves to be, can we REALISTICALLY not expect to be treated, from time to time, and subjected to the SAME treatment Christ received? Of course not; it goes with the territory of God's Realm.

BACKSLIDER / INDULGING IN WILFUL SIN {KNOWINGLY}

Prov 14:14 The SCOUNDREL suffers the consequences of his ways.

Jer 2:5 &: 19 What was the fault you found in God ??? What caused you to withdraw from God ??? You went after emptiness, and became empty. Can you SEE {via reasoning} this ??? Isa 5:4 What was it God failed to do ??? Did God decree wrong results or information ???   Jer 2:13 & :19 The impenitent backslider is in fearful danger. You have done 2 evils: forsaken God, and have digged for yourself broken cisterns that hold no water. Your own wickedness will reprove you, and your apostasy will rebuke you.

Know and see {via reasoning} that it is an evil and bitter thing for you, to have left God, and that the fear of the Lord is not with you. Wis. 16:15-24 Jer 15:6 Heb 10:30-31 Rev 3:19-22 Rev 3;15-16.   1 Kings 11:19 (3)   God gets angry when we turn our MIND away from Him, even though He 'appeared' to us before. Luke 11:24-26 Our last state becomes worse than the first...going from worse to worse. Matt 15 :7-8 HYPOCRITE... honouring God with your lips, but your heart is far from Him.

Jer 8:5-6 What caused you to rebel with obstinate resistance ??? What are the deceptive idols ??? What causes you to refuse to turn back to Him ??? Seeing what is not true, you don't repent of your wickedness, saying "what have I done ?" You keep on running your course like a steed dashing into battle. Luke 21:34 & 36   Take heed of yourself, lest your heart be over-burdened with self-indulgence and drunkenness, and the cares of this life, and the day or reckoning comes upon you like a whirlwind, suddenly. (Prov 1:22-33).

Jer 3:12-14 Return to God...He will not turn His Face away

from you. But yet, acknowledge your iniquity; that you have transgressed against God; and have scattered your ways; and not listened to The Lord... return to God, and He will take you back. You will again see Him, as He says. (Mark 16:7). Hosea 11:7; 14:1-4 You have stirred up God to bitterness because you have fallen by your iniquities. Take with you words, and return to The Lord, and say to Him: take away all iniquity, and receive the good, and I will render my lips to you; and ask Him to have mercy on you.

2 Chron 7:14 What God demands in order to effect reconciliation... being converted, humble yourself. Make supplications to Him, and seek His Face. Do penance (ASCETICISM) for your most wicked ways...THEN will He hear from Heaven, and forgive your sins, and heal them. (Psalm 51: Ezek 36:25-38).

1 John 1:9 If we acknowledge our sins, He is faithful and just to forgive us our sins, and to cleanse us from all iniquity. (Psalm 103:11-18). Isa 3:13-19 God is willing to receive ALL who will come back to Him...even those who have devoured the vineyard; and the spoils of the poor are in your house; you consume the poor; grind the faces of the poor; haughty, walking with stretched neck; wanton glances of your eyes; made a noise as you walked; moving in a set pace. 2 Chron 7:14 Ezek 33:14-16 Isa 55:6-9 Mal 3:7-8.

Luke 15:11-24 Came to himself; reasoned it out. John 6 :37. Christ will not cast out ANYONE who comes to Him. Heb 5:12 After being reconciled to God, take heed that no evil spirit dwell within you; and also that an unbelieving heart, that would turn you away from God again, dwells NOT within you. Mark 14:38 Watch and pray that you may not enter into temptation... the spirit is indeed willing, but the flesh is weak.

Matt 24:10-12   Remember, we ARE in the 'last days'... false teachers will arise, and WILL lead MANY astray. MANY will fall away, betraying one another and hating one another. Because iniquity will abound, the charity (love) of' MANY will become cold.

2 Pet 2:20-22   BUT REMEMBER, if, after being reconciled to God again, escaping the defilements of the world through the knowledge of our Lord and Saviour, Jesus Christ, you are AGAIN entangled therein and overcome, your latter state will become worse for you than the former. For it were better for you NOT to have known 'the way' of justice (Luke 12:47-48), than having known 'the way', to turn back from Precepts, Oracles and Commandments delivered to you. For what the true Proverb says has happened to you.. "a dog returns to his vomit" and "a sow even after washing, wallows in the mire". (Prov 26:11 Heb 3 :12).

Luke 21:36 Watch then, (after being reconciled to God), praying at all times, that you may be accounted worthy to escape all the torments of the end of time, (and the torments of an eternity in hell), that are to be, and to stand before Jesus Christ. God's part we CANNOT do; our part God WILL NOT do.

John 3:16 God's part ; Rom 5:8 Christ's part ; John 6:37 Man's part. There must be a DECISION...there must be a RESOLVE.

SLACK ABIDING produces BACKSLIDING.

Wis 16:26 It is God's WORD (the Bible) that preserves those who believe in Him.
   IMM Book 3:30   But now, having recovered after the storm...
   Prov 23:7 We are not what we think we are, but what we think, THAT we are.

   TURN FROM YOUR BACKSLIDING

1. IF you set your heart (& spirit) aright and stretch out your hands toward Him;
2. IF you remove all iniquity from your conduct, and let not injustice dwell in your tent, surely THEN you may lift up your face in innocence; you may stand firm and unafraid. For THEN you shall forget your misery, or recall it like waters that have ebbed away.
3. THEN your life shall be brighter than the noonday; it's gloom shall become as the morning, and you shall be secure, because there IS hope; you shall look around you and lie down in safety, and you shall take your rest with none to disturb. Many shall entreat your favour, but the wicked, looking on, shall be consumed with envy. Escape shall be cut off from them, they shall wait to expire. JOB 11 : 13 –20

FAITH

VISUALIZATION OF, AND BELIEF IN, ATTAINMENT OF DESIRE.

Faith Is the head chemist of the mind. When Faith is blended with the 'vibrations' of THOUGHT IN THE HEART, the subconscious mind instantly picks up the 'vibrations', translates them into their Spiritual equivalent, and transmits it to Infinite intelligence, as in the case of Prayer.

Love and Faith are psychic; related to the Spiritual side of man. The mixing, or blending, of the three emotions of Faith, love and sex, has the effect of opening a direct line of communication between the finite, thinking mind of man, and Infinite Intelligence.

Repetition of affirmation of orders to the subconscious mind is the only KNOWN METHOD of voluntary development of the emotion of Faith.

ALL thoughts, which have been emotionalized (given feeling) and blended with Faith begins immediately to translate themselves into their physical equivalent or counter- part, via GOD'S help, grace, blessing, power and might.

Not only THOUGHT impulses which have been blended with Faith, but those which have been blended with ANY of the POSITIVE emotions, (or any of the NEGATIVE emotions), may reach and influence the subconscious mind.

Conduct yourself just as you would if you were ALREADY IN POSSESSION OF THE THING THAT YOU DESIRE, WHEN YOU CALL UPON THE SUBCONSCIOUS MIND.

Faith is the 'external elixir' that gives life, power, and action to the impulse of THOUGHT IN THE HEART.

Faith is the basis for all 'miracles' and all mysteries that cannot be analysed by the rules of science. Faith is the only known antidote for failure. Faith is the element, (the chemist) that, when blended with Prayer, gives one direct communication with God (Infinite Intelligence). Faith is the only agency through which the cosmic forces of Infinite Intelligence can be harnessed and used by man. Faith is a state on mind that may be induced by auto-suggestion. HEB 11: 1.

AUTO- SUGGESTION

USING THE THINGS THAT ARE NOT, TO BRING TO NAUGHT THE THINGS THAT ARE. 1 COR 1:28.

AUTO -SUGGESTION WORKS: it can be used for the glory and success of, man if it is used CONSTRUCTIVELY. On the other hand, if used DESTRUCTIVELY, it will destroy just as readily. If we fill our minds with DOUBT, FEAR, and UNBELIEF, auto -suggestion will take that spirit of UNBELIEF, and use it as a pattern by which the subconscious mind will translate it into it's physical equivalent.

Like a wind that carries one ship east and the other west, in the same locality, the law of AUTO -SUGGESTION will LIFT US UP or PULL US DOWN, according to the way WE set our 'sails' of THOUGHT. NO THOUGHT, whether, POSITIVE or NEGATIVE, can enter the subconscious mind without the aid of the principle of AUTO -SUGGESTION.

The subconscious mind takes ANY orders given it, in a spirit of ABSOLUTE FAITH, and ACTS upon those orders, although the 'orders' must be presented over and over again, through REPETITION, before they are interpreted by the subconscious mind. Your subconscious mind is the most FAITHFUL and LOYAL SERVANT you can possibly have in your lifetime.

Know, understand, and use, the ENERGY and EXTRA ABILITY and POWER that is ours through TRANSMUTATION OF THE SEX DRIVE.
If we will not ACCEPT the pain of SELF -DISCIPLINE, we will be GIVEN the pain of REMORSE and REGRET ... GUARANTEED.
PAINT THE PICTURE;
REHEARSE THE PART;
PLAY THE ROLE;
DO NOW WHAT YOU WOULD DO THEN.
WE ARE NOT WHAT WE THINK WE ARE, BUT WHAT WE THINK,
THAT WE ARE

REPENTANCE...FAITH...DISCIPLINE...CHRIST-LIKE... CHARITY...HOLINESS... RIGHTEOUSNESS.

AUTO- SUGGESTION ... WORD IT.

FAITH IN GOD:*BELIEVE GOD...*TRUST GOD...*LOYAL TO GOD.

I CAN DO ALL THINGS THROUGH CHRIST, WHO STRENGTHENS ME.

THANK YOU LORD JESUS; **YOU** ARE MY VICTORY.

I CAN'T LOSE... WHY??? I'LL TELL YOU WHY... BECAUSE I HAVE: GOD'S GRACE; HELP; BLESSING; POWER; AND MIGHT!

THE SAPIENTIAL LITERATURE OF PAGAN NATIONS AND RELIGIONS

Despite numerous resemblances, (usually exaggerated), to the Holy Bible of God's Realm, the sapiential literature of pagan nations and religions, is replete with vagaries, and abounds in polytheistic conceptions.

The Wisdom Books of the Sacred Scriptures of God's Realm remain profoundly Human, Universal, fundamentally Moral, and essentially Religious and Monotheistic.

Under the influence of The Holy Spirit, the Law, and the Prophets of God, the Wisdom of God is Piety and Virtue, identified with The Holy Spirit of God, intended to enlighten Mankind of God's Realm. Impiety and vice are folly in the sapiential literature of the pagan religions and nations of Lucifer's realm.

SAPIENTIAL: Literature Appearing to be wise and full of deep knowledge.

POLYTHEISTIC: Belief in the existence of more than one god.

OUR 12 APOSTLES
1. SOUL
2. HEART & SPIRIT

3. TALENTS & GIFTS
4. BRAINS & MEMORY
5. MIND, EMOTIONS, & WILL
6. EYES
7. EARS
8. MOUTH & TONGUE.
9. HANDS
10. FEET
11. TIME
12. MONEY

DUTY TO GOD

*FAITH IN GOD
*BELIEVE GOD
*TRUST GOD
*LOYAL TO GOD
LOVE GOD
FEAR GOD
TAKE REFUGE IN GOD
HOPE IN GOD
SUBMISSION TO GOD
OBEDIENCE TO GOD
WITH A GOOD, AND A GLAD HEART; WILLINGLY.

THE TATE FAMILY
DICK TATE –Want to run everything.
RO TATE -Tries to change everything
AGI T ATE -Stirs up trouble whenever possible
IRRI TATE -Always-helps AGI TATE
HESI TATE & VEGI TATE -Pours cold water on new ideas.
IMI TATE -Will mimic everyone
DEVAS TATE -Loves to be disruptive

POTEN TATE -Wants to be a big shot
FACILI TATE -COGI TATE -MEDI TATE -Always save the day and get everyone pulling together (Quoted from OUR DAILY BREAD booklet d/ 18 August 2004)

I know you believe you understand what you think I said, but I am not sure you realize that what you heard is not what I meant.

"STRONG IN FAITH" (Romans 4:20).

Remember faith is the only way you can obtain blessings. Prayer cannot draw down answers from God's throne except it be the earnest prayer of the man who believes. Faith is the angelic messenger between the soul and the Lord Jesus in glory. If faith is withdrawn, we can neither send up prayer nor receive the answers. Faith is the telegraphic wire which links earth and heaven--on which God's messages at love fly so fast that before we call, He hears us. But if that telegraphic wire of faith is snapped, how can we receive the promise? Am I in trouble? I can obtain help for trouble by faith. Am I beaten about by the enemy? My soul leans by faith on her dear refuge in God. But take faith away-in vain I call to God. There is no road between my soul and heaven. Faith links me with divinity. Faith clothes me with the power of God. Faith engages on my side the omnipotence of Jehovah. Faith insures every attribute of God in my defence. It helps me defy the hosts of hell. It makes me march triumphant over the necks of my enemies. But without faith how can I receive anything of the Lord? Let not him that wavereth expect that he will receive anything of God!" "If thou canst believe, all things are possible to him that believeth" (Mark 9:23). JAS 1:5-8 (An irrese1ute person who entertains (holds) conflicting sentiments) HEB 11:6 Without FAITH, it is IMPOSSIBLE to please God. C. H. SPURGEON.

See also DECLARARI ISBN 1-4120-8974-3 TRAFFORD PUBLISHING 06-0730 2006

RELIGIO DELENDA EST

(RELIGION MUST BE DESTROYED)

Ron Pratt

Religio Delenda Est Index

The Surrender to Secularism	135
God is Banned	138
Mysticism; Paganism; Secularism/Humanism/Nominal Pagan Christianity	139
The Bad/Good News	143/144
What can/must we do?	147

    1. Education;
    2. Media and Entertainment;
    3. Apologetics;
    4. Evangelism;
    5. Family Productivity;
    6. church Leadership;
    7. Government

Roll – Your – Own Religion	152
Spiritism	153
Shamanism	155
Animism; Mystery Religions	156
Idolatry	157
Sympathetic Magic	158
Law of Similarity	158
Hinduism	159
Syncretism	160
New Thought	161
Humanism:	163

1. Collective Humanists;
2. Individualistic Humanists;
3. Feminism;
4. Scientism Humanism

Babylon	165
Babylon Today, Babylon Yesterday	167/168
The Mighty Babylonian Empire; The Dark Side of Babylon	170
Assyria, the Armpit of the "New Age"	174
Showdown with Israel's God	177
Egyptian Religion	178
In Cannon Land (It's Not So Grand)	183
The Iniquity of the Amorites. El vs. Baal	184
Babylon Jerusalem	188
Tolerating/ compromising with the Canaanites; Judgement follows	189
Hidden Teachings of Hinduism and Buddhism; The beginning of Hindu Religion	191
Out of the Blue- Aztec Empire	208
The Dear, Sweet Mayans	214
Greece: The Beautiful Side of Evil	217
Here comes De goddess;	222

1. Cybele
2. Dionysian Bacchanalia

God's Judgement on Pagan Greece	230
Rome: Christians and Pagans take off the Gloves	231
Christ vs. Caesar	233
Paganism A.D.	241
France Goes Pagan	248

John Wycliffe; Self-Appointed English Religious reformer.	250
England Goes Christian	253
Christians make some mistakes	255
First Fruits of the "Enlightenment".	260
The First American "New Age"	262
The Depression Knocks back the "New Age".	264
Pagans are Now Accrediting the Christians	266
Epilogue	270
God's Realm Thinking; Lucifer's Realm Thinking	280
Strangers are come into theSanctuaries of the Lord's House; Polluted Scripture, Pulpit, Sanctuary and Tabernacle.	281
What does it mean to Be Saved and Born Again?	284
The A.B.C'S of Being Saved.	287
Hypothesis	292
How to Read the Scriptures.	293
Spiritual Growth	297
Let's Re-build	301
Putting first things first	307
Vocations for the Church of Jesus Christ	311

RELIGIO DELENDA EST
(RELIGION MUST BE DESTROYED)

THE SURRENDER TO SECULARISM; The cornerstone of secularism is Darwinism. The first fundamental lesson given was man's descent from the ape – DARWINISM, promoted via propagandists.

The PR FLAKS of the day utilized brutal and numbing MONOTONY, and AGGRESSIVE ANTAGONISM which was found in their 'tool box'.

Spontaneous outbursts of righteous indignation became fewer and fewer. The unwholesome universal academic mood became perplexing and challenging.

The FREE THOUGHT FEDERATION, with many affiliated Societies, developed their platform of 'NINE DEMANDS OF LIBERALISM (1848) i.e. 5 of these were:

- **All religious teaching in Public Schools must be prohibited;**
- **Use of the Bible in Public Schools must be prohibited;**
- **Theological oaths in all Governmental Departments and Courts must be prohibited;**
- **Laws toward enforcement of Christian Morality must be abrogated**
- **There must be separation of Church and Education**, headed by **BRADLAUGH** (an atheist) and **HOLYOKE** (an agnostic)…both were ANTI - RELIGIOUS PR FLACKS.

The first use of the term **'SECULARISM'** (about 1846), coincides with the endeavours of **HORACE MANN** (PR FLACK), known as "THE FATHER OF AMERICAN PUBLIC SCHOOLS".

As Secretary of the first STATE BOARD OF EDUCATION, MASSACHUSETTS, in 1837, he worked perseveringly to establish Public Schools WITHOUT RELIGIOUS INFLUENCE. Obviously, both Horace Mann and John Dewey plagiarized the teachings of the ancient pagan Greek Empire, passing them off as their OWN "wisdom".

That Horace Mann's EXTREME programme for Public Schools made RAPID and CONSIDERABLE progress may be gathered from Abraham Lincoln's PROCLAMATION (RE divorce of Education from Religion) issued in March 1863, when he said: "We have been recipients of the choicest bounties of heaven; We have been preserved, these many years, in peace and prosperity...but we have forgotten God. We have forgotten the gracious hand which preserved us in peace, and enriched and multiplied us; we have vainly imagined, in the deceitfulness of our hearts, that all these blessings were produced by some superior wisdom and virtue of our own. Intoxicated with unbroken success we have become too self - sufficient to feel the NECESSITY of Redeeming and preserving Grace; too proud to pray to the God who made us".

The American Hierarchy, in their annual statement issued 15 Nov 1952 aptly quoted Lincoln's words (above) as a description of their present (current) situation, then said: "These words of Lincoln not only recall to us our National, current traditions relative to the importance of Religion; they also remind us of the CONSTANT INCLINATION of this Country to turn away from God, and to be immersed in material pursuits. In OUR day, widespread yielding to this TEMPTATION (from whom ??? (Lucifer)), has given rise to an even GREATER danger - the way of life we call -**"SECULARISM"**.

Those who follow this way of life, DISTORT and BLOT OUT our Religious Traditions, and seek to REMOVE **all** influence of Religion from public life. Their main efforts are centered (**again**...**STILL**), on the divorce of Religion from **EDUCATION**. Their strategy seems to be: FIRST to secularize COMPLETELY, education, and THEN to claim it, a total monopoly of the Educational "ELITE"

To teach MORAL and SPIRITUAL VALUES divorced from SCRIPTURE, and based solely on SOCIAL CONVENTION, as these men **claim** to do, is NOT enough. Unless man's conscience is ENLIGHTENED by the KNOWLEDGE of PRINCIPLES that express GOD'S LAW, (**PRECEPTS, ORACLES** and **COMMANDMENTS**), there can be **NO FIRM AND LASTING MORALITY**. Without **RELIGION**, MORALITY BECOMES SIMPLY A MATTER OF INDIVIDUAL TASTE; OF PUBLIC <u>OPINION</u>; OR MAJORITY VOTE.

The moral Law must derive it's validity, and it's **binding force** from the **TRUTHS OF SCRIPTURES**. Without Religious Education, **MORAL EDUCATION IS IMPOSSIBLE**.

"To educate a man in mind, and not in morals, is to Educate a **MENACE TO SOCIETY**" Theodore Roosevelt, 11 NOV 1902.

Why this SHARP contradiction between the American tradition (the need of Religion/Scriptures in Education as expressed by Lincoln and the American Hierarchy), and **OUR** Canadian present day **ALARMING** condition of affairs (Scripture/Education) ??? The **CHIEF** factor contributing to this DEPLORABLE situation, is **UNDOUBTEDLY** the Educational Philosophy of **JOHN DEWEY** - the man who, for over 50 years, has been accepted as the **PHILOSOPHER OF AMERICAN EDUCATION**. (FOUNDER OF THE "DEWEY DECIMAL CLASSIFICATION" SYSTEM OF CLASSIFYING BOOKS). What Lucifer snared America with, spilled over into Canada.

In Dewey's teachings, man is no more than a biological organism; he has no separate soul or mind; man's natural inclination, instincts, and impulses grow and develop under controlled and directed experience. Traditional Religious (Scriptural) and cultural values, according to Dewey, **CANNOT**, therefore, be the basic material for the **SCHOOL CURRICULUM. There are no ABSOLUTES in the Dewey philosophy.** "Man **MUST** grow and develop INDIVIDUALLY and SOCIALLY, **SOLELY** by meeting or adopting himself to his present **PROBLEMS** and **ENVIRONMENT**". (John Dewey, 1888).

Dewey was **deeply** impregnated with DARWINISM. His teaching is **MONIST; (SINGLE...EMPIRICAL);**IT HAS NO PLACE FOR GOD OR FOR A SEPARATE SOUL - it is sheer, rampant **SECULARISM, and PAGANISM.**

GOD IS BANNED; Secularism/Humanism/Paganism/ Mysticism/ Witchcraft are evils that menace us from without; a deadly cancer eating at the very vitals of our National life. These corrosive influences have already made TREMENDOUS inroads into every phase of our Canadian National existence. BUSINESS AND GOVERNMENT; LABOUR AND EDUCATION; RELIGION; THE ARTS; THE SCIENCES; all these have felt their base impact. **No department of our national life is immune.**

Consciously or unconsciously, they are being preached and taught in our Secular/Humanistic Universities, and who will dare deny that these evil influences are not felt even in the SUPPOSEDLY guarded environs of our Christian institutions of higher learning. Most terrible of all, secular/humanism/paganism is APOTHEOSIZED IN THE LIVES OF OUR PEOPLE.

EVERY organ of our society, the stage; television; radio; moving pictures; the press; **ALL** CARRY THEIR 'MESSAGE' OF RAW MATERIALISM. No Spiritual values; no fixed canons of morality; what the majority wants and do, determines the acceptable **'norms'** of conduct. **DARE** to question these **'norms'**, and you are at once branded as 'OLD FASHIONED', 'STUPID/DUMB', 'FUNDAMENTALIST', 'REACTIONARY' 'A SQUARE'.

Basically, secularism/humanism are one; **both** are predicated on the same premise - **THE MATERIALISTIC/ANTI - RELIGIOUS CONCEPT OF LIFE.** They are one in their MATERIALISM; one in their PRAGMATISM; one in their ATHEISM. It is high time that our general population, **especially** our Christian population awoke to this fact, and **REALIZED** it's malevolent implications, **ACCORDING TO GOD'S NATURAL LAW,** which **WILL** (whether we like it or not; whether we believe it or not) **PREVAIL, AS IT HAS DONE SINCE THE BEGINNING OF TIME.**

If man is all animal; if there is nothing in his make-up but matter; if man's soul is not immortal; if man's only motivation is materialism, sensuality/lust, and pleasure seeking; no Eternal destiny; no absolutes (that are non-negotiable); no God; then the secularists/humanists are right, and more logical to follow. But they are **NOT** right…and they **DO** try to force us to follow THEIR false philosophies, to THEIR ultimate hideous conclusion; the **COMPLETE** degradation of the human population, as we have already seen, **in history**, when God's Natural Law is/was unleashed in consequences and vengeance. In other words, we are nourishing in our National breast, at home, the very VIPER whose head, with so much fanfare and sinister hypocrisy, we set out to crush in the four corners of the globe, i.e. pornography, abortion, child prostitution, cannibalism, sensuality/lust etc.

Politically, Canada is a member nation of the so-called Christian West, as opposed to the mystical East. Ideologically speaking, an impassable gulf lies between these two worlds. One might reasonably expect to find at least a stalemate existing between these two camps. But such IS NOT the case.

MYSTICISM; PAGANISM; SECULARISM; HUMANISM; NOMINAL PAGAN CHRISTIANITY **ruthlessly advances**, while our Nation just as **steadily** and **cravenly** gives way. Paganism, Mysticism, Atheism, secularism/humanism, lesbianism, homosexuality, idolatry, sensuality, drug/alcoholism, immaturity, impaired rationale, arrogance, rebellion, malicious cunning, gnosticism etc., are **UNRELENTING** and **UN-RELAXED** IN THEIR MILITANT ASSAULT, WITH THE ASSISTANCE OF EVIL, GRACE, and BLESSINGS, (provided by Lucifer), to his ANGELS, SPIRITS, DEMONIC SAINTS, INSTRUMENTS, and SERVANTS, **always and everywhere they OPENLY** profess and consistently practice their evil and empirical thinking. They are **RESOLUTE** in their policy of **EXPANSION,** whether by **intrigue** or **force**; dogged in their determination to **conquer our Nation and the world.**

On the other hand, the supposedly Christian West, because of the pervading and corroding secular/humanistic miasma, **compromises** on it's basic Religious principles and traditions, and makes dismal appeasements on **established policy.** Obsession with these vitiate hallowed principles and traditions, corrodes **NATIONAL PATRIOTISM.** DESPITE the brutal, murderous profligate history of their "ISMS", we **PERSIST** in doing 'business' with them; we sit at table with them and drink to their health; and when their high officials, with crime-soiled records are pleased to visit our 'territories', we spread out the plush red carpet for them. Notwithstanding the fact of history regarding their vitiates; we still **persist** in making 'agreements' with them. WHAT HAVE WE TO LEARN FROM THEM??? We stand by **silently** while every Spiritual value our forefathers fought for, and built our Nation on, are mocked and trampled into the dirt. What is our response to this ??? we condescendingly shrug our shoulders, and produce a smile that says **"o well; what the hell; let it go; nothing to get riled up about".**

Why this exasperating, shameful **inconsistency** ??? The answer is very plain. The brutal, murderous "isms" were monotonously drilled into our ears and brains via their PR FLAKS. i.e. there is no God...no soul...no after life...no virtue; there is but one meritorious attitude of mind - complete submission to their "ISMS".

In class rooms and on platforms, the SAME brutal, murderous "ISMS" are being continuously expounded before our youth. i.e. there is no God; no soul; no after life; no absolutes; no stable morality; and what the majority decrees and does, however outrageous to our Christian morality, or contradictory to the teachings of Christ or the Scriptures, **IS** TO BE THE ACCEPTED STANDARD OF MODERN MORALS AND GOOD MANNERS.

If this seems too severe stricture on our school system - listen to the words of a saintly Churchman and a great Scholar, Pope Pious XII, in an address on the "progress" and problems of the church in our Country; he declared: "We raise our voice in strong complaint, that in so many schools of your land, Christ is often despised or ignored; the explanation of the universe and mankind is forced within the narrow limits of secularism/materialism or rationalism, and new educational systems are sought after which cannot but produce a sorrowful harvest in the intellectual and moral life of the Nation". 1935.

Personally, I have come to see more and more clearly what the 'champions' of the infamy of the 'ISMS' meant when they boasted, SO OFTEN, that they had MANY friends and adherents and sympathizers in Canada; that all would go well for them (the champions) and their bedfellows. Their gross theosophies and spurious speculations have been anti-religious. This explains why, if a choice has to be made between Christ and His Church, the majority of Professors in our Provincial and secular Universities, together with a large number of our citizens would choose THEM AND THEIR 'ISMS', not Christ and His Church. This is my considered opinion on this question.

Their 'ISMS' **DOMINATE** our Provincial and National centres of learning, and from those 'Ivory Towers', their **LETHAL** FALLOUT filters into every crack and cranny of our Nation's life. This mortal VIRUS penetrates even into the mind, and destroys the Soul.

Pope Paul VI called for a crusade against modern, practical atheism. At an Audience with 224 Jesuit delegates in the spring of 1965, he made the following pronouncement: "Atheism is a fearful danger threatening all mankind. Atheism manifests itself variously under changing aspects, among which militant impiety is undoubtedly to be regarded the most terrible. For it does not limit itself to denying the existence of God in thought and mode of life, but it takes up arms against theism to uproot every Religious sentiment and value. 'Practical' atheism is professed by those who place every value in pleasure; who reject all religious worship because they regard it as superstitions; useless and tiresome to worship and to serve the Creator, and to obey His Laws. They live without faith in Christ, without hope, and without God"

Pope Paul concludes: "This is the atheism which prevails in our time- sometimes openly, sometimes hidden and disguised, most often under the guise of progress in culture, economics, and the social field".

The naked atheism that I personally heard so brutally and blasphemously proclaimed; the cruel denial of God that was forced down the throats of students, via PR FLACKS, was the supposedly "SCIENTIFIC EVIDENCE" and 'FINDINGS" of Darwin. A most basic example of atheism.

Pope Paul made it very clear that when warning against atheism, he is not referring to atheism as a mere abstraction, as some philosophical transcendental principle, but as a concrete phenomenon ever spreading in the country in which we live. Atheism permeates modern society in a thousand subtle and devious ways. It makes no difference whether the harder words are used i.e. **PAGANISM/ATHEISM**, or the EUPHORIC terms **SECULARISM /HUMANISM** be used. And since **paganism/atheism bears so many DISGUISES**, we must learn to UNMASK it, in it's various shapes and forms.

SOME of the **various shapes and forms** unmistakably are: *atheism in the Supreme Court barring God from our national education system; *atheism expresses itself in obscene literature, plays, TV shows, and advertising; *atheism powers the drive in our universities and technical institutions for the total elimination of all absolutes; *atheistic fall-out influences the thinking and attitudes of **religious** teachers, students, clergy (both secular and religious), attending notoriously godless institutes of higher learning; *atheism is effectively furthered by the deliberate caricature of Christ's Church by slick theologians and non-theologian writers who exaggerate, and hold up for ridicule the picayune foibles of Ministers/Priests, Nuns and the LAITY. The damage in this field can be immense, and include gross theosophy and spurious speculation; *atheism or dynamic materialism is the solid foundation for the unbelievable development of the Birth Control/Planned Parenthood campaign; the only parallel to the startling success of this movement, is the growth throughout the world of atheistic propaganda itself, as orchestrated by the PR FLAK.

All these things add up to MILITANT IMPIETY, which is to be deplored and warned against. We must decide what action is to be taken to meet and overcome the ever pressing menace of atheism in the 'modern' world. If God's Servants and Instruments do not do this, Almighty God will do it Himself, utilizing **HIS** way of dealing with atheistic Nations as illustrated via the history of past Nations. Here I cannot help but recall the reflections of a friend, Whittaker Chambers, when he was pondering over the amazing progress made (in less than 50 years), from total chaos to world dominance by Russian Communism, and the parallel developing palsy of the once all powerful and so-called CHRISTIAN WEST during the same brief period of time. 1967.

What our age needs is LESS MINDS and MORE MARTYRS - less useless information and more WISDOM and KNOWLEDGE BESTOWED VIA THE HOLY GHOST. (PARACLETE). Isa 8:19-20 - consulting *mediums, spirits, horoscopes, astrology, necromancers, 'new age' gurus', roll your OWN religion western paganism, teachers that say "each person must,do what is right for 'YOU'"*.

THE BAD NEWS: Our Nation at one time was a Western Christian Culture. For instance, the Canadian Government IS committed to fighting murder and rape. That helps, because any religion that did such things could be OUTLAWED on account of it's practices without ever referring to it's religious aspects. Today, the leaders of our Canadian Society PROUDLY proclaim their **commitment** to abortion, infanticide, euthanasia, sexual immorality, pornography, and the like. Therefore, it is no longer possible to count on the Christian moral consensus. If a group of people appeared in court, claiming their **right** to sacrifice living aborted fetuses as on offering to their goddess, it would **not** be possible to predict which way the court would rule. (PR FLAKS).("TOLERANCE", "COWARDICE", and "COMPROMISE" is **FORBIDDEN** by ALMIGHTY GOD).

THE GOOD NEWS: WHY should we Canadians let them make the Rules??? Canadian Christians do **NOT** have to play the game according to their **pagans'** rules. The rule that **ALL** religions, even satan worship, must be given equal treatment under the law is **not in the Bible.** The rule that we must obey Supreme Court decisions that forbid our children to pray in school is **not in the Bible.** The rule that we Christians must not impose our Christian morality on other people is **definitely not in the Bible!** The **whole point** of Civil Government is to impose morality on **unwilling people.**

WHOSE MORALITY ??? Pagans have MORALS too, **(even if they don't like to use the word)**, and THEY **do their best** to impose their morals on everyone else. The same people who are so worried about Christians imposing OUR morality on them, support compulsory attendance laws; compulsory organ donation laws, compulsory sex education, and **censorship** of Christian practice in the public arena.

What pagans **REALLY** mean by **"DON'T IMPOSE YOUR CHRISTIAN MORALITY ON US"**, is, **"let there be no limits to OUR tyranny".** If there is no absolute law of God saying, **"THOU SHALT NOT KILL"**, then rulers and their henchmen can murder all they like. If no law says **THOU SHALT NOT COMMIT ADULTERY"**, then the elite can corrupt our sons and daughters at will. If **'THOU SHALT NOT STEAL"** is no longer an unbreakable rule, then you can bet the elite, WILL take bribes, confiscate property, and use their power in every way they can to enrich themselves. THIS is EXACTLY what happened in **EVERY** Country where the rulers have cast away **GOD'S LAW**. And what happens to those who protest this **oppression ???** THEY END UP DEAD OR IN JAIL.

> "YOUR LAWS IGNORE OUR DEEPEST NEEDS
> YOUR WORDS ARE EMPTY AIR;
> YOU'VE STRIPPED AWAY OUR HERITAGE,
> YOU'VE OUTLAWED SIMPLE PRAYER;
> NOW GUN SHOTS FILL OUR CLASS ROOMS,
> AND PRECIOUS CHILDREN DIE;
> YOU SEEK FOR ANSWERS EVERYWHERE,
> AND ASK THE QUESTION WHY ?
> YOU REGULATE RESTRICTIVE LAWS,
> THROUGH LEGISLATIVE CREED, AND YET YOU FAIL TO UNDERSTAND, THAT GOD IS ALL WE NEED.

That little poem was written by DARNELL SCOTTE, 20 APRIL 1999, and expresses these thoughts to "NEW AGERS", to help them, but unfortunately, due to their impaired rationale, the "NEW AGERS" cannot begin to comprehend what Darnell is trying to help them with.

True freedom is only possible for the people when they, **AND** the rulers are **bound** by the same righteous, unchanging, absolute Laws. As long as the ruler gets to make up whatever rules **HE** wants, he CANNOT be held accountable by **ANYONE.** In Biblical terms, he has declared himself a god, just as Caesar was declared a god in ancient Rome.

Our founding fathers were keenly alive to the possibility of **DESPOTS** arising who would want to play god. That is why they made such an effort to promote **total freedom for Christianity in our Country.** In the U.S.A., in his famous FAREWELL ADDRESS, George Washington said, "Religion and morality are the two great pillars of human happiness. Nor can it be expected that national morality can prevail in exclusion of Religious principles". 1789. Freedom FOR religion; not freedom FROM religion.

There **WERE** ABSOLUTE Religious principles, namely those of traditional nondenominational Christianity which America should follow. So it was with Canada also. John Dewey, the philosopher of American Education said "surely, the freedom of religion mentioned in the American Bill of Rights means the founders intended to create a free bazaar of religions, where everything from satanism to Ba hai gets equal promotion". ***NOT A CHANCE***.

May I suggest that what the American Founding Fathers meant by "FREEDOM OF RELIGION" was "FREEDOM OF **BIBLICAL** RELIGION"…i.e. freedom **FOR** Religion; NOT freedom **FROM** Religion. i.e. CHRISTIANITY and it's associated sects. It is **obvious** they were worried that one of the sects might become an established State Religion, but they were not at all opposed to GENERALLY PROMOTING CHRISTIANITY.

As American Supreme Court Justice Joseph Story wrote: "The real object of the Founding Fathers was not to countenance, much less to advance, Mohammedism, or Judaism, or infidelity by promoting Christianity, but to exclude all rivalry among Christian sects, and to prevent any hierarchy of any national ecclesiastical establishment from receiving the exclusive patronage of the national Government" 1905.   **OBVIOUSLY**, America was intended to be a Christian nation, with it's laws based on the Bible. This would avoid the anarchy of having no settled authority on which to base the Laws. In fact, if one were to study early American law, it is **crystal clear** that the Law **WAS** based on **THE BIBLE.**

There is no such thing as a Country without a State Religion (which is **NOT** the same thing as a State Denomination). The louder a Country proclaims it's commitment to Religious neutrality, the surer you can be that you will find a system of **vigorous** indoctrination in the **UNDECLARED** Religion. Canada, America, and the other Western Nations are **INEVITABLY** going to be either

CHRISTIAN or **PAGAN. WE**, the citizens, must choose which. If we do not choose, **THE CHOICE WILL BE MADE FOR US.**

What will happen if we keep on playing by **THEIR** RULES ??? In **ALL** of **HISTORY, ALL** pagan empires have had the choice of only TWO FATES:
1. Surrender to The Lord;
2. Be used by the Lord to Judge His unfaithful People...**and then be crushed.**

If the Church does NOT stand and fight, I **CAN** tell you what will happen...**THERE WILL BE A PERIOD OF PERSECUTION... BY GOD.**

But if we stand **FIRM**, either The Lord will take us all away, and then Judge the cultures which refused to hear Him, **OR**, He **WILL** GIVE US BACK OUR COUNTRY. According to the Bible, this is a sign to non-believers; true Christians **WILL be delivered**, but **GOD** will destroy our opposition. (As long as the true Christians REMAIN faithful **AND** courageous. Phil 1:27-29).

The INGREDIENTS of Christian Victory have never changed: Boldness; Conviction of TRUTH and intolerance of error; Selflessness and service to others; Humility; Holiness; Hope for the future; Belief in a God who can do great things; Spread of the Gospel in our Nation; and not wait to be fodder for pagan fires.

WHAT CAN/MUST WE DO ???

1. EDUCATION; Once again, Education must become a Church function. **ALL** Education, from kindergarten through graduate university. We Christians cannot hope to even hold our present position, let alone advance, while we hand our children over to people imbued with pagan ideals. Our children should be either home - schooled or in private Christian schools run under Church authority, or that somehow, the children be able to get a Christian Education, **AND** act like Christians in Public Schools. Christian children in Public schools should **REFUSE** to attend classes where pagan doctrines are taught i.e. evolution; witchcraft; that ALL Religions are alike. Christian students should pray and preach exactly as if praying and preaching (witnessing) have never been banned. The Christian Public school teachers we hear about, should liberate their lights from under the bushel, and feel free to explain the Christian point of view on **ANY** subject, and to pray with and for the children, run Bible studies, and so on.

2. MEDIA AND ENTERTAINMENT: It is time for Christians to **STOP** supporting media that insults Christians and Christ while promoting paganism. How can **WE** win, or even hang in there, while we let **THEM** preach to us for hours every day, and **WE** are not available to preach to **THEM** because we are too busy listening to **THEIR** message??? i.e. TV; magazines; newspapers; movies; radio; music; and live entertainment. As for news, we have plenty of good Christian media that will be happy to supply even more, if we would just support them.

3. APOLOGETICS: It is time to **STOP** trying to prove the truth of Christianity on pagan terms, and treating pagans to a taste of the power of God. Christians should **STOP** presenting medical ethics in terms of "it really IS cheaper to save handicapped people than to kill them", and legal ethics in terms of the cost of prison construction. We **KNOW** what is RIGHT. Let's admit it is RIGHT. Let's talk about selfishness and justice, and what the Bible says about current issues. Let's STOP flinching away from the prospect of being called **UNLOVING** and **JUDGEMENTAL.** Pagans define love as totally accepting people as they are, NEVER pressuring them to change their evil ways. Pagans call us **UNLOVING**; let's NOT go along with this, and actually **BE** unloving by letting them travel, unimpeded, down the road to hell, **IF** they are ADAMANT in their decision to serve in Lucifer's realm, as instruments and servants of Lucifer.

4. EVANGELISM: Let our Canadian Priests/Ministers and Evangelists **START** believing that 5,000 really **CAN** be converted by a single sermon/homily, in a single hour. Let's **STOP** the fiddle-faddle with Church growth statistics and demographics and projecting our niddling little 2% per annum Church growth rate out into the future. When a denominational spokesman makes an outrageously faithless statement, let's call him up on the carpet.

5. FAMILY PRODUCTIVITY: Let's **STOP** treating the Christian family as some pathological growth, and start **TRAINING** it. If we could simply manage to have more than the average 1.8 children, AND RAISE THEM TO BE CHRISTIANS, We would eventually overtake the pagan element with OUR numbers. The Churches should make it **TOP PRIORITY** to train parents how to train their children, to train **THEIR** children.

6. CHURCH LEADERSHIP; The Church must **RIGOROUSLY** enforce Biblical Standards for Church Leaders, and make it a goal to train every man **NOT** disqualified because of divorce etc. to become an Elder, and his wife to be an **ELDER'S** wife. If this was done **CONSISTENTLY** for one generation, it would go far to eliminate the divorce plague in our Churches. We must not ALLOW the Clergy to POLLUTE our Sanctuaries, Pulpit, or Tabernacles. We must either CONVERT them or TURF THEM OUT.

7. GOVERNMENT: Throwing all our efforts into electing "OUR" guys is **NOT** the best way to advance our cause. Taking away the market for GOVERNMENT INTERVENTION, by **DOING** the job **OURSELVES** IS. So is standing up for what is right, even if it **DOES** CUT INTO OUR CHEQUES. We will find support in government, for our goals, if we are willing to put our money where our mouths are. Strategies for how to accomplish these goals are discussed in BILL PRIDE'S book 'FLIRTING WITH THE DEVIL' (Crossway Books 1988) and MAY PRIDE'S book 'ALL THE WAY HOME' (Crossway Books 1989). God **CAN** HELP US.

A motley collection of fishermen, tax collectors, and illiterate Galileans took over the pagan Roman Empire. A group of insignificant young men kicked off a **REVIVAL** that changed the face of England. GOD wiped out the Assyrian armies surrounding Jerusalem. All this **CAN** happen again **TODAY**. All we have to do, is to take what we learned in Church, about Missionaries converting pagan tribes, and **APPLY IT TO OUR OWN COUNTRY**. Challenge the idols. Do what you can to replace ungodly pagan laws, and social structure, with good, sound, time-tested CHRISTIAN Laws and Social Structures. And **WHATEVER** you do, **DO NOT** go around repeating the **LIE** that PAGAN BELIEFS AND PRACTICES ARE JUST AS VALID AS CHRISTIAN BELIEFS AND PRACTICES! **DON'T** MAKE A BARGAIN TO LEAVE THEM ALONE IF THEY'LL LEAVE YOU ALONE. (For one thing, **THEY** won't keep it).

We are **NOT** HERE TO HOLD PEOPLE'S HANDS UNTIL THEY ARRIVE SAFELY IN HELL, BUT TO SHOW THEM THE WAY TO HEAVEN. **THIS** is why **YOU** got SAVED; not to hold down a pew, but to **SERVE** in the Lord's Army. **GOD** HAS GIVEN US OUR WEAPONS: **PRAYER, SCRIPTURES, HOLY LIVING,** AND **BOLD PREACHING OF RIGHTEOUSNESS.**

Pagans may have PR FLAKS, MEDIA, EDUCATORS, and even many LAWMAKERS, in their pockets, but our God has **HIS** INSTRUMENTS and SERVANTS and THE WHOLE WORLD in **HIS HANDS.** They have their CONSPIRACIES, but no conspiracy can succeed against THE LORD. **WE** ARE HERE FOR A PURPOSE… **GOD'S PURPOSE.**

Those of us who have had our heads in the sand, **NOW** have a chance to taste what **CONTINUING** apathy will bring upon us. **WE** MAY BE THE VERY WEAPONS God uses to finally unite Christians of **THIS** DAY, into an army to fight **GOD'S** BATTLES. If our fear of a pagan future for Canada is enough to pry us away from our TV sets and computers, let's get serious about raising our children as CHRISTIANS. As parents **GOD** imposes on us to raise and train OUR children, how to raise and train THEIR children, in the PRECEPTS, ORACLES and COMMANDMENTS. Remember well; THE HUSBAND/FATHER IS CULPABLE, BEFORE GOD, FOR THE SPIRITUAL AND MATERIAL WELL-BEING OF HIS WIFE AND THE CHILDREN, NOT THE WIFE/MOTHER. We **WILL** have reason to look back, and Bless GOD FOR GETTING IT OUT INTO THE OPEN.

But if we refuse to come when THE LORD summons us (by name), and to fight as **HE** directs, we **CAN** look forward to sharing in the Judgment God **WILL** rain down on our pagan culture and nation. The mess we now face, is the **DIRECT RESULT OF CHRISTIAN INDIFFERENCE.** For all intentions and purposes, in keeping with God's Natural Law, our GRANDPARENTS did this to us...**NOW** it's **OUR** duty to clean up the mess for **OUR** grandchildren. We **HAVE** the "BROOM"; let's start sweeping! ISA 30:9-11.

During the Renaissance...(14th to 17th Century) THEOLOGIANS, SCHOLARS, PHILOSOPHERS and ANTIQUARIANS became interested in uncovering new proof of the glories of Greece and Rome. These so-called "SCHOLARS" were Christians interested in "SPOILING THE EGYPTIANS". In other words, they wanted to glean whatever wisdom, knowledge, and insights they could, from the "ACHIEVEMENTS" of the ancients, "WITHOUT BECOMING ENSNARED BY PAGAN PHILOSOPHY OR EVIL"

1. They opened their hearts to pagan gods and evils **THEMSELVES**;
2. Then they mourned the demise of the pagans;
3. They then **SECRETLY** decided the gods were no longer to be mocked, and were to reign BESIDE Christ, but not to REPLACE Christ.

Satan hit "PAY DIRT"; **RICH, FERTILE SOIL.** Want to know what the end result was??? Read on...

Via malicious cunning, satan led these "SCHOLAR'S" to his pagan gods, goddesses, women whose great charm and beauty induced swoon or trance, somnolent, sophisticated, arousers/inducers to adoration. Satan gave them the grace to be cunning, delusional, pseudo, fallacious, sham, vanity, false belief regarding themselves, made them schizophrenic, and gave them demiurge, hallucinations, retroversions, and they thought themselves to be "admirable". And this became the source of polluted scriptures, sanctuaries, tabernacles and pulpits. ISA 3:16 etc.

PRECEPTS, ORACLES and COMMANDMENTS are **NON-NEGOTIABLE** re TRADITIONS, PRINCIPLES, CEREMONIES,

RITUALS, and CUSTOMS. ISA 1:11-20 ISA 5:20-25 EZEK 18:25 etc. Argue with GOD??? HOW **DARE** YOU...**FORGET IT**.

The so-called "**NEW AGE**" is nothing but microwave PAGANISM. It is nothing more, or LESS, than a conglomeration of WORN-OUT pagan doctrines of **FAILED ANCIENT EMPIRES**.

We will begin with a brief recap of a few favourite "NEW AGE" beliefs...(we must be SURE to recognize them).

ROLL-YOUR-OWN RELIGION: Western paganism preaches that each person must "do what is right for HIMSELF". People tend to select bits and pieces of various practices, (i.e. crystals and witchcraft etc); then glom them together as their FANCY suits them. This is the way "POPULAR" religion, (opposed to the OFFICIAL Religion of GOD), has been practiced in ancient cultures, and the culture of OUR Nation, these days. They are NOT loyal to any one type of teaching, preaching, or practice. Most pagan practices fit into several different categories at once. For instance, much of what a shaman does falls under SPIRITISM; magic is tied closely with ANIMISM...you roll-your-own Religion.

DIVINATION; Astrology, (ASTROLABE) the teaching that the stars in the sky guide our lives, is the most popular form of DIVINATION in the West. It is the **"GATEWAY"** to paganism (pagan religion) for MANY people.

Like **ALL** other techniques for predicting the future, (Horoscope), astrology puts NATURE in control, and dispenses with the **Sovereignty of God.** DIVINATION is completely amoral. The stars **NEVER** guide us to make **RIGHTEOUS** choices, or even hint that RIGHTEOUSNESS exists. The PERVERT, REPROBATE, and the UPRIGHT all receive their readings on an **equal basis**. The BIBLE **PROHIBITS (FORBIDS)** astrology etc **ABSOLUTELY** and **COMPLETELY**. In fact, part of the reason for God's JUDGEMENT

OF BABEL was the towers built **"UNTO THE HEAVENS".** GEN 11:4.

In ancient times, the future was divined by sheep livers and chicken entrails. The BABYLONIANS devoted THOUSANDS of volumes to the "**SCIENCE**" of liver DIVINATION. To THEM, those **COPIOUS** 'observations' constituted the **PINNACLE** of "**SCIENCE**".

TEA-LEAF diviners; PALM READERS; THE "CURIOUS"; and the "SERIOUS"; mostly favour **TAROT CARDS** and I CHING in our day and age.

SPIRITISM: The "ancient" **"SCIENCES"** and **"CHANNELLING"** have taken the WESTERN world **'BY STORM'**. The DARK ROOM, TRUMPETS, FLOATING TABLES, ECTOPLASM, and "DEAD 'UNCLE HARRY'S' VOICE, have been replaced by BRIGHT LIGHTS and "VOICES" that speak in Near East accents with a dash of King James English.

Today, one of the most-used forms of **SPIRITISM**, is contact with a "**SPIRIT GUIDE**". You empty your mind and **BINGO**! Something is speaking to you, or even appearing before you. (THIS IS QUITE DIFFERENT FROM CHRISTIAN PRAYER, WHERE YOUR MIND STAYS **ACTIVE** AND **FOCUSED** ON GOD'S WORD).

Exactly **WHAT** are those "**SPIRIT GUIDES**" ??? TRUE CHRISTIANS recognize so-called "SPIRIT GUIDES" as old fashioned **DEMONS**, and the process of emptying one's mind to receive a **DEMON**; an **INVITATION** to **DEMON POSSESSION**. However, "**DEMON POSSESSION**" does not sell, so the **DEMONS** are being 'billed' as **WONDERFUL HELPERS** who will lead you to godhood, as long as you are **WILLING** to "**TOTALLY SURRENDER**" to **THEIR LEADERSHIP**.

Mystic "NEW AGERS" see their 'GUIDES' as "one of the gods; an angel; a dead person; or an ascended master like Buddha. A HUMANIST will see it as **HIMSELF** TALKING TO **HIMSELF** - a hidden part of his **OWN** mind. Under the **PRETENCE** that "SPIRIT GUIDES" are simply "**IMAGINARY FRIENDS**", PUBLIC SCHOOL TEACHERS are leading little children to invite such 'guides' INTO THEIR LIVES.

Most adult "new age" types view the 'GUIDE' as "**the god within**". For some, this allows them to skip the **gurus** and **swamis**, and go directly to the "SOURCE" (the demons), and become "**SELF-GUIDED**". One writer explains: "I KNOW THIS SOUNDS FAR-FETCHED...PART OF THE FADDISH TREND TOWARD SELF-ACTUALIZATION WORKSHOPS; PSYCHICS; CHANNELS; and SPIRIT MEDIUMS LIKE RAMTHA; SETH; (and BOAPSIE'S "HUNK-RA" in DOONESBURY). ALL THESE THINGS CAN BE EXPENSIVE AND **ADDICTIVE**. BUT THE GUIDE MEDITATION IS FREE AND DONE IN SOLITUDE, MAKING ME DEPENDENT ON NO ONE BUT MYSELF, AND SOLELY RESPONSIBLE FOR MY OWN "MOVIE", (as the jargon has it). THE PHRASE "WE CREATE OUR **OWN** REALITY "IS DEMONSTRATED BY ME, TO ME, THROUGH THIS MEDITATION"**.** MURRAY HOPE, NEW YORK 1984.

The Bible PROHIBITS seeking contact with spirits other than God's Realm - be they billed as dead people; demons; ascended masters; spirit guides; or aliens. These contacts, whether made by Ouija Boards, automatic writing; channelling; meditation; or centering; are ALL **DANGEROUS**; opening the 'door' to EVIL SPIRITS.

"NEW AGERS" fail to take into account that they have no way to check the accuracy of the spirits' claims. Generally, they ASSUME the 'spirit' is a GOOD SPIRIT. In fact, they assume ALL spirits are good. The BIBLE, on the other hand, **FLATLY** STATES THAT **ALL such contacts are EVIL.**

Over and **over**, CHANNELLED SPIRITS offer the same basic teachings. The first is "thou art god". THIS familiar LIE, dating back to the Garden of Eden, is then linked with the teaching that "ALL YOU NEED FOR SALVATION (enlightenment, or whatever), is within YOU.

Oddly enough, the ground rules then state that you have to TOTALLY surrender to the control of the spirit in order to experience this "WONDERFUL GODHOOD" and FREEDOM. All you need, to become free, is to MAKE YOURSELF THE SPIRIT'S SLAVE.

SHAMANISM: A SHAMAN is a person who serves as a spiritual leader because of his ALLEGED ABILITY to contact and control spiritual forces, often within the use of "POWER ANIMALS" or TOTEMS (i.e. your basic black cat). This is also the textbook definition of a **SORCERER**, but "SHAMAN" still sounds better than **"SORCERER"** to the man in the street.

The visual image of the SHAMAN is that of a **WITCH DOCTOR** with feathered headdress and bone ornaments. Most 'modern' SHAMANS skip the feathers.

Like the channelled entities (and, as we will see, like certain popular psychologists), shamans often refer the "seeker" to his **OWN** inner guidance as 'the way to truth'. Acting on IMPULSE in this manner, just like you did when you were a baby crying in dirty diapers, is called **"INTUITIVE" by "New Age" pagans.** They make MUCH of the difference between the "FREEDOM OF INTUITIVE LIVING, as opposed to the STRICTNESS of "living by rigid rules" (although, oddly enough, no "new ager" so far, has come out against toilet training).

The shaman himself attempts his "CURES" and other "SPIRITUAL" processes by "INTUITIVE" ceremonies and spells.

Classes are offered in shamanistic dancing and drumming; the making of "medicine" bags; peyote beading; and power animal contacts, coming SOON to a University near you.

ANIMISM: Here is the good old-fashioned all-african

paganism, with which we are so familiar. ANIMISM is the belief that SPIRITS or POWERS inhabit objects and "ANIMATES" them. **PANTHEISM,** the belief that ALL NATURE IS GOD, falls under this category, as does the belief that INDIVIDUAL SPIRIT BEINGS INHABIT THE TREES, ROCKS, WIND, ETC. A deeper look at most of these teachings reveals a belief in "MANA", a nameless, faceless power, not dissimilar to "THE FORCE" as portrayed in the "STAR WARS" series.

The use of AMULETS, TALISMANS, CRYSTALS, or SYMBOLS TO BRING POWER, LUCK, or "ENERGIES" TO BEAR, is an extension of this belief. This, of course, is UNBIBLICAL AND DENIES THE SOVEREIGNTY OF GOD. If "powers" reside in objects to be used at will by ANY individual, then God is unnecessary.

MYSTERY RELIGIONS: Mystery religions do not necessarily focus on a particular god or goddess, but they THRIVE ON CLAIMS; that they hold **"SECRET KNOWLEDGE"** that leads to GOD, HAPPINESS, NIRVANA, or WHATEVER.

Most of these **CULTS** APPEAL TO THE **"WISDOM OF THE ANCIENTS".** ROSICRUCIANS claim to possess the wisdom of Egypt and Babylon. **Mainline "New Agers" are fond of ASSERTING THEY HAVE THE GOOD WORD FROM ATLANTIS.** (A NEAT TRICK SINCE THEY HAVE NOT EVEN FOUND ATLANTIS YET). MORMANS **VIGOROUSLY** maintain that **they** and **they alone**, have the records of otherwise unknown **ancient American civilizations.**

Secret INITIATION RITES and SPECIAL KNOWLEDGE are the earmarks of these **CULTS**. Often, Christianity is accused of being just another of the **mystery religions** that sprang up around the time of Christ.

Those who SAY this, CLAIM that Baptism and Communion were the INITIATION RITES. But there is NOTHING **HIDDEN** or

SECRET about BAPTISM or COMMUNION - in fact, outsiders are **URGED** TO ATTEND CHRISTIAN WORSHIP.

The Apostle PAUL speaks ELOQUENTLY about the "MYSTERIES OF THE FAITH," but ONLY in the context of being **"revealed" mysteries. Most of this "mystery" was hidden until Christ came.** Unlike the MYSTERY CULTS, the mysteries the Apostle Paul speaks of were even hid from the Prophets who proclaimed them…hidden **FROM** the chief initiates.

The MYSTERY CULTS are designed to **EXCLUDE** PEOPLE FROM GOD, HAPPINESS, NIVARNA, or WHATEVER, **unless** they qualify in INTELLEGENCE, WISDOM, or SOME OTHER ABILITY. JESUS CHRIST was sent to **INCLUDE** PEOPLE.

IDOLATRY: When people think of PAGANISM, they usually think first of IDOLATRY. They picture wood or stone figures surrounded by dancing and bowing people; a fat smiling Buddha with clouds of incense or smoke rising before him; or the superheated arms of a brass Molech awaiting the tiny, squirming infant sacrifice.

But idolatry, by GOD'S definition, is when ANYTHING is placed ahead of GOD. For this reason Scripture condemns **COVETOUSNESS** as idolatry. **CAREER, WEALTH, CONVENIENCE, POSSESSIONS,** and **POPULARITY** can **ALL** fill the bill of IDOLATRY. The common element of them all is **SELF**. In ALL of these, **(and MANY others)**, man vaunts **HIS** WILL before **GOD'S WILL**.

The most common idol worshipped in the WEST today, lives in the **MIRROR.** Even the **ATHEIST** does his homage at the silvered glass alter. People say there is NO GOD because they think **THEY** are God. Both Scripture and experience **WILL** bear out this simple truth.

Now being layered over this **CULTURAL SELFISHNESS** is the **'THOU ART GOD'** teaching of the 'NEW AGE' PAGANS.

"TO FIND GOD" intones THOMAS E. MAILS (1988), "BE YOURSELF". Another says "I'VE FOUND HUMILITY IN ACKNOWLEDGING THE POWER I HAVE IN CREATING ALL THAT COMES TO ME. THE 'BEING' AND 'DOING' OF MY LIFE, AS WRETCHED AND WONDERFUL AS IT IS, IS THE PERFECT UNFOLDING OF ME". KAY RIES, 1988. (Lord, preserve us from such "HUMILITY").

Have you fallen down and worshipped 'NEW AGER' CHRIS PRINGER today ? He thinks you should. He says, "MY PART OF THE PLAN FOR EARTH IS BEING RESTORED, I AM THAT I AM, (through me) THE POWER OF ALL LIFE IS MANIFESTED". 1989.

TRADITIONAL **(EASTERN)** IDOLATRY **IS** being practiced in the WEST today. MANY 'NEW AGE' writers and speakers now recommend resurrecting the 'ancient' **PANTHEONS,** and **ESPECIALLY** THE WORSHIP OF THE MOTHER GODDESS. But so far, it's easier to tease people into mooning into their mirrors, than into investing in bulky statues that clutter up their busy living rooms.

SYMPATHETIC MAGIC: Often called **"EARTH MAGIC",** claims that natural laws as seen in the visible sphere affect the spiritual realm, as well. i.e. Since dirt (earth) brings about growth in seeds, then dirt may be selected for any **SPELL** or **MEDICINE BAG** related to growth. So if you want to grow tall, eat some dirt, or roll in the dirt, or rub dirt in your hair. For **REAL** power, use the dirt off a tall basketball player's sneakers. **YUM!** It is a practice associated with **SHAMANISM.**

"THE LAW OF SIMILARITY" is the basis of all **"SYMPATHETIC MAGIC"** i.e. VOODOO DOLLS etc. Actions done to an OBJECT also effects the OBJECT or ENTITY that is **LIKE IT**. The **ASSOCIATION** may only exist in the mind of the **MAGICIAN**". JAMES FAUBEL 1989.

Unhappily, the more hard-core 'NEW AGERS' have discovered that in ancient **OCCULT** THINKING, **BLOOD** is the most POWERFUL substance one can use.

"BLOOD HAS THE MOST POTENT VIBRATION OF ANY SUBSTANCE ON THE PLANET, AND IS USED IN MOST MAGIC WORK. TIBETAN LAMAS STILL USE IT TODAY. WHEN YOU RELEASE BLOOD FROM YOUR BODY, YOU GET POWER; MANY MEN WHO WERE IN VIET-NAM CAN ATTEST TO THIS "MAGICAL" POTENCY OF THE SPILLING OF "THE DARK FORCES". THE PLANET NEEDS BLOOD TO BE RELEASED, IT NEEDS IT IN SOME WAY TO FEED THE PLANET (THE GODDESS, MOTHER EARTH), AND MAINTAIN NATURAL BALANCE". EILEEN SHAVELSON. 1988.

Interesting ecology, this. Our planet wants BLOOD. It is a big planet and must have a big appetite. Releasing blood from YOUR body (we're NOT talking chicken blood here) gives POWER. Human blood = power. Mother Earth wants to eat **YOU**.

Watch out where this blood-thirsty trend leads. **IT COULD GET NASTY!**

HINDUISM: We will have more on Hinduism later, but we must mention it quickly here because the two most basic **"NEW AGE" DOCTRINES ARE REINCARNATION** (the notion that you will be REBORN into many future lives), and **KARMA**(the notion that the good and ill in your present life comes as a DIRECT result of your actions in a PREVIOUS life). These two doctrines are at the root of a whole series of **ABUSES.**

The cycle of REINCARNATION and KARMA **presupposes** a **"WORKS"** Salvation, and an **UNLIMITED NUMBER** of 'TRIES' for the goal. **Unfortunately,** the "GOAL" is not worth having, since

Hindu heaven is to **ESCAPE** THE CYCLE OF REINCARNATION AND BECOME **"GOBBLED UP"** INTO THE god **BRAHMIN**, avoiding the endless misery of suffering and dying in LIFE AFTER LIFE. Hindu's have not yet realized that REINCARNATION is NOT really a 'cute' way to avoid the Hebrew/Christian doctrine of **HELL**, it **IS** hell.

Within Hinduism, this life isn't the greatest either, since **everything** bad that happens to you is **YOUR OWN FAULT** AND DESERVES NO SYMPATHY FROM OTHERS. If you are in POVERTY; SICK; or AFFLICTED, **YOU DONE IT TO YOURSELF**. (a result of your response and behaviour patterns (good or bad) in your **PREVIOUS** life on earth. On the other hand, **if you are rich and healthy, you have no obligation to spread the "BLESSINGS" around. ANY suffering you inflict on your social inferiors is THEIR OWN FAULT for having BAD KARMA**. Such is the **compassionate** "NEW AGE" TEACHING. (hence the **CASTE** SYSTEM of India).

SYNCRETISM: The attempt to blend MANY religions into an **AMORPHOUS MASS**. It's the teaching that, since **ALL** 'roads' lead to God, you might as well try them all out.

The MYSTIC RELIGIONS; PHILOSOPHERS; GNOSTICS; AND OTHERS, **ALL** TRIED TO ABSORB Christianity into their happy little **SYNCRETISM…BUT WITHOUT SUCCESS**.

Pagans today try to imply that BIBLICAL JUDAISM and CHRISTIANITY are actually **SYNCRETISTIC RELIGIONS**. They point to the SIMILARITIES between CREATION and FLOOD LEGENDS of **BABYLON**, and the **BIBLICAL ACCOUNTS,** then IMPLY THAT THE BIBLICAL ACCOUNTS WERE BORROWED FROM THE PAGAN NATIONS…it **ACTUALLY** HAPPENED **THE OTHER WAY AROUND.** The pagan versions are DISTORTED, with their totally impossible adventures of **emotional gods** and mythical beasts, **IN CONTRAST TO THE RESTRAINED SENSIBLENESS OF THE BIBLICAL ACCOUNT.**

SYNCRETISM demands **TOLERANCE** OF DIFFERENCES in pagan teachings via the teaching that each person **HAS HIS OWN PATH**...it makes little difference since **ALL** paths lead to the same place.

Western pagans can simply select **ANYTHING** from a smorgasbord of religious ideas, and concoct their OWN private religion. They can even toss out old pieces, and add new ones with abandon, and it is viewed as part of their **OWN** EVALUATION... their **OWN** path. The only way you can come up with anything these pagans will look upon with contempt, is to CLAIM to know the "ONE AND ONLY RIGHT WAY" (It's O.K. to know the "ONE BEST WAY", as long as it's only best for YOU). Once you claim to KNOW the "**ONE RIGHT WAY", the gloves come off**; you will be LABELLED:

"UNENLIGHTENED"; (Maharishi Mahesh Yogi 1975)
"FUNDAMENTALIST FASCIST"; (Psychic Guide Sept-Nov 1986)
"A DARK POCKET OF RESISTANCE" (John Price 1984)
"AN IDOLATER" (Matthew Fox 1981)
"NEGATIVE" (Moira Timms 1980)
"INFERIOR" (Richard M. Bucke 1901)
"UNFIT" (Maharishi Mahesh Yogi 1975)
"ANTICHRIST" (John R. Price 1984)

All in the name of universal LOVE and PEACE and BROTHERHOOD, of course.

NEW THOUGHT: "NEW THOUGHT" teaches what has come to be called "THE POWER OF POSITIVE THINKING" - that man may shape his OWN reality with his THOUGHTS. This is ALSO a perfect example of how satan perverts GOD'S NATURAL LAW.

Is "NEW THOUGHT" a "NEW AGE" teaching ? NEW AGERS themselves think so. "FROM AN OCCULT POINT OF VIEW, THE POWER OF POSITIVE THINKING, WHICH UNDERLIES MANY SELF-HELP PHILOSOPHIES, IS SIMPLY **WHITE MAGIC**" (Nevill Drury 1989).

"TRADITIONAL" appearing religious figures have prepared the religious public for this OCCULT belief. Like KARMA, this belief tends to STIFLE COMPASSION. "AFTER ALL", a "NEW THINKER" will argue, "I CAN'T **REALLY** HELP HIM UNTIL HIS THINKING CHANGES".

Some 'extras' have been added to the practice, such as **USING SPEECH** to **"AFFIRM"** the truth of the SELF-CREATED; SELF-DESIRED reality. "THE LAW OF REPETITION INVOKE OFTEN! THE SUBCONSCIOUS MIND IS IMPRESSED BY REPETITION" (James E. Faubel, 1989, ("LAWS OF MAGIC").

The ALEISTER CROWLEY we are urged to follow, was a notorious SEXUAL PERVERT and WITCH OF THE EARLY TWENTIETH CENTURY. (just to give you an idea of the "ROOTS" of **"NEW" THOUGHT).**

ANOTHER way to turn your cloudy thoughts into real hard cash or health, or WHATEVER, is the technique of **VISUALIZATION**. SHAKTI GAWAIN, a PROMINENT 'New Ager', explains how it works: "WHEN WE CREATE SOMETHING, WE ALWAYS CREATE IT FIRST IN A THOUGHT FORM. THE IDEA IS LIKE A BLUEPRINT; IT CREATES AN IMAGE OF THE FORM, WHICH THEN MAGNETIZES AND GUIDES THE PHYSICAL ENERGY FLOW INTO THAT FORM, AND EVENTUALLY MANIFESTS IT ON A PHYSICAL PLANE". (Shakti Gawain's book "BASICS OF CREATIVE VISUALIZATION").

Shakti says: "THE MORE CLEARLY YOU CAN PICTURE WHAT YOU WANT, IN YOUR MIND, THE MORE POWERFUL THE FORCE TO BRING IT INTO REALITY". Supposedly, THIS is the driving force behind the "VISUALIZE WORLD PEACE" bumper stickers seen across Canada and the United States. (You will note that we do NOT yet have world peace).

1 COR 1:28 must be taken into consideration and juxtaposed within this pagan scenario.

HUMANISM: Most people have difficulty recognizing HUMANISM as a pagan practice. This is due to the MISCONCEPTION that HUMANISM is merely a FORM OF ATHEISM, with no particular teachings of it's own. In reality, HUMANISM is a sophisticated form of **IDOLATRY**.

HUMANISTS can be religious or non-religious; it amounts to the same thing in practice. In HUMANISM, man collectively OR individually, is the center of all things. The HUMANISTS get to tell the rest of us what we want, and FORCE it on us. (**ANOTHER** distortion of God's Natural Law). i.e. in a relationship with God, there is no democracy…it is an emphatic dictatorship (in a sense)…it's HIS way or the highway…PERIOD. The **PRECEPTS, ORACLES, COMMANDMENTS AND GOD'S NATURAL LAW ARE TOTALLY NON-NEGOTIABLE.** There is **NO ROOM** FOR WHEELING, DEALING, BARGAINING or TRADE-OFFS…To reiterate, they are **TOTALLY NON-NEGOTIABLE.** The non-religious humanists tell us that **"IF** God exists, He has left us to our own devices".

    1. **COLLECTIVE HUMANISTS:** Tend toward **POLITICAL** and/or **TOTALITARIANISM,** MOSTLY as MARXIST COMMUNISTS. They seek the long-range evolution and betterment of society - UNDER **THEIR** CONTROL, of course. CHRISTIAN Socialists ARE, in spirit and truth, saints, instruments and/or servants of God, indwelt by the Holy Spirit, TRULY walking the path God created them to walk for **HIM**. i.e. Jesus Christ.

"Religious Humanism considers complete realization of human personality to be the end of man's life, and seeks it's development and fulfillment in the here and now. This is the explanation of the HUMANIST'S Social passion" (The Humanist Manifesto 1, eighth affirmation).

2. **INDIVIDUALISTIC HUMANISTS:** Tend to seek **SELF-FULFILLMENT,** whether SPIRITUAL or MATERIAL. They seek the improvement of their **OWN** LIVES, and PERHAPS the lives of a few close friends. **PERSONAL FULFILLMENT**, however, can mean anything from being a RUTHLESS businessman, to a SERIAL KILLER. HUMANISM offers no particular moral concepts.

"Believing that Religion must work increasingly for joy in living, religious humanists aim to foster the CREATIVE in man, and encourage **ACHIEVEMENTS** THAT ADD TO THE SATISFACTIONS OF **LIFE**". (The Humanists Manifesto 1, Twelfth affirmation).

The above two quotes emphasize subjective things like **"REALIZATION OF THE PERSONALITY"** and **"SATISFACTIONS OF LIFE"**, leaving **EVERYONE** to define what this means **TO HIM/HER.** What if someone feels "CREATIVE" and finds "SATISFACTION" from being a BUM or a RAPIST ???

3. **FEMINISM:** Is humanism with **"WOMAN"** replacing **"MAN"** as the 'CENTRE". This form of HUMANISM holds all the same political and social goals, but emphasizes that a **MATRIARCHAL** society is more likely to achieve those IDEALS than the **PATERNALISTIC** society.

4. **SCIENTISM HUMANISM:** Humanism also includes the subheading of SCIENTISM - the INORDINATE workshop of 'science'. This is only true, however, when 'science' agrees with **IT'S PRESUPPOSITIONS.** Any AMOUNT OF EVIDENCE FOR **BIBLICAL** CREATION, FOR EXAMPLE, IS **TOTALLY IGNORED AND REJECTED.** If the FACTS do not support the hypothesis, the FACTS are set aside, allowing the hypothesis to reign supreme. (DUMB EMPIRICAL THINKING).

*"Religious Humanists regard the universe as self-existing and not created".

*"Humanism believes that man is part of nature and that he has emerged as a result of a continuous process".

*"Humanism asserts that the nature of the universe depicted by modern science makes unacceptable any supernatural or cosmic guarantees of human values".

*HUMANIST MANIFESTO, AFFIRMATIONS 1, 2, and 5.

Quite old-fashioned, these humanists quotes. They could have come straight out of ancient Greece or Rome. In brief, humanism is simply upper-class PAGANISM. If you are rich enough and/or arrogant enough, you can do whatever you want, without even consulting the gods. Morality is irrelevant - or at least subject to change without notice.

BABYLON: (ISA 13:19-22) What has ancient Babylon got to do with modern Canada, U.S.A., Australia, New Zealand, and/or European nations??? Precious little - UNLESS you read the supermarket tabloids, or the astrology (horoscopes) in your local paper; UNLESS you have seen the movie STAR WARS, or recently donated to, or attended, a secular college or university; UNLESS you are a buyer or seller of crystals and/or other semi-precious stones; UNLESS your life has been at all affected by the "modern" philosophy that ALL religions are equally valid; UNLESS a majority of your fellow citizens believe that the Government is the proper agency to solve all social problems.

MANY heads of Government, or their spouses, are in the HABIT of consulting an astrologer re their horoscopes; i.e. Mc Kenzie King; Nancy Reagan; Hillory Clinton; Jean Chretian, etc.

ASTROLOGY, a "NEW AGE" practice, if there ever was one, was invented by the ancient Babylonians, (via the grace and blessings of Lucifer). See the book "ASPECTS OF RELIGIOUS PRACTICE IN BABYLON AND ASSYRIA" WRITTEN BY BENJAMIN BLOM, 1911, (page 260). Let's start there, and see how many "NEW AGE" beliefs come straight from the ancient empire of pagan Babylon. We will see WHY **GOD** DESTROYED THIS ANCIENT (cesspool) EMPIRE.

Today's astrologers candidly admit their debt to the Babylonians. While the Greeks refined and personalized the practice, (via the same grace and blessings of Lucifer), it STARTED in Babel. So did EVERY TYPE of **DIVINATION** and **MAGICAL PREDICTION** that has been used THROUGHOUT HISTORY, from DREAM INTERPRETATIONS, through OBSERVATIONS OF OUTWARD BEHAVIOUR, and OBSERVATIONS OF INNER ENTRAILS OF BIRDS AND OTHER ANIMALS. See "FIRE FROM STRANGE ALTERS" by J.N. FRADENBURGH, 1891.

Babylonians also invented the idea of **"THE FORCE"**, a pantheistic god-energy; the WORSHIP OF SACRED ANIMALS, called **"TOTEMISM"; "WITCH DOCTORING",** now known in AVANTEGARDE "NEW AGE" circles as **"SHAMANISM", and "WORSHIP OF THE EARTH MOTHER",** which, in it's up-dated version today, can be seen in **"FEMINIST"** courses or classes on **"WOMEN'S SPIRITUALITY"** at local tax supported universities. See **"FIRE FROM STRANGE ALTERS"** pages 54, 131, and 132.

See also, the 1984 Bulletin of Washington University, St. Louis, Missouri, in which will be found listings for SEVERAL courses featuring **"THE ANCIENT GODDESS TRADITIONS"**, and their **"SIGNIFICANCE FOR WOMEN TODAY"**. Since 1984, these courses have become MORE widespread, and spawned the woman Priest/Minister movement of OUR day, as a **"NEW THINKING" APPROACH, THAT IS NOW POLLUTING SCRIPTURES, SANCTUARIES, PULPITS AND TABERNACLES.**

From **PET ROCKS** to **GOD ROCKS**, TODAY'S **"NEW AGE"** is wrapped up in a THEOLOGY of AMULETS, SYMBOLS, TALISMANS, and BODY PARTS, (the idea that such objects contain residual powers, was an **IMPORTANT** part of BABYLONIAN THINKING), <u>**DIRECT** FROM THE ANCIENT "WISDOM" AND "KNOWLEDGE" OF BABYLONIAN DAYS, BEING PASSED OFF AS "NEW AGE" AND "MODERN THINKING" OF "TODAY", JUST "RECENTLY DISCOVERED" BY INSTRUMENTS AND SERVANTS OF LUCIFER, BY THE grace and power OF LUCIFER.</u> SHEER, ABSOLUTE **PAGANISM.**

Many of these **<u>CHARMS</u>** are being revived today. Shops have sprung up nationwide; they sell small beaded leather bags designed to hold the ingredients for SPELLS of **PROTECTION, STRENGTH** or **POWER**. They also sell PRECIOUS and SEMI-PRECIOUS **STONES** and **CRYSTALS** that are **ALLEGED** to either CONTAIN or ATTRACT ENERGY.

One store flyer lists the STONES/CRYSTALS and their **MAGICAL PROPERTIES**...the flyer claims "**AMETHYST;** Reflects the amethystine love ray of the **AQUARIAN AGE.** Wearing it attunes one to love energies. Promotes development of INTUITIVE FACULTIES". In this, the shop owner was following Babylonian teaching, since the Babylonians EXTENSIVELY used stones/crystals in healing rituals, though not their chapter and verse, since the Babylonians actually used AMETHYST as a cure for DRUNKENNESS and GOUT, **NOT** as love-energy tonics. ("AMULETS" pages 53-55, MICHAEL HOWES, 1975). The main idea is that you should buy as many expensive stones/crystals as possible, and wear them all at once. This **IS** in tune with the Babylonian spirit.

The BABYLONIANS were MERCHANTS, SALESMEN, and HUSTLERS. Whereas the ASSYRIANS were NASTY WARRIORS WITH NO SENSE OF HUMOUR.The EGYPTIANS were PRAGMATIC SOPHISTICATES, the BABYLONIANS believed in getting in there and SELLING. This, too, is an important **"NEW AGE"** doctrine, as virtually NOTHING in the **"NEW AGE"** is free. You must pay the Guru, pay the channeler, pay the Swami. You pay for the MAYAN WALL CALENDAR, for the MIND BUILDING SESSIONS at the universe of the shop, for the CUTE LITTLE IMAGES OF BUDDHA and ISHSTAR. You get to keep on paying forever for all your un-enlightened behaviour, through the magic of KARMA and REINCARNATION.

BABYLON TODAY; Let's check out exactly what the Babylonians had going for them, to see **IF** their example is worth following.

Since ALL **"NEW AGE"** roads seem sooner or later to lead to Babylon, one would expect this mighty empire to be a major world force today. After all, the **"NEW AGE"** claims to be the LATEST, GREATEST SOURCE OF SPIRITUAL POWER AROUND...FAR **SUPERIOR** TO THE **"OLD, OUTDATED, PATRIARCHAL RELIGION OF CHRISTIANITY"**, for example. With all that Babylon had going for it...**mighty spells, powerful amulets, goddess worship, shamanism,** and so on...surely Babylon must be an inspiring place to visit.

NOT EXACTLY...in the words of archaeologist CHARLES SEIGNOBOS: "Near the ruins of Babylon, the only people to be seen today are a few fever-stricken wretches of Bedouin bandits from the desert, who roam the countryside looking for travelers to rob. In the swamps of the Euphrates, a few Arabs live in huts made of reeds and muck, built on low islands which they can leave only on flat-bottomed boats, along the narrow channels they made through the dense thickets of reeds. This land, now a desert, used to be one of the most fertile places on earth...for thirty centuries, this land supported one of the largest population groups in the world". (THE WORLD OF BABYLON, CHARLES SEIGNOBOS, 1975).

WHAT HAPPENED??? If all these **"NEW AGE"** practices are so mighty, how could an ENTIRE EMPIRE, **DEVOTED** TO THEM, fall so low ???

BABYLON YESTERDAY: Actually, I should have asked "How could SEVERAL empires devoted to them fall so low ??? Babylon was the site of two major empires and a number of minor ones.

During the first two thousand years of it's history, Babylon was ruled by "A SUCCESSION OF KINGS, OF WHOM WE KNOW NOTHING, NOT EVEN THEIR NAMES" (The world of Babylon, CHARLES SEIGNOBOS, 1975, page 12). **THIS IS NOT TRUE**...

The BIBLE names **NIMROD**, great-grandson of NOAH, as the founder of Babylon **AND** THE OTHER major cities in **SHINAR**, and **ALSO** the major cities of **ASSYRIA**, including NINEVEH and CALAH, both of which have been DISCOVERED and EXCAVATED. Babylon was one of "THE FIRST CENTRES OF HIS (NIMROD'S) KINGDOM", according to GEN 10:10.

NIMROD WAS THE **FIRST** DICTATOR. His kingdom did not last, but his religion did. (to the third and fourth generation scenario...(remember ???)). During this early period of **CHALDEAN** history, foreigners conquered the country twice, only to find that Babylon was the **ORIGINAL** ETHNIC and RELIGIOUS melting pot. Each time, the invaders ended up accepting the Babylonian's language, religion, and customs...in spite of the **proven fact,** that Babylonian gods and goddesses had not been able to keep **THEM** (the invaders) out in the first place. (The World of Babylon, CHARLES SEIGNOBOS, 1975).

Meanwhile, the sister city of Babylon, UR was built. Ur was important not only because it has been excavated, giving us a very good look at Chaldean life of that time, but because it was the hometown of ABRAHAM, father of the Jewish Nation, which Abraham left at the Command of God.

The inhabitants of Ur followed similar traditions of the Babylonians, including rampant IDOLATRY and SORCERY. As usual, these "magical practices" didn't help, and Ur was sacked (not for the first time) not too long after Abraham left.

The next great king of Babylon was the famous **HAMMURABI**, seventeenth century. Hammurabi's law code is still used in LIBERAL **SEMINARIES** as a textbook example of **"HOW THE ANCIENT HEBREWS STOLE THEIR RELIGIOUS IDEAS FROM THE PAGANS AROUND THEM". (???).**

Hammurabi is also known for his TEMPLE BUILDING and his MASSIVE PROGRAMME of CANAL and DIKE construction. Less well known are Hammurabi's contributions to (our) modern life...The PROFESSIONAL ARMY and the STATE BUREAUCRACY. (A HISTORY OF RELIGIOUS IDEAS, VOL 1, page 68).

Hammurabi's dynasty lasted for less than a century; northern barbarian's took over the area. (as MIRCEA ELIADE says, "THE HISTORY OF MESOPOTAMIA SEEMS TO REPEAT ITSELF; THE POLITICAL UNITY OF **SUMER** (the land of Babylon), and AKKAD (the site of Assyria) IS DESTROYED BY BARBARIANS FROM WITHOUT; IN TURN, THESE ARE OVERTHROWN BY INTERNAL REVOLTS" (A HISTORY OF RELIGIOUS IDEAS, VOL 1, page 67). The "all powerful gods" couldn't keep their own empire going.

Eventually, the king of Babylon rebelled against the Assyrians, who at that time controlled the area. SARGON, king of the Assyrians, took Babylon. Babylon rebelled AGAIN, and Sargon's son, SENNACHERIB, decided to put an end to "this nuisance, Babylon". He burned the city to the ground, including it's walls and temples, and threw the rubble in the canal that went through the city. Sennacherib's son ESARHADDON, then made the fatal mistake of rebuilding Babylon, going so far as to lay the first brick himself.

THE MIGHTY BABYLONIAN EMPIRE; We now enter the period of NEBUCHADNEZZAR, son of NABUPOLASSAR. Nebuchadnezzar was the mightiest sovereign on the face of the earth (via Lucifer's grace, blessing, power and might). He beautified Babylon and designed it's famous HANGING GARDENS. He also conquered Judah and brought it's people into captivity. Truly, THIS was the PROOF that pagan gods were MORE powerful than the God of the BIBLE, who obviously "OUT PROMISED HIMSELF; COULD NOT SEE/ FORESEE WHAT WAS ABOUT TO COME ABOUT; AND WAS **NOT** POWERFUL ENOUGH TO DO ANYTHING ABOUT IT" right ???

Nebuchadnezzar, to his **EXTREME** embarrassment, was FORCED to learn the lesson that **GOD** ruled over the kingdoms of men, **INCLUDING** pagan empires such as Babylon (and Assyria).

As Nebuchadnezzar was walking on the roof of his palace, boasting about HIS great achievements in establishing Babylon, a voice from Heaven announced that GOD was about to execute Judgement on him. Nebuchadnezzar would lose his mind, and run in the fields like a wild animal, until he acknowledged that **GOD** ruled over **ALL** kingdoms and kings. **AND SO IT HAPPENED.** Nebuchadnezzar was reduced to the state of an animal, until he learned to, in his OWN words, "EXALT AND GLORIFY THE KING OF HEAVEN, BECAUSE EVERYTHING HE DOES IS RIGHT, AND ALL HIS WAYS ARE JUST. AND THOSE WHO WALK IN PRIDE HE IS ABLE TO HUMBLE" (The whole story is found in the fourth chapter of the Book of Daniel).

Today the Jews are still here and the Babylonians are not. The Jewish Prophets had foretold that their nation would go into captivity in Babylon, as a punishment for their sins against God. The Prophets also foretold that Babylon itself, (the mightiest empire the earth had ever seen) would be destroyed BY GOD. A coalition of MEDES and PERSIANS took the city in 539 B.C. After ALEXANDER THE GREAT captured Babylon (as the Prophet Daniel had foretold he would), Babylon passed through a number of hands, and eventually FELL INTO RUIN.

According to Biblical prophecies of more than two thousand years ago, Babylon will NEVER be rebuilt and inhabited.

THE DARK SIDE OF BABYLON: Babylon is now an ancient empire. Today, it is nowhere EXCEPT in the deluge of "NEW AGE" teachings that have their roots in Babylon. The REASON for this is quite plain if you believe what the BIBLE says about Babylon. It's **RELIGION** and **CULTURE** was **ODIOUS** to God. The Babylonians worshiped everything in sight, **EXCEPT** God. They also indulged in VILE practices ...as usual, "THE FORCE" has it's "DARK SIDE"...(**POWER, HELP, GRACE AND BLESSINGS FROM LUCIFER).**

CHALDEAN **SORCERERS** developed CHARMS and a SPIRITUAL POISONER'S ART much like **VOODOO**, via Lucifer's power and might. (FIRE FROM STRANGE ALTARS, pages 46, 48, 49). **SELF-MUTILATION** was a Babylonian RELIGIOUS VIRTUE. (FIRE FROM STRANGE ALTARS, page 920). For the not-so-virtuous, PROSTITUTION was established. (HUBERT SAYCE LECTURES, 1887, pages 266 & 267, as quoted in FIRE FROM STRANGE ALTARS, pages 131 & 132). The interesting wrinkle on PROSTITUTION was that it was **COMPULSORY** FOR **EVERY** BABYLONIAN WOMAN TO BECOME A TEMPLE PROSTITUTE **AT LEAST** ONCE IN HER LIFE, PROVIDING FUNDS FOR THE CHURCH. (SEIGNOBOS, THE WORLD OF BABYLON, page 97).

GOD had instituted animal sacrifice as an atonement ritual, but **AS USUAL**, (via Lucifer, the great copy-cat and counterfeiter), those who found Almighty God "TOO STRICT" very soon were loading heavier burdens on themselves and their children. **HUMAN** sacrifice became an **IMPORTANT** FEATURE of Babylonian religion. Consider this Babylonian hymn to the god TUTU: "Thou art exalted in the heaven; in the world thou feedest on mankind; thou art princely in the earth, the flesh of their hearts thou eatest, the flesh in abundance thou eatest" (FIRE FROM STRANGE ALTARS, page 40). Those chosen for this "HONOUR" were slaves, prisoners, and children. (A. R. W. GREEN, "THE ROLE OF HUMAN SACRIFICE", page 86).

When building houses, devotees would hollow out shrines for one or several of the *igigi* (the pantheon of gods and goddesses) in a wall. To protect the shrines (and the houses), they would place an infant in an earthen jar, then seal the jar into the wall as a sacrifice to whatever **IGIGI**.

SANITIZING BABYLON: As **OUR** Canadian culture, under "NEW AGE" influence, slides closer and closer to Babylon, those gruesome (GOD FORBIDDEN) practices are being sanitized. It is now possible for a writer like **NIGEL DAVIES**, author of "HUMAN

SACRIFICE IN HISTORY AND TODAY", to write a book that has been offered through major book catalogues and bookstores, to say, "BOTH SACRIFICER AND VICTIM KNEW THAT THE ACT WAS **REQUIRED**, TO SAVE THE PEOPLE FROM CALAMITY, AND THE COSMOS FROM COLLAPSE. THEIR OBJECT WAS, THEREFORE, MORE TO **PRESERVE** THAN TO **DESTROY** LIFE". (NIGEL DAVIES, "HUMAN SACRIFICE IN HISTORY AND TODAY", 1981 page 13).

NIGEL DAVIES even goes so far as to say, "FACED WITH THE MASS BRUTALITY OF OUR CENTURY, **REAL** AS WELL AS **SIMULATED** (here he is referring to the "VIOLENCE ON TV AND IN THE MOVIES"), "ONE MAY ASK WHETHER, IN ITS PLACE, MAN MIGHT NOT DO BETTER TO REVERT TO THE RITUALIZED KILLINGS OF THE PAST. TRADITIONAL (he means "PAGAN")SOCIETY FOR BOTH MATERIAL AND SPIRITUAL NEEDS; SACRIFICE AND RELIGIOUS RITUALS WERE A **VITAL** UNITING FORCE IN THE COMMUNITY. HUMAN SACRIFICE THUS PLAYED ITS PART IN MAN'S STRIVING TO LIVE IN HARMONY WITH THE COSMOS". (NIGEL DAVIES, "HUMAN SACRIFICE IN HISTORY AND TODAY", 1981, pages 289, 290).

"HOW ODD IT IS THAT TOTAL RELIGIOUS TOLERANCE (AS PRACTICED IN BABYLON AND MANY OTHER ANCIENT EMPIRES) **ALWAYS** WENT HAND-IN-HAND WITH HUMAN TORTURE AND SACRIFICE. A SOCIETY THAT IS TOO "LOVING" TO CONDEMN ANYTHING AS EVIL, ENDS UP **SPONSORING** THE EVIL IN THE NAME OF "COSMIC HARMONY". (PAUL DE PARRIE and MARY PRIDE, "UNHOLY SACRIFICES OF THE NEW AGE", 1988).

PLAYING WITH FIRE: Many people are attracted to the "NEW AGE" by **FLASH** and **GLITZ**. It's fun to play with PRETTY CRYSTALS, and to sleep under a PYRAMID. It's exciting to chat with an ancient TIBETAN MASTER. "NEW AGE" books like "COMMUNION", read like science fiction thrillers, and there is

always the FORBIDDEN THRILL OF ALL THE EXOTIC SEXUAL PRACTICES "NEW AGERS" PROMOTE.

But WHOEVER starts out playing with CRYSTALS **WILL** end up "playing with fire". ALL those titillating "NEW" ideas ("NEW" ONLY TO THOSE WHO AREN'T ACQUAINTED WITH CLASSIS PAGANISM), have **AGONIZING** consequences.

The "NARROW MINDED, PURITANICAL, **PATRIARCHAL**" Jews went on to FLOURISH, while the "BROAD-MINDED, PLURALISTIC, SEXUALLY LIBERATED, **MATRIARCHAL**, BABYLONIANS **ARE NO MORE**. Their empire has crumbled.

In his play JULIUS CAESAR, Shakespeare made BRUTUS say "THE EVIL MEN DO LIVE ON AFTER THEM; (to the third and fourth generation), THE GOOD IS OFT INTERRED WITH THEIR BONES".

The Babylonians may have invented debased paganism, but their neighbours, the **ASSYRIANS**, turned PAGANISM into an ART form. Lucifer, via his power, might, counterfeiting, grace and blessings used those tactics to snare the Babylonians and the Assyrians, and is using those SAME TACTICS, to ensnare **OUR** generations and Canadian culture, and the pseudo Christian Church.

ASSYRIA, THE ARMPIT OF THE "NEW AGE": An ORACLE concerning NINEVEH... "Woe to the city of blood, full of lies, full of plunder!...never without victims!... "I am against you", declares The Lord Almighty...I will treat you with contempt and make you a spectacle. All who see you will flee from you and say, 'Nineveh is in ruins - who will mourn for her ?...Nothing can heal your wound; your injury is fatal. Everyone who hears the news about you claps his hands at your fall, for who has not felt your endless cruelty ?" NAHUM 1:2, 3:1, & 5-7, & :19.

If there was ever a competition for the title 'MISS ANCIENT

EVIL EMPIRE', Assyria would be the winner, hands-down. They were VILE characters. Imagine Stalin with fangs or Hitler with a rattlesnake tail, and you've just about got it. ALL that they accomplished, was a direct result of the grace, blessings, counterfeiting, power, subtleties, and might of Lucifer. This is **WHY**, SO FAR, THE "NEW AGERS" have passed **QUIETLY**, over the Assyrians' contributions to MODERN, PAGAN, "NEW AGE" consciousness.

But we CANNOT ignore Assyria as easily as all that. Assyria was a sister nation to Babylon, **BOTH** founded by the same person, and **BOTH** OFTEN RULED BY THE SAME LEADERS. In **MOST** matters, the Assyrians SIMPLY FOLLOWED BABYLONIAN CUSTOMS, which, as we have seen, are now the basis of the **CURRENT** "new age" PACKAGE.

Whereas modern "NEW AGERS" only visualize a ONE-WORLD GOVERNMENT, THE ASSYRIANS **DID** SOMETHING ABOUT IT, and for a while, did it more effectively than the Babylonians.

Briefly, their story was that "THE GODS MADE THEM DO IT". TIGLATH PILESER, the most famous Assyrian conqueror, inscribed on his capital City,"THE GOD ASHUR ORDERED ME TO BEGIN MARCHING...(CHARLES SEIGNOBOS, "THE WORLD OF BABYLON", 1975, page 23).

Today, a question nobody seems to be asking those who dabble in contacting or resurrecting ancient gods, ascended masters, and the like is '*what do you do if the god (or whatever) orders you to start committing crimes ?*'

Once people get the idea that it is their DESTINY to usher in the "NEW AGE" by force (**as opposed to the Christian way of gaining ground by PRAYER and GOOD DEEDS**), all sorts of UNPLEASANTNESS tends to develop, like, for example, in the case of Assyria.

CRUSH! KILL! DESTROY! When the Assyrians moved in, there went the neighbourhood. As a robot villain in an old episode of "LOST IN SPACE" used to chant **"CRUSH! KILL! DESTROY!** This was the Assyrian motto.

"Every spring, the king of Assyria commanded his troops

to assemble and set off on an expedition; they would invade a region and lay waste EVERYTHING IN THEIR PATH...When the battle was over, they chopped the heads off the dead, and put the prisoners in chains, often killing them too. Then they laid siege to the capitol city, looting everything within it, if they succeeded in taking the capitol...they then set fire to the whole city and withdrew with their loot and captives. The king was an ABSOLUTE MASTER who called himself "the shepherd of the people"; and in fact, his subjects **DID** OBEY HIM JUST LIKE SHEEP...the popular belief was that the god ashur made him king to command the Assyrians, and also to subdue the kings of other nations...Those who refused to declare allegiance to Assyria were treated as insurgents; if they were captured, they were flayed alive, crucified, or impaled. (SEIGNOBOS, "THE WORLD OF BABYLON, 1975, pages 42 & 43).

The Assyrians were not, in the least, ashamed of their behaviour. Consider Assyrian king ASHURNASIRPAL'S OWN account of how he treated the inhabitants of SURU in MESOPOTAMIA, who had rebelled against Assyria. As Ashurnasirpal approached, the people became afraid and BEGGED him to forgive them. "I killed every other one of them and led the survivors into captivity; I built a pyramid outside the gates of the city, flayed alive some of the ringleaders and had them stretched out on the pyramid. Others were buried alive as part of the masonry, while others were impaled along the ramparts. I had many of them flayed alive in my presence, and then lined the walls with their skins. I made crowns with their heads and wreaths with their corpses". The remnant were removed as slaves to Assyria, along with their cattle and the booty. (SEIGNOBOS, "THE WORLD OF BABYLON", pages 44 & 45).

Ashurnasirpal was so proud of his treatment of captives that he even inscribed the gory tales on his palace walls. HENRY LAYARD, the discoverer of several important Assyrian cities, found this inscription, which was first translated in 1870, on the walls of the Northwest Palace at NIMROUD, the Assyrian city of CALAH:

"Their men, young and old, I, Ashurnasirpal, took prisoner. Of some I cut off the feet and hands; of others I cut off the noses, ears, and lips; of the young men's ears I made a heap; of the old men's heads I built a tower. I exposed their heads as a trophy in front of their city. The male children and the female children I burned in the flames". (ROBERT SILVERBERG, "THE MAN WHO FOUND NINEVEH", 1964, page 145).

Yet, Assyria was fated to be humbled before the God of Israel, in spite of the Israelites' VASTLY INFERIOR MILITARY FORCE. See JONAH and NINEVEH, the Book of JONAH, CHAPTER 3.

SHOWDOWN WITH ISRAEL'S GOD: Between the Assyrian god of Ashur and the God of Israel, SENNACHERIB'S ARMY had worked its way to Jerusalem, subduing the countryside as it went. The entire country around Jerusalem was studded with the tents of the Assyrian army. Inside Jerusalem, those Jews who had managed to escape the Assyrians were huddled together like sheep...and not very many sheep. (the Assyrians came down like wolves, on the sheep fold).

The Field Commander of the Assyrian army was urging the Jews to surrender, boasting that no god had EVER delivered his/her people from the hands of the mighty Assyrians.

HEZEKIAH, King of Judea, asked God to avenge the insult done to His Name. That night the Angels of The Lord killed **one hundred and eighty five THOUSAND** Assyrian warriors. Jerusalem was besieged alright...by dead bodies. Sennacherib **hastily** withdrew to NINEVEH. There, while he was worshiping his powerful god, his own sons killed him in their temple. (2 KINGS 18:17-19).

The Assyrians' magic (and they were **FAMOUS** FOR THEIR MAGIC), didn't help them. Their gods couldn't save them. YET, magicians through the ages, up to and including the **"NEW AGE"**, have maintained a naïve trust in their power. (They actually use Assyrian words).

'SCHOLARS' today ooh and aah over Assyrian art and architecture, managing somehow to ignore its meaning. Some are even trying to rehabilitate the culture by claiming only the Assyrian kings were crazy. (They suppose then, all the soldiers who obeyed the king's orders to burn little children, and to skin children alive etc,. were **"NORMAL").** But THEIR "NEW AGE" petered out, (just as OURS will), into the desert sands of CHALDEA...gone with the wind. Assyria is gone...the vicious hordes before whom the earth once trembled, are no more. **GOD** blew them away, and His people didn't have to raise a finger. (God is no respector of persons or paganism, if necessary, He will "blow" US away also).

EGYPTIAN RELIGION: The EARTH and the SUN became the major gods of Egypt. Those were the only consistent things about their religion.

The Egyptians never developed a coherent theology. Their spiritual life was guided by a combination of old village tales and minor gods. As often as not, the stories conflicted. This resembles today's "NEW AGE" movement where REALITY is supposed to be only an illusion and ABSOLUTES disappear.

When Egypt became more politically unified, a priestly guild arose. The priest/priestesses overlaid the religious confusion with several main teachings which revolved around RA, the mostly inactive SUN god, and the story of OSIRIS, the NILE god, and his sister/wife, ISIS, the EARTH goddess. The other important doctrine was that of the elevation of the Pharaoh to the level of a god...the SON of RA. This set the doctrine of state-worship in 'concrete', in a way that had not been attempted even by the Assyrians and the Babylonians, whose kings had been merely the FAVOURITES of the gods, not their children. ("ASPECTS OF RELIGIOUS PRACTICE, pages 15 & 24).

Religion and State among the Egyptians were completely identified. God himself was the ruler, and the king was his son. ("FIRES FROM STRANGE ALTARS", page 295).

This separation between the people and the god (Pharaoh) caused difficulties for the state religion. The common folk felt little affinity with the aristocratic gods and government. It didn't take long for the priests and the priestesses to see the value of integrating popular religion and its practices into their official teachings. Soon Egypt boasted a MULTITUDE of gods and goddesses...one for every conceivable plant, animal, or insect. The divine couple of OSIRIS and ISIS formed the centerpiece. The incestuous marriage of OSIRIS to ISIS was further compounded and complicated by the introduction of OSIRIS' brother SET, and SET'S wife, NEPHITHIS.

NEPHITHIS greatly resembled her sister ISIS in character. She was also called the MOTHER GODDESS and the MISTRESS OF HEAVEN. She bewailed the murdered OSIRIS (killed by SET), and is the GUARDIAN OF THE PIOUS DEAD. NEPHITHIS becomes by OSIRIS the mother of ANUBIS, whom ISIS adopts and brings up, while, on the other hand, ISIS is sometimes designated as the wife of SET. (This ancient soap opera gives new meaning to the phrase "KEEPING IT IN THE FAMILY"). ("FIRE FROM STRANGE ALTARS", page 256).

Today, SET, the Egyptian "god of evil", has been revived as a god under the auspices of THE TEMPLE OF SET, A SATAN WORSHIPING CULT, and ISIS is the centrepiece of both TV shows and serious worship. The ROSICRUCIAN ORDER claims to trace their roots to this ancient Egyptian mystery religion. One "NEW AGE" promoter, DR. TOBY WEISS, offers to help you "EXPLORE INNER EGYPT" by a "POWER PLACES TOUR", where you "TRAVEL BACK INTO ANCIENT EGYPT TO EXPERIENCE THE gods/goddesses AND THEIR SACRED TEMPLE SITES". WEIS claims to "LEAD MANY PEOPLE INTO THEIR OWN INITIATION INTO THE INNER ESSENCE OF EGYPTIAN LIFE". ("THE NEW TIMES" VOL 4, No. 2, 1988, page 16).

The Egyptian fascination with AMULETS, CRYSTALS, and SYMBOLS, is STILL with us today via the "NEW AGE". The ANKH appears frequently today as jewelry, and is PROMINENT in "NEW AGE" LITERATURE and PARAPHERNALIA. The eye of ISIS's son HORUS (he only had one eye, SET having destroyed the other) has become another popular symbol in modern PAGANISM).

OSIRIS, however, is not terribly popular. OSIRIS was definitely the WIMP OF THE Gods. As the story goes, SET captured OSIRIS and cut OSIRIS into thirty six pieces, scattering them around the earth. ISIS (SISTER/WIFE OF OSIRIS) tracked down most of the pieces, and managed to fix OSIRIS up enough to get her (ISIS) pregnant with HORUS, but not enough so OSIRIS could move around or speak or anything like that. Like the CANNANITE god EL, this put OSIRIS conveniently out of the picture, so younger gods could take over.

Although OSIRIS and ISIS are strikingly similar to the other god/goddess combinations in other cultures, the Egyptians took the position that the sexual rites, so common in BAAL/ASHTEROTH worship, were reserved for the INITIATES INTO THE PRIESTHOOD.

So the people watched as the seal on the door leading into the holy of holies was broken. The people gazed in wonder while the awesome priests/priestesses and 'initiates' entered the sanctuary to pay homage to the god of the temple. As the doors swung shut behind the privileged few, the masses (congregation) turned and left, each carrying his/her own thoughts as to what was going on behind the closed doors. Gradually, the sexual aspect of the great god persuaded the people to include the PHALUS (image of the male penis; a phallic symbol) in their public ceremonies, and to emphasize the symbol ever more frequently in their festivals.

OSIRIS/ISIS worship eventually degenerated into the PAGAN ORGIES seen in other lands, probably driven by the people's jealousy over the libertine indulgences of the priests/priestesses. It was not enough for them any longer, to have their popular religion recognized; they wanted to PARTICIPATE in the "MYSTERIES". (MARCUS BACH,"STRANGE SECTS AND CURIOUS CULTS", pages 28 &29).

MARCUS BACH points out: "The first ISIS was the 'VEILED ONE'; the concealer of hidden truth. ISIS's naked form was draped with scarlet cloth. Her right breast was a cluster of purple grapes, a hint of the lust of man's eternal passion; her left breast was a sheaf of wheat, symbolizing that in the grain is hidden the sperm of life. The priests/priestesses said all this was a high and noble meaning, but the disenfranchised multitudes made ISIS a COURTESAN (a prostitute with a courtly, wealthy, or upper-class clientele).

OSIRIS became a confused and divided figure. Sex was his emphasis and sexual orgies were introduced until OSIRIS was once more dismembered, not by cruel SET (as in the myth), but by the priests/priestesses and the people.

Disenchanted, the people turned to anything or anyone who would bring them good fortune, whether it was an ANKH (a cross having a loop for its upper vertical arm; an emblem of life in ancient Egypt); an APIS (a sacred bull worshiped by the ancient Egyptians); or an ordinary animal. The priesthood, as well, began to doubt the heretofore unquestioned power of their gods. The man in the field realized that his grain grew just as well without the corn god's aid; the masses, convinced that OSIRISM was but an excuse for LICENTIOUSNESS (disregarding sexual restraint), turned their rituals into unabashed sexual orgies. The priest/priestesses, degraded by rumours that they, too, held indecent sexual ceremonies in secret chambers of the temples, found themselves shorn of any holy illusion, so far as their once awed worshipers were concerned. (MARCUS BACH, "STRANGE SECTS AND CURIOUS CULTS". Pages 30, 31, 33, & 34).

Pharaoh AKH-EN-ATON tried to reform matters by elevating his personal SUN cult to a new state religion. Some have speculated that this was a form of primitive MONOTHEISM (doctrine that there is only ONE God), similar to (and perhaps influenced by) Jewish Monotheism (PLAGERIZED ???). But it was also like a return to Babylonian PANTHEISM (pantheon of gods). In any case, Egypt plunged back into LICENTIOUSNESS, LEADING TO DEGENERACY.

This pantheon told on Egyptian morality. The ethical system was practically destroyed...If everything be an emanation from god, and hence part of god, then sin is impossible. This was a hopeless fall, and resulted in those features so disgusting to Jews, Greeks, and Christians. (J. N. FRADENBURGH, "FIRE FROM STRANGE ALTARS", 1891, page 288).

Egypt, once the mightiest nation on earth, by the time of the fall of Jerusalem to the Babylonians, was reduced to the state of a "REED WHICH PIERCES A MAN'S HAND...IF HE LEANS ON IT" (2 KINGS 18:21). Egypt would enjoy a brief renaissance under CLEOPATRA, thanks to her intrigues with Roman leaders, but was doomed thenceforth to dwindle to its present status of a third-rate world power, with the native Egyptians ruled by the Arabs. OSIRIS was finally exported to Greece as DIONYSUS, and to Rome as BACCHUS...two hedonistic (pleasure and happiness is the SOLE or CHIEF good in life) gods who greatly aided the destruction of their various cultures. In Egypt, native Egyptian religion itself has been wholly replaced by COPTIC (Afro - Asiatic) CHRISTIANITY and ISLAM.

The pyramids sit crumbling in the desert. Their treasures have been extracted and carried around the world for the amusement of museum crowds. The native Egyptians are ruled by Arabs whose religion has nothing but contempt for the gods of Egypt. Still, the Egyptians "WORDS OF POWER", their "BOOK OF THE DEAD", and even their gods are being REVIVED, as the "LATEST and GREATEST SPIRITUAL FORCES". It is beginning to look like the "NEW AGE" has an obsession with FAILURE. (MURRAY HOPE, "PRACTICAL EGYPTIAN MAGIC", 1984, page 32).

IN CANNON LAND: (It's not so grand)... "THEN THE LORD SAID (to Moses) "I AM MAKING A COVENANT WITH YOU. BEFORE ALL YOUR PEOPLE I WILL DO WONDERS NEVER BEFORE DONE IN ANY NATION IN ALL THE WORLD. THE PEOPLE YOU LIVE AMONG WILL SEE HOW AWESOME IS THE WORK THAT I, THE LORD, WILL DO FOR YOU. OBEY WHAT I COMMAND YOU TODAY. I WILL DRIVE OUT BEFORE YOU THE AMORITES, CANAANITES, HITTITITES, PERIZZITES, HIVITES, AND JEBUSITES. BE CAREFULL NOT TO MAKE A TREATY WITH THOSE WHO LIVE IN THE LAND WHERE YOU ARE GOING, OR THEY WILL BE A SNARE AMONG YOU. BREAK DOWN THEIR ALTARS, SMASH THEIR SACRED STONES AND CUT DOWN THEIR ASHERAH POLES. DO NOT WORSHIP ANY OTHER GOD, FOR THE LORD, WHOSE NAME IS JEALOUS, IS A JEALOUS GOD". EXODUS 34:10-14.

For miles the tents spread over the desert. People milled about them; warriors trying on their armour; women chasing small children; girls carrying water to the flocks. Even from a distance the people radiated strength, health, and youth. Not an old man or woman was to be seen...every one of that generation, EXCEPT for JOSHUA and CALEB had perished in the wilderness. (after wandering fourty years with Moses, (in the desert), until they all died off, their just recompense from God).

BALAK's spies watched them (the Israelites), TREMBLING, and then scrambled back to tell their master, king of MOAB, the dreadful news..."THE ISRAELITES HAVE COME!"

Before the next ten years were over, EVERY PAGAN TRIBE IN CANAAN felt the heavy hand of God's people. Yet those Canaanite tribes had cities "FORTIFIED UP TO HEAVEN", and manned by STRONG pagan armies. Some of the people who lived there were GIANTS. The land was full of WITCHES, SORCERERS, and WORSHIPERS of supposedly "POWERFUL gods". 'Mother' nature was courted and appeased with innocent blood. The Canaanites had CRYSTALS, AMULETS, CHARMS, SPELLS, and IDOLS to fall back on, and were as sexually liberated as the writers of HUSTLER magazine could wish.

SO, HOW DID THE ISRAELITES, WHO LACKED ALL THOSE "NEW AGE" ADVANTAGES, CONQUER THE LAND ???

The answer of HOW the Israelites conquered Canaan, is the same reason WHY the Israelites conquered Canaan.

THE INIQUITY OF THE AMORITES: As the BIBLE so eloquently puts it, the iniquity of the AMORITES (the chief tribe of Canaan) was FULL. It had not been FULL in the time of ABRAHAM, and therefore God had refused to give ABRAHAM the land at that time. (GEN 15:16). But now the Canaanites had rotted. They were not only SINNING, but had **GLORIFIED** and **INSTITUTIONALIZED** their SINS. Even tiny children and animals were used for their LUSTS. They had become as "MODERN" as God was going to let them.

People today like to complain that the OLD TESTAMENT is "**UNLOVING** and **HARSH**" because of COMMANDING the Israelites to destroy the CANAANITES (among other tribes). Such people ought to watch some of the older movies and the present day movies and TV shows, ESPECIALLY the children's shows. Such evils cry ALOUD to be DESTROYED.

If you would like to try to understand WHY the Israelites were RIGHTEOUS back then in destroying the Canaanites, instead of imagining DEVOUT, NATURE-WORSHIPING pagans, with flowers in their hair, REALIZE we're talking about ENTIRE TRIBES of CHILD MOLESTERS, CANNIBALS, and people who DELIGHTED in watching helpless human beings SUFFER, via the grace, blessings, help, power and might of SATAN, whom they CHOSE to FOLLOW and SERVE, as his (satan's) servants and instruments.

Only under the influence of psychology/psychiatry, which has been the back door for introducing rampant paganism to the west, (via satan's angels, saints, spirits, instruments and servants i.e. "PRINCIPALITIES", (remember, psychology/psychiatry is NOT a 'SCIENCE', it IS a **PAGAN RELIGION**)), the concept of the DEATH PENALTY has been replaced by the concept of "REHABILITATING" such criminals, and letting them loose to commit their VILE crimes AGAIN and AGAIN. DEUT 7: 1 - 6 and DEUT 21:18 - 21.   We ARE closer to Canaan Land than we think.

EL vs BAAL; The battle of the gods RAGED in Canaan. BAAL and EL, via their followers (in satan's realm), vied for the worship of the people.

EL was a kind, generous god...the last remnant of the Canaanites' memory of the God of NOAH. Over the years, that memory had slipped into **pagan distortion**, and EL acquired a wife and a pantheon of lesser gods, to alternately HELP then HARASS.

EL was called "creator of heaven and earth", and yet, during the Israelites' stay in EGYPT, it seems that the younger, more virile BAAL stole the hearts of the CANAANITE people. BAAL also stole the heart of EL's wife, ASHTEROTH; finally, she dumped EL for BAAL. MARCUS BACH describes BAAL as "the god of sun and sex" ("STRANGE SECTS AND CURIOUS CULTS", page 12).

Throughout the SHRINES and/or GROVES erected to BAAL, (the sun/sex god), and ASHTEROTH, (the earth goddess, and BAAL'S mother/wife), stood obelisks of obvious PHALLIC character. The tribes of Canaan were COMPLETELY, **100%,** OBSESSED with every kind of DEVIANT SEX, from TEMPLE PROSTITUTION of **both** GIRLS and BOYS, to INCEST and BESTIALITY. 'Modern' sociologists of religion like to refer to the "DEVOUT" nature of these 'beliefs'. They mean that the Canaanites SINCERELY believed that those practices were approved by the gods. THAT, of course, justifies the Nazi death camps and every other horror of history, since the more evil the deed, the more likely the doer is to justify it. (MARCUS BACH, "STRANGE SECTS AND CURIOUS CULTS", pages 13 & 14.

Today, both PLAYBOY types and MODERN feminist goddess worshipers would love to reintroduce BAAL-like thinking.

One such female, BARBARA G. WALKER, author of a book inappropriately titled "THE SKEPTICAL FEMINIST", recommends MANDITORY sexual initiation of young boys and girls by older men and women, in specially designated "LOVE TEMPLES". In her thinking, adding religious overtones would justify this CHILD MOLESTING. At least she is honest enough to point out that such "MODERN" sexual "LIBERATION" really goes back to the ancient goddess worship of thousands of years ago. "SUCH OFFICIAL SEX EDUCATION OCCURS IN A RELIGIOUS OR SEMI-RELIGIOUS SETTING, BECAUSE SEX IS VIEWED AS A SOLEMN SACRAMENT...LOVE TEMPLES ARE FOUNDED ON MUCH THE SAME RATIONALE AS WERE ANCIENT SHRINES OF THE "GREAT MOTHER" (ASHTEROTH (ISHTAR/ASHTER)). (BARBARA G. WALKER, "THE SKEPTICAL FEMINIST - DISCOVERING THE VIRGIN MOTHER" 1987, pages 268 - 270).

The goddess rites of ASHTEROTH were INSEPARABLE from those of BAAL. The goddess had a bad case of SEXUAL IDENTITY CRISIS. Some of the 'priests' appeared in women's garb during the temple services. (TRANSVESTITES). The MOABITES made ASHTEROTH a divinity "A FEMALE AT SUNSET AND A MALE AT SUNRISE (lesbian-'butch').("FIRES FROM STRANGE ALTARS", Pages 130 & 131).

Their ceremonies included GLUTTONY, DRUNKENNESS, FORNICATION, ADULTERY, PROSTITUTION, CHILD MOLESTING (BOYS AND GIRLS), HOMOSEXUALITY, LESBIANISM, INCEST, and BESTIALITY...and EVERYONE participated. BAAL was "THE LORD OF LICENTIOUSNESS". BAAL IS PORTRAYED IN UGARITIC MYTHOLOGY AS IMPREGNATING A HEIFER TO SIRE THE YOUNG BULL GOD. See LEV 18: 22 - 27.   ("FIRES FROM STRANGE ALTERS", pages 130 - 131). The CANAANITE population practiced those "RITES", that the JEWS rejected as ABOMINATIONS, according to GOD'S NATURAL LAW. (PRECEPTS, ORACLES and COMMANDMENTS).

If the land was dry, or if in a drought, the priest/priestess enacted other MIMETIC RITES; simulating rain by slashing bodies with knives until the blood gushed out. This was to show BAAL how he should pour rain upon the fields, while they chanted:
"where is the victor BAAL,
where is the prince lord of the earth ?
The virgin mother earth is awaiting him!".
("STRANGE SECTS AND CURIOUS CULTS", pages 15 - 16).
So too, sexual confusion is PRIZED in today's 'NEW AGE' utopia. (BARBARA G. WALKER, "THE SKEPTICAL FEMINIST", 1987 page 270.

ASHTORAH/ANATH was CANNIBALISTIC and VICIOUS. BAAL was Canaan's most popular export. BAAL's 'SEXUAL REVELATION/REVOLUTION' was as immensely widespread THEN as it is NOW. As MARCUS BACH noted…"the popularity of the god of SUN and SEX *attracted* other SEMETIC (Jewish) tribes FROM FAR BEYOND IT'S (Canaan's) BORDERS".

Even the ancient ORGIASTIC rites were not enough to satisfy BAAL. As usual, when men and women turn sex into an EXCUSE for ORGIES, the **PRODUCTS** OF THAT SEX, (NAMELY THEIR *OWN* CHILDREN), BEGAN TO BE SACRIFICED TO THE god OF THEIR LUSTS. It is here that we seen WHY the God of Israel cried out through His prophet JEREMIAH. JER 19:4 - 6 & 1 KINGS 17:1 & 18:1 - 46.

Developing BIBLICAL Doctrine and Practice from the Canaanites, would be like Christian morality evolving from the pages of HUSTLER/PLAYBOY magazines. *IT SIMPLY CAN'T BE DONE.*

Israel was NOT just a little bit different from the other nations when they (Israel) were following the God of Israel, they were going 180 degrees in the opposite direction. UNHAPPILY, ISRAEL (and her sister nation JUDA), DOOMED THEMSELVES, by making the same FATAL mistake about the Canaanites, that the Christian Church is now making about the "NEW AGE".

***BABYLON JERUSALEM:** "BE CAREFUL NOT TO MAKE A TREATY WITH THOSE WHO LIVE IN THE LAND (of Canaan); FOR WHEN THEY PROSTITUTE THEMSELVES TO THEIR gods AND SACRIFICE TO THEM, <u>THEY</u> WILL INVITE YOU, AND YOU <u>WILL</u> EAT THEIR SACRIFICES". EXODUS 34:15.*
"...SEE IF THERE HAS EVER BEEN ANYTHING LIKE THIS; HAS A NATION EVER CHANGED ITS gods ? (yet, they are not gods at all.) BUT MY PEOPLE HAVE EXCHANGED THEIR GLORY FOR WORTHLESS IDOLS". JER 2:11.

With the words from the mouth of JEREMIAH **G O D INDICTED J U D A!** None of the idolatrous nations had ever abandoned their god, no matter how powerless they proved to be in time of need. Yet, **J U D A** had traded the **TRUE GOD** for stocks of wood and pillars of stone. **J U D A** was sacrificing their own children to the Canaanite idols. In a few short years, (giving Juda room and time to repent), the TRUE GOD would show **HIS** TERRIBLE JUDGEMENT on those practices by delivering HIS OWN PEOPLE over to the **BABYLONIANS**. Only one third would survive the horrors of the PLAGUE, the SWORD, and the SIEGE. JUDA would be dragged out of their OWN LAND, and taken as DESPISED CAPTIVES into the country that was **THE WORLD CENTER OF PAGANISM**. Those who had run after foreign gods would suffer HORRIBLY for their CHOICE. **GOD IS NO RESPECTER OF PERSONS**. DEUT 10:17, JOB 34:19 - 21, WISDOM 6:7, SIRACH 35:12 & :22, ACTS 10:34, ROM 2:11, EPH 6:9, COL 3:25, 1 PET 1:17.

When God delivered Israel from slavery in Egypt, He sent Plagues to judge OSIRIS and ISIS, the Egyptian version of BAAL and ASHTEROTH, and afflicted the ENTIRE land. Then God miraculously made a division between GOSHEN, (where HIS people dwelt), and the rest of Egypt. The plagues never touched Israel. Wondrous works followed miracles, and finally YAHWEY divided the Red Sea and allowed the MILLIONS of Israelites to cross on dry ground, as the waters formed "A WALL ON THE RIGHT HAND AND THE LEFT".

YAHWEH THEN JUDGED THE "LIVING god" of Egypt; PHARAOH, crushing and drowning under those collapsing walls of water.

TOLERATING/COMPROMISING WITH THE CANAANITES:
It took over 40 years for the Israelites to make the short journey (11 days DEUT 1:2 - 3) to Canaan...LONG ENOUGH FOR THE REBELLIOUS TO DIE OFF, and FOR THE CHILDREN TO GROW UP FEARING THE LORD. Then, just before the Israelites were about to enter Canaan, MOSES **ONCE MORE** reminded the Israelites to keep COMPLETELY separate from idolatry/paganism. EXODUS 34: 11 - 17.   *No tolerating... no compromise...no mixture.* DEUT 12: 30 - 31.   God sent His Angels before Israel and victory was assured. JOSH 17: 13. But Israel **"LACKED THE WILL"** and *tolerated...compromised...temple prostitutes...forced labour...covenants of trade...intermarriage...accepted paganism...*a little LEAVEN worked its way through the whole dough. Israel's unwillingness to obey God led them to the position where **"EACH MAN DID WHAT WAS RIGHT IN HIS OWN EYES"**. A **GREAT** and **GOOD** TEN-WORD DEFINITION OF PAGANISM. Soon the Israelites were serving the CANAANITES. JUDGES chapter 7.

God delivered Israel into bondage to the AMORITES...God delivered them in bondage to MOAB...God delivered them into bondage **AD INFINITUM.** Israel could not escape the cycles that THEIR tolerating/compromising built. JUDGES 11: 30 - 40.

Attached to all of those IDOLATROUS ways, were a

MULTITUDE of other **FORBIDDEN PRACTICES**, MORE AKIN TO A **"FOLK RELIGION"**, fully acceptable by the 'official religious' priests/priestesses. DEUT 18: 10 - 11. Israel showed a GREAT talent for embracing all those ***ABOMINATIONS***.

WE WANT TO BE LIKE THE OTHER KIDS: So Israel had forsaken **YAHWEH**, and served other gods, priests/priestesses. 1 SAM 8:7-8.

IDOLATRY INSTITUTIONALIZED BY THE JEWISH KINGS: Solomon married foreign wives, against the Law of Yahweh. Jewish royalty were leaders of the cults of MOLECH and/or BAAL. 1 KINGS 11:7

JUDGEMENT FOLLOWS; It was not long before the IDOLATRY split the kingdom between ISRAEL and JUDAH. JEROBOAM 1st, king of the new northern kingdom of Israel instituted IDOLATRY as his official state religion, in order to PREVENT his subjects from making the annual pilgrimage to JERUSALEM. This spelled **D O O M** for Israel. God sent the ASSYRIANS to destroy the northern kingdom in 722 BC, (no worse fate was possible!) it's survivors were scattered throughout the nations.

JUDAH, was the southern kingdom. Under king JOSIAH, the valley of TOPHET was DECOMMISSIONED as a child-killing centre. 4 KINGS 23:10, and the pagan alters were defiled. JOSIAH turned the valley into the PERPETUALLY burning city dump, called the VALLEY OF HIMMON or GEHENNA. This name became synonymous with HELL and ETERNAL DAMNATION. It was the term Jesus used for HELL.

But neither JOSIAH'S or HEZEKIA'S reforms could hold off GOD'S Judgement forever. HEZEKIA'S own son MANASSEH, was responsible for so disgracing Israel with lewd and bloody practices that God, from that time forward, absolutely REFUSED to forgive them. The Israelites had become MORE evil than the Canaanites they had replaced. 2 KINGS 21: 9.

When God could bear it no longer...when He would no longer put up with the INSULTS to His NAME and His HOLINESS...He handed JUDAH over to BABYLON. The remnant of God's people would learn to FEAR and OBEY Him, as SLAVES in the land of their ENEMIES. Israel was the 'football' of the nations; tossed to and fro by one conqueror after another, until they (the Jews), rejected their OWN **MESSIAH,** which resulted in the destruction of JERUSALEM in 70 AD. LUKE 21: 24.

HIDDEN TEACHINGS OF HINDUISM AND BUDDHISM:
ROMANS 1:18 & :21 - 25 refers.

A vast cloud appeared over the plain of SHINAR. Tribe after tribe of FIERCELY PROUD, light skinned ARYANS were migrating from the west, and settled for several centuries in the vicinity of **BABYLON.**

The ARYANS stood out among the MESOPOTAMIANS with their PALE SKIN and POINTED NOSES...which WERE, as often as not, HELD ALOOF from the DARKER SKINNED inhabitants. From here, the ARYANS scattered throughout the plains and hills of CENTRAL EUROPE. Their PROUD names appeared in places as widely separated as IRELAND (AYAR-LAND) and IRAN (AYAR-AN),

Some of the ARYANS moved EAST from MESOPOTAMIA, after adopting large portions of the religion of BABYLON, *"THE MOTHER OF HARLOTS AND ABOMINATIONS OF THE EARTH".* REV 17:5.   The DRAVIDIANS, the DARK SKINNED ancient people of the INDIAN SUBCONTINENT, were soon overwhelmed by the ARYIAN hordes, as was the RANDOM, ANIMISTIC religion of the DRAVIDIANS.

THE BEGINNING OF HINDU RELIGION: The DRAVIDIANS lived in TERROR of SPIRITS, and only felt safety through following RITUAL OBSERVANCES in aspect of DAILY LIFE. "HOLY" men, IN CONTACT WITH EVIL SPIRITS, uttered

ORACLES and brought the OPPRESSION of the SPIRIT WORLD into the family home. AMULETS, CRYSTALS, ICONS, and COLOURED POWDERS, served as limited protection from DEMONS, and FOCAL POINTS OF UNIVERSAL 'ENERGIES'

To this HAPHAZARD system, the NEWLY ARRIVED ARYAN'S added their OWN ancient tribal SUPERSTITIONS, now POWERFULLY ORGANIZED and ENERGIZED by BABYLONIAN religion. Local deities were soon overshadowed by the TRIAD of BRAHMA, VISHNU, and SHIVA...a virtual COPY of the BABYLONIAN gods EA, MARDUK, and ISHTAR.

HINDU RACISM: The ARYANS viewed the DRAVIDIANS with DISDAIN, calling the DRAVIDIANS, in their OWN territory, ASURAS (demons), DASAS (blacks), ANASCHS (people with no nose), AYAJUAH (without sacrifices), ADEVA (godless), AVARATAH (without purpose in life). (TROY ORGAN, "HINDUISM", 1974, page 41).

This was the first RECORDED attempt in human history, to IMPLEMENT racism as part of a religion...AND IT WAS SUCCESSFUL. Even today, in Canada, where racism is almost the only UNIVERSALLY ACKNOWLEDGED SIN, "NEW AGERS" don't feel the need to apologize for HINDU RACISTS...instead, they are COPYING the ARYANS/HINDUS.

Today, "NEW AGE" teaching INSISTS that two races inhabit the earth. (SEE CHAPTER 10 OF TEXE MARRS, "DARK SECRETS OF THE NEW AGE", for a COMPREHENSIVE, well-documented discussion of "NEW AGE" doctrine). Early in the 1900's, NAZIS, like the ancient ARYAN WARRIORS, used the OCCULT belief to divide between GERMANIC ARYANS, and all other people, subjecting all others to SUBHUMAN SLAVERY. Today's PAGANS ascribe the differences between races, to SPIRITUAL TRAITS, rather than PHYSICAL TRAITS. Some say that one group is descended from the warlike ATLANTEANS, but the more advanced spirits are those of LEMURIAN DESCENT. "NEW AGE" spokesman WILLIS W. HARMON calls this newly-evolved man *HOMO*

NOETICUS. ("RATIONALE FOR GOOD CHOOSING", JOURNAL OF HUMANISTIC PSYCHOLOGY, WINTER 1981).

The difference between the OLD and NEW races, by all accounts, seems to be "in one's ability to accept ALL beliefs as VALID; TOLERANCE and COMPROMISE for ungodly religions and practices". In other words, "don't upset the applecart"..."don't denounce injustice"..."let those in power do their thing, without complaining".

KEEPING THE POOR IN THEIR PLACE: For the last 50 years, INDIA has been presented as a GENTLE, PEACE-LOVING PLACE, WHERE NOBODY WOULD EVEN STEP ON AN ANT.

The ENTIRE HINDU SOCIETY is ACTUALLY designed toward one goal...KEEPING THE BRAHMIN CASTE IN POWER. Whatever/whoever gets in the way of this goal, is RUTHLESSLY CRUSHED.

The superior fighting abilities of these ARYAN TRIBES, puts them SUDDENLY and FIRMLY IN COMMAND!

INDIAN SOCIETY was then divided into TWO CASTES...the FREE (ARYA) and the SLAVE (DASA). (ORGAN, "HINDUISM", page 190). The primary difference was based on SKIN COLOUR. This obvious PREJUDICE was justified by the TWIN DOCTRINES of REINCARNATION and KARMA. Later, the CASTES or VARNAS became four DISTINCT GROUPS.

Westerners are repelled by the idea that by BIRTH one is BRAHMIN, KSHATRIYA, VAISHYA, or SHUDRA (OUTCASTS). Hindus will remind westerners that a BRAHMIN is NOT a BRAHMIN because of his birth, but rather because of his birth into a BRAHMIN family, which WAS a result of his having attained that status, because of his VARIOUS (perhaps MANY) REINCARNATIONS. VARNA is determined by KARMA. Birth into a VARNA is no accident. It is a NATURAL RESULT of KARMIC causes.(ORGAN, "HINDUISM", page 194). They give no credence whatsoever to the FACT that CHILDREN LEARN WHAT THEY LIVE, usually.

As a man is CONTINUALLY REBORN, he is born into the

CASTE he DESERVES, because of the GOOD or EVIL done in his past lives. His troubles are of his OWN doing…(a cosmic survival-of-the-fittest).

CHRIS GRISCOM, "NEW AGE" teacher, seen this REBIRTH CYCLE as a GUIDED TRIP TO PERFECTION. Along the way, GRISCOM says, "it's O.K…even BENEFICIAL …to murder other people. At this time, we are living with the imprint of addiction and emotional body response patterns of many lifetimes. Experience is the only way to find another blueprint. Perhaps the soul says, 'you need to understand PERMISSION, so go in and kill a few people, and you will begin to understand the cosmic law of PERMISSION…In that killing, the soul will begin to understand the law of PERMISSION, the recognition that the VICTIM and the VICTIMIZER are one, the understanding that there is no separation between us. If we experience a killing in some lifetime, something in our own body is activated. It responds to that, and we get in touch with the REALITY that this experience is a part of us". (CHRIS GRISCOMB, "ECSTASY IN A NEW FREQUENCY", 1987, pages 15 & 48).

To GRISCOM, it is all to the good that some are DOWNTRODDEN, POOR, DISEASED, PERSECUTED, or KILLED. Those are roles of the person's OWN CHOICE. "The victim and the victimizer are one, and we don't need to attach ourselves to either of these polarities. Rather, we need to free ourselves from the grip, and the limitations, of each of these roles, because they are simply roles decided upon freely by all players, agreed upon unanimously. (GRISOM, "ECSTASY IN A NEW FREQUENCY", page 55).

Such CALLOUSNESS is typical "NEW AGE" thinking. This leaves the afflicted *"IN THEIR PROPER PLACE"* in the "NEW AGE", in the same way as the CASTE system of INDIA. If the VICTIM of the OPPRESSION objects, that is only because he is UNENLIGHTENED, and his oppressors don't have to pay any attention to him.

In INDIA each of the four CASTE divisions was divided into

millions of degrees. "The SANSKRIT (ARYAN) word for the TRADITIONAL CLASSIFICATION is "VARNA", and VARNA means COLOUR. But it ALSO meant SPECIES, KIND, CHARACTER and NATURE of the individual. The COLOUR HYPOTHESIS claim that the LIGHT-COMPLEXIONED INDO-ARYANS wished to avoid assimilation with the DARK-COMPLEXIONED ABORIGINES whose land they invaded. To this day, FAIR SKIN is prized in INDIA.Colour has long been associated with the four VARNAS...WHITE with BRAHMINS; RED with KSHATRIAS; YELLOW with VAISHYAS; and BLACK with SHUDRAS. (ORGAN, "HINDUISM", pages 190 & 191.

So those relegated to the lowest class, could rightly be POORLY-TREATED...and the NON-CLASS, called UNTOUCHABLES or OUTCASTS, could be treated worst of all. DR. AMBEDKAR says "TO THE UNTOUCHABLES, HINDUISM IS A VERITABLE CHAMBER OF HORRORS" (ORGAN, "HINDUISM", page 192).

The CASTE system, a result of PAGAN BELIEFS, serves as a RELIGIOUS excuse for ignoring the PLIGHT of the POOR and the AFFLICTED...the very people Scripture COMMANDS Christians to SERVE.

THE CORE OF HINDUISM; KEEPING THE ELITE IN POWER. Hinduism has CORE DOCTRINES: REINCARNATION; KARMA; and CASTE. These are ESSENTIAL for MAINTAINING the POWER of the BRAHMIN ELITE. To prevent the possibility of discussion as to whether these doctrines are TRUE or FALSE, HINDUISM also CLEVERLY presents itself as a SUPERMARKET OF BELIEFS. You can believe ANYTHING you want to, and worship any god you choose, so long as you acknowledge the SACRED BRAHMIN CASTE.

The BRAHMINS were quick to EXPLOIT their position as the PRIESTLY CASTE. By the time of the BRAHMINS (800 - 700 BC), the BRAHMINS had become a HEREDITARY PRIESTHOOD. In charge of ALL sacrificial duties, for which they were PAID FEES, by the people. The BRAHMINS were saying that via the RIGHT

SACRIFICES, which they ALONE could offer, they could PROCURE the favours of the gods; various temporal blessings; and a good place in heaven. MEN, GOVERNMENTS, and gODS...were ALL under THEIR PRIESTLY CONTROL...

The fruit of this CONTROL became increasingly hard to bear, as the 'PRIESTS' loaded heavy burdens on the people. In INDIA, as in other places, CHALLENGES to the 'ELITE appeared in the sixth century BC. ("THE NEW ENCYCLOPEDIA BRITANNICA", VOL 18, page 912).

In the sixth century BC, there was a tidal wave of revolt against the priest crafts of the ancient world. This tidal wave shattered the power of the old pagan religions, though their cults continued to exist as BACKWATERS for centuries (even to this day), via the help, grace blessings, power and might of satan, through his angels, spirits, saints, instruments and servants.

Six world religions appeared within fifty years of each other. (Hebrewism was already well established at the time of CREATION, and reinforced, and carried on via NOAH and his descendants). ZOROASTRIANISM; BUDDHISM; JAINISM; CONFUCIANISM; VEDANTA MONISM; and TAOISM. (One OBVIOUS source of the six religions is the preaching of ISAIAH (740 BC onwards), and the other EIGHTH CENTURY BC PROPHETS OF ISRAEL, with the refrain from JEREMIAH and EZEKIEL a century or so later), via the power and might of satan, the master counterfeiter and duplicator; the father of deceit and deception, in an attempt to revive his religions, PAGANISM.

We can find the ethical emphases of ZOROASTER and BUDDHA (563 - 483 BC), MAHAVIR (599 - 527 BC), and CONFUCIUS (551 - 479 BC), in the Great Prophets of THE ONE TRUE GOD OF ALL CREATION.

The actual spark of the sixth century revolution probably came from ISRAEL, via PERSIA. It is significant that the revolt was SIMULTANEOUS in both INDIA and CHINA. (ROBERT BROW, "RELIGION: ORIGINS AND IDEAS", 1972, pages 27-29). Like a COBRA, HINDUISM was able to finally open its mouth wide enough to SWALLOW UP ALL SIX CONTENDERS, for the most part.

THE *REAL* TEACHINGS OF HINDUISM: (EVERY ONE OF WHICH IS NOW ACCEPTED AS A "NEW AGE" DOCTRINE).

ESCAPE FROM REINCARNATION: The GOAL of Hinduism is to finally EXHAUST the RESERVOIR of KARMA, and become one with the great god BRAHMAN (which amounts to becoming part of the void (nothingness). Similarly, in Buddhism one desires to attain the state of NIRVANA, to escape from the dreary wheel of life. This is called "LIBERATION".

In higher HINDUISM, BUDDHISM, and JAINISM, man is not just interested in a better reincarnation. One life is bad enough, and the thought of an eternity of reincarnations is intolerable. The JAINS offer an escape by good deeds to destroy the evil in the soul. Buddha preached that desires and passions held man in the vicious wheel of reincarnation. The Hindu VEDANTISTS (see VEDANTA), teach the release is found by "UNION WITH THE ABSOLUTE". (BROW, "RELIGION: ORIGINS AND IDEAS", page 96).

Hinduism may be characterized as a system of means appropriate for the attainment of "LIBERATION".

The non-liberated man is subject to "COMMON DESTINY": enslaved by his actions which follow him INDEFINITELY "as a calf follows its mother", he is CONDEMNED to be re-born; and as most human actions are tainted with malice, the risk of being re-born into a lower CASTE (condition), ultimately as an ANIMAL, is greater than the possibility of ACHIEVING an EXALTED state. (BROW, "HINDUISM", pages 41-43).

"NEW AGE" teachers generally don't focus on the undesirableness of reincarnation. By PROMOTING both REINCARNATION and SEARCH FOR VIRVANA at the same time, they manage to appeal both to THE DESIRE FOR SPECIAL KNOWLEDGE and THE DESIRE TO ESCAPE GOD'S JUDGEMENT. The 'teachers' also don't stress the possible NEGATIVE CONSEQUENCES of REINCARNATION.

All "NEW AGERS" seem to expect to be a PRESIDENT in their next lives. WHY NOT ??? at least several thousand of them have been CLEOPATRA before.

THE SEXUAL REVOLUTION: Some Hindus try to reach NIRVANA by assiduous NAVEL-GAZING. Others hope to PARTY their way to LIBERATION. A look at ancient Hindu temples IMMEDIATELY reveal the INTENSE SATURATION of sexual themes running from simple PHALLIC IMAGES of veneration, to INTRICATE carvings of naked gods and goddesses.

The temple is dedicated to a particular god. The image of this god is accompanied by a particular attribute, which becomes AUTONOMOUS. In the SHAIVITE context, this 'attribute' is often a LINGS, a PHALLIC emblem. The LINGA is a short pillar of black stone, bare or engraved, around which is performed PUJA of a votive character. (BROW, "HINDUISM", page 31).

Ancient teachers of TANTRIC (a SECT) YOGA had discovered the doctrine of the ARYAN SUPER-MAN, the man who is a law unto himself.

The TANTRIC places HIMSELF above the conventional law. What others CONDEMN, he assumes as a badge of NOBILITY. What poisons others, nourishes him. What sends others to hell, ASSURES his salvation. Hence, prohibited acts are used as "rungs of a ladder" by which he ascends to the 'HEIGHTS': alcoholic liquor must be drunk; meat, (taboo to other Hindus) MUST be eaten; forbidden SEXUALITY i.e. INCEST and ADULTERY **MUST** BE PRACTICED. (CAVENDISH, "ENCYCLODEDIA OF THE UNEXPLAINED", pages 242-243).

TANTRIC YOGA has MANY followers in the West today. Not surprisingly, its proponents have found the idea of "SALVATION THROUGH SIN", to be a CONVENIENT means of JUSTIFYING evil. For an example, one book quoted earlier suggests that one might "NEED" to kill another (in one incarnation or another), in order to learn some VALUABLE SPIRITUAL LESSONS. **How handy for the SON OF SAM.**

VIOLENCE: Thanks to MAHATMA GANDHI, (a Hindu who admits he was STRONGLY influenced by CHRISTIANITY), Hinduism in the West has a reputation of GENTLENESS and NON-VIOLENCE. Hindus are SUPPOSED to be too tender-hearted to even step on an ant, let alone harm another human being.

THIS, however, is an absolutely false picture of Hinduism.

EXTREME vegetarianism was incorporated into some sects of Hinduism, but it is important to remember that INDIA'S WARRIOR CASTES have NEVER held this doctrine. For three thousand years, DEVOUT Hindu soldiers have had no hesitation about killing men in war, and eating VENISON, MUTTON, and POULTRY. (BROW, RELIGION: ORIGINS AND IDEAS", page 109).

Consider what kind of ETHIC springs from the doctrine that any suffering you inflict on your fellow man is HIS fault...He ASKED for it. If he suffers, that is a result of BAD KARMA, HIS PENALTY FOR WRONGDOING IN A PREVIOUS LIFE. In any case, HIS suffering is merely an ILLUSION that should NOT touch your conscience.

So INDIA has HARBOURED the THUGEE CULT, which caught and strangled UNSUSPECTING VICTIMS as offerings to MOTHER KALI and the KHONDS, who kept human beings to be SLAUGHTERED AS SLOWLY AS POSSIBLE, IN THEIR NATURE-WORSHIP RITUALS. For CENTURIES it was LAW that widows would be ROASTED ALIVE on their HUSBAND'S FUNERAL PYRE. HUMAN SACRIFICE was RITUALIZED and CODIFIED in SACRED INDIAN BOOKS. None of this aroused ANY COMPASSION until the great uprising at the time of BUDDHA, because, as the author of "HUMAN SACRIFICE IN HISTORY AND TODAY" (NIGEL DAVIES, 1981) says, "the 'underlying conditions' that breed human sacrifice were present: Lack of any benevolent redeemer, absence of a truly human ethic, and finally, belief in a ceaseless cycle of re-birth that turned death of a human into a TRIVIAL INCIDENT".

AND TODAY, INDIA HAS 'THE BOMB'.

DRUGS: Drug abuse is ANOTHER "precious inheritance" the West has received from our "ENLIGHTENED FRIENDS", the

HINDUS. The older among us might recall how that FAD really took hold when THE BEATLES CAME BACK FROM VISITING AN **INDIAN GURU**, AND BEGAN TO **PROMOTE**, **(AS A FAVOUR TO THE WEST), DRUG USE AS A RELIGIOUS ACT**...(A PAGAN RELIGIOUS ACT). Until that time, there had been VERY LITTLE drug abuse in Western nations, even among the "FLAPPERS" of the late 20's etc.

The **RIG VEDA**, a HINDU SCRIPTURE, presented drug-taking as "THE GREATEST SPIRITUAL EXPERIENCE EVER". One particular drug, SOMA, is called "THE SOUL AND CENTRE OF SACRIFICE". (ELIADE, "A HISTORY OF RELIGIOUS IDEAS" VOL 1, page 211). **"all the virtues of SOMA are bound up with the ecstatic experience brought on by its ingestion...The revelation of a full and beatific existence, in COMMUNION with the gods, continued to haunt INDIAN spirituality long after the disappearance of the original drink. Hence, the attempt was made to attain such an existence by the help of other means: other drug substitutes; asceticism; orgiastic excesses; meditation; the techniques of YOGA, and mystical devotion".**

The QUEST for a **"HIGH"** that now entangles, and binds tighter and tighter, and destroys the lives of millions, in every Western nation, **STARTED RIGHT THERE.**

BEING 'COOL': ANOTHER nearly universal phenomenon among youth today, is the desire to be "cool". This is in contrast with the FIERCE LOYALTIES shared by Western children OF THE PAST...**LOYALTY** to FAMILY; RELIGIOUS GROUPS; COMMUNITY; PROVINCE; and COUNTRY. Youth today seek to act as if they care about nothing at all. This, **too,** is straight out of the HINDU/BUDDHIST grab bag.

From 200BC to AD100, Many HINDU youths were abandoning the ways of their fathers, to follow the teachings of BUDDHA. To change this state of affairs, the **BHAGAVADGITA** was written by KRISHNA HINDUS.

The problem was ACUTE/SERIOUS. BUDDHA had REJECTED

the whole idea of the CASTE system, AND the need for SACRIFICES as well, which ALSO excluded the need for BRAHMIN PRIESTS. BUDDAH'S teachings were spreading like wildfire. Even a great king of INDIA had become a BUDDHIST.

The GITA is a dialogue between a hero of the WARRIOR CASTE, that had been foremost in the revolt against BRAHMINISM, and KRISHNA, an incarnation of the god VISHNU.

The hero, ARJUN, is about to go into battle, and wonders why he should bother. As a BUDDHIST, he does not want to kill; he does not NEED the victory, and he FEELS COMPASSION for his enemies.

KRISHNA counters those arguments with an appeal to ARJUN'S DUTY to his CASTE. How can ARJUN think of overthrowing all civilized society by refusing to behave according to his CASTE ??? Further, the enemy only APPEAR to be people. REALITY IS AN ILLUSION. Thanks to reincarnation, death is no tragedy anyway. Finally, KRISHNA informs ARJUN that he is right to not feel any desire to fight, but that he should wade out there and kill. Anyway, the BUDDHIST ideal of renouncing the world, and accepting NON-VIOLENCE is WRONG. "DESIRELESS ACTION" is the RIGHT way...obeying the BRAHMIN rules of CASTE without caring terribly about the outcome. (BROW, "RELIGION: ORIGINS AND IDEAS", 1972, PAGES 42, 43, AND 53).

This explanation stopped BUDDHISM, in INDIA, IN ITS TRACKS. Two versions of HINDUISM have also stopped the Christian Church in IT'S tracks. The version for adults, PIETISM, causes CHRISTIANS to care nothing about what happens to other 'Christians', (or the world, for that matter), as long as THEY are (they imagine) "SAVED" and "BORN AGAIN", contrary to the Teachings of Jesus Christ. The version for children, BEING COOL, causes them to care only about NOT CARING.

Desireless action is NOT Christian. Jesus Christ neither established a Monastery, nor a COMMUNAL SETTLEMENT, NOR CALLED His Disciples to abandon their DESIRES. Desires were to be PURIFIED, RE-DIRECTED, and FANNED TO INTENSE

PASSION. GOD was to be LOVED with ALL one's heart; Christians were to love one another with a PURE HEART, FERVENTLY; COMPASSION was to be INTENSELY PRACTICAL...

If a Christian separates from secular involvement, because of a PREOCCUPATION with his OWN Salvation, he may name Christ in his prayers, but his teacher is BUDDHA.

DEMON POSSESSION AND INTOLERANCE: 'POSSESSION' by the gods is another SOUGHT-AFTER experience. Whether this is done through MEDITATION, RITUAL DANCE, or OTHER means, the gods are INVITED to INHABIT the worshippers. Today's "NEW AGE" catalogue offers SEVERAL books to teach you HOW to receive a spirit to "channel". ("NEW AGE CATALOGUE", 1988, page 2).

The worshippers of the various CULTS, submit themselves to considerable preparation: preliminary ablutions; corporal postures and gestures; control of breath; 'possession' (NYASA) by the god of the body of the worshippers; etc. The notions of pure and impure are everywhere evident. "PURITY" is the essential watchword of HINDUISM, and its religious practices of 'purification' are INFINITELY diversified.

But what does 'PURITY' mean to a HINDU ???

To the TANTRICS, drunkenness, sensuality/lust, incest, and even cannibalism are "PURIFYING". Another group thinks eating feces and drinking urine "PURIFY" them. Still other groups regard all these things as IMPURE. None of these beliefs is HERESY.

In truth, HERESY is nearly impossible in HINDUISM. One of the few discernable HERESIES is making the claim that YOUR WAY to BRAHMIN...or ANY one way, is the ONLY way...nearly the same kind of HINDU *FAUX PAS* is claiming that there is only ONE God.

A 19th century attempt by RAMMOHAN ROY, (at a kind of Unitarian/one god religion called BRAHMO SAMAJ (ONE god SOCIETY), or the THEISTIC CHURCH OF INDIA), caused a furor with the orthodox Hindus of Calcutta. They were furious with the establishment of the BRAHMO SAMAJ, and immediately organized a rival association; the DHARMA SABHA. (RENOU ORGAN, "HINDUISM", page 32).

So while "TOLERANCE" 'appears' to be one of the highest virtues of HINDUISM, it is ONLY tolerant of anything that does NOT present CHRISTIAN SALVATION. RAMMOHAN ROY had NOT 'crossed the line' when he touted the Teachings of Jesus... so long as RAMMOHAN continued to claim that it was not the PERSON, but the TEACHINGS of Jesus that were unimportant. RAMMOHAN had said "I REGRET ONLY THAT THE FOLLOWERS OF JESUS, IN GENERAL, SHOULD HAVE PAID MUCH GREATER ATTENTION TO INQUIRIES AFTER HIS NATURE THAN TO THE OBSERVANCES OF HIS COMMANDMENTS".

These sentiments are often expressed by "NEW AGE" adherents who are APPALLED that anyone would claim that there is only ONE WAY to God. Neo-pagans are more than willing to ascribe the title of TEACHER, AVATAR, or MASTER to Jesus, and to acknowledge that Jesus is the equal of BUDDHA, KRISHNA, and others, but utterly REFUSE to consider the CLAIMS that Christ Himself made, THAT HE IS VERY GOD. When RAMMOHAM insisted on an OMNIPRESENT GOD, who "IS THE ONLY PROPER OBJECT OF RELIGIOUS VENERATION", THAT created the furor. The local HINDUS could NOT **tolerate** such an assertion...IT WAS HERESY.

Another doctrine HINDUS can't tolerate is the claim that GOD is the source of Salvation.

A Hindu, even if he belongs to a group, considers HIMSELF ALONE to be responsible for his Salvation.

But even RAMMOHAN had to admit that "Christianity, if properly inculcated, has a greater tendency to improve the MORAL, and POLITICAL state of mankind, THAN ANY OTHER KNOWN RELIGIOUS SYSTEM". (a Monarchy).

This TRUTH became more and more evident as Christianity took its TENUOUS foothold in INDIA. Although the percentage of Christians in INDIA is, to this day, almost negligible, the ENTIRE national mind-set was changed by their arrival. It was the

INTOLERANCE of CHRISTIANS that brought about this change... CHRISTIAN INTOLERANCE of IGNORANCE; UNTREATED DISEASE; NEGLECT OF THE POOR; and of SQUALOR.

Throughout the 19th century, Missionaries POURED into INDIA, and founded CHURCHES, HOSPITALS, ORPHANAGES, TUBERCULOSIS SANITORIUMS, HOMES FOR LEPERS, SCHOOLS FOR THE BLIND, PRINTING PRESSES, AGRICULTURAL INSTITUTES, INSANE ASYLUMS, ELEMENTARY AND SECONDARY SCHOOLS, COLLEGES, and MANY other institutions for the improvement of the life of the people...

HINDUISM was 'STIMULATED' by CHRISTIAN EXAMPLE to do more than had previously been done for the POOR; SICK; and the NEEDY. i.e. there were no homes for the lepers before Christianity came to INDIA...much more defensible (than claims that HINDUS COPIED CHRIST WITH KRISHNA) is the HYPOTHESES that the BHAKTI developments, with their emphasis on the sinfulness of man, and the Grace of God, may reflect the impact of Christianity, and there is no doubt that Christianity was partly responsible for the appearance of the great modern HINDU REFORMERS such as: RAMMOHAN, SWAMI, DAYANADA, KESHUB CHUNDER SEN, RAMAKRISHNER, VIVEKANANDA, and GANDHI, each of these **acknowledged** his debt to Christianity. (RENOU ORGAN, "HINDUISM", pages 312 - 313).

When the English took over INDIA, they brought an end to ALL legally sanctioned human sacrifice, including SUTTEE (burning the widow, alive, on her husband's funeral pyre). The amazing courage of just one British Major saved over fifteen hundred men, women, and children, who were being kept as sacrificial victims by the KHOND tribe.

Through the work of Missionary AMY CARMICHAEL, temple prostitution of young girls, (some only three and four years old) was finally SUPPRESSED.

These were ALL common-place before the introduction of the Christian "HERESY".

HINDUS never produced a world empire like those of EGYPT

and BABYLON, but HINDU TEACHINGS have survived, INTACT, to this day. Hindu PRACTICES, on the other hand, have been CLEANED UP, due to CHRISTIAN INFLUENCE. Even so, "NEW AGERS" should think twice, before going into pagan "RAPTURES" about Hindu teachings, because HINDUISM is the religion that HAS produced the POOREST, MOST DEGRADED, and UNCOMPASSIONATE culture on earth today.

MOHAMMED: The founder of the Islamic religion. Moslems believe Mohammed was the last messenger of God. They believe Mohammed completed the sacred teachings of such earlier prophets as Abraham, Moses, and Jesus. Moslems say that they respect Mohammed, but they do not worship him..

Most of Mohammed's countrymen worshipped many gods, and prayed to idols and spirits. Mohammed brought a new message to his people from God. God requires men to make ISLAM (submission) to Him.

Mohammed replaced the old loyalties to tribes, with a new loyalty/tie of EQUALITY and BROTHERHOOD among ALL Moslem's. He preached against the iniquities of the wealthy class, and tried to help the poor. Mohammed led his countrymen to unite in a great religious movement. Today, there are more than 460,000,000 Moslems throughout the world.

Mohammed was born in Mecca, South-western Arabia. His father died before his birth, and his mother died when he was a child. His grandfather, and later his uncle became his guardians and raised him. Mohammed lived with a desert tribe; he learned to tend sheep and camels.

At the age of 25, Mohammed entered the service of Khadija, a wealthy widow. She was 15 years older than Mohammed; he later married her. They had 2 sons and 4 daughters. The sons died young. One of his daughters, Fatima, married Ali, son of Abu Talib. Many Moslem's trace their descent from Mohammed through this couple.

When Mohammed was 35, he was meditating alone in a cave on Mount Hira; a vision appeared to him. Moslems believe the vision was the Angel Gabriel, who called Mohammed to be a Prophet and proclaim God's message to his countrymen.

At first, Mohammed doubted that his vision had come from God. His wife Khadija assured him that it did, and she became his first disciple. No more revelations came, and Mohammed grew discouraged. Then the Angel Gabriel came once more and told him "Arise and warn; magnify thy Lord".

Mohammed told only relatives and friends, of the revelations, at first. But soon he began to preach in public. Most people ridiculed him, but some believed him. Alu Bakr, a rich merchant, became a disciple.

Omar, a leader of Mecca persecuted Mohammed at first, but later accepted him as a prophet. Mohammed continued to preach in Mecca until calamities took place; his wife and Abu Talib (son-in-law) died. Then the people of Mecca began to hate Mohammed again, for his claims, and his attacks, on their way of life. Some of them even plotted to kill Mohammed.

In 622 AD Mohammed fled north to the nearby city of Medina (then called Yathrib). The Moslem calendar begins from that date (Friday 16 July 622 AD (in 30 year increments). The people of Medina welcomed Mohammed. His preaching and Statesmanship won most of them as followers. This emigration to Medina is called the HEGIRA.

Mohammed was now the head of a religion and a community. He made his religious message into Law. He abolished the customs of worshipping idols, and killing unwanted baby girls. He also prohibited WAR and VIOLENCE, **EXCEPT** in cases of SELF – DEFENCE, and FOR THE CAUSE OF ISLAM.

Mohammed expected Jews and Christians to accept him as a prophet. At first, he was friendly toward them. But the Jews in Medina broke their alliance with him, and conspired with his enemies against him. Mohammed angrily drove them from the city, and abandoned many of the Jewish traditions he had followed, He established FRIDAY, rather than Saturday as the Moslem sabbath.

In 630 AD Mohammed and his followers returned to Mecca and occupied the city. They destroyed all the idols in the heathen temple (the KABBA), and turned the area surrounding the KABBA into a Mosque. they entered Mecca in triumph. He died 2 years later in Medina. His tomb is located in the Prophet's Mosque in Medina.

After Mohammed died, in 632 AD, ABU BAKAR was elected CALIPH, (the Muslim ruler). He and his successors encouraged the JIHAD (holy war). Within 100 years, they built an empire that stretched from Northern Spain to India. The spread of Islam engulfed the Persian Sassanian empire and much of the Christian Byzantine Empire.

Moslems united millions of different people into one great Brotherhood. They established a civilization in Iraq, Persia (now Iran), Palestine, North Africa, and Spain. They transmitted much of the classical knowledge of the ancient world.

The Caliph Othman, who ruled from 644 AD to 656 AD, and ordered the first official edition of the Koran, and sent a copy to the chief Mosques in each of the capital cities of the Moslem provinces.

Moslems consider the Koran to be the words of God Himself, spoken to Mohammed by an Angel. Parts of the Koran resemble the Bible, the Apocrypha, and the Jewish Talmud. The Koran contains many of the same stories about the Prophets that appear in the Old Testament. The Koran also has stories from the New Testaments about Jesus Christ, whom it calls THE WORD OF GOD. They believe that God sends Prophets with sacred books to teach man his duty to God and his fellow man.

The Moslems believe that Mohammed was the last of the Prophets, and that Jesus Christ and the Old Testament Prophets were his predecessors.

Like all religions, Islam has it's SECTS. In the 900's AD, the Moslem world split into two great divisions, SUNNITES and SHIITES. The BAHAI faith grew out of the SHIITE group.

European ideas penetrated into Moslem countries and brought

about many changes. "MODERN" education and economic reform spread. The Moslem people wanted to be up-to-date, strong, and independent of their European masters. As a result of their conquests, Moslems came into contact with Greek, Roman, and Persian sciences and philosophies; history and literature. Moslems honored LEARNING; they founded MANY Universities and academies. They translated major 'WORKS' into LATIN, the language of "LEARNING".

The Muslims threatened Europe until the King of the Merovingian Franks, Charles Martel, defeated them, at the battle of TOURS in 732 AD.

UNHOLY SACRIFICES (AZTECS AND MAYANS):
ISA 14: 20 - 21, spoken of BABYLON, but applicable to **ALL** cultures which are the "SONS" OF BABYLON.

MONTEZUMA hid deep in the bowels of the "BLACK HOUSE OF MAGIC AND WITCHCRAFT". A ritual of MONTEZUMA was where countless human hearts were offered to the SETTING SUN, and the blood, (FOOD FOR THE god), oozed in sticky waves to cover the black volcanic rock of the pyramid TENOCHTITLAN.

As with **ALL** WITCHES and BLACK ART (MAGIC) PRACTITIONERS, Montezuma's **DOOM** approached, disguised as HERNANDO CORTES.

OUT OF THE BLUE; "METEORIC" best describes the rise of the AZTEC EMPIRE. In a few brief centuries, the AZTECS went from a pitiful band of OUTCASTS, from the wastelands of northern Mexico, to SAVAGE and SOPHISTICATED rulers of the central jungles.

At first, they proved useful, to the established kingdoms, as MERCENARIES. They were UTTERLY RUTHLESS...(their greatest sales pitch). But those who HIRED the AZTECS, failed to cover their OWN backs, and soon the CRAFTY NEWCOMERS were a

GREATER THREAT than the enemies they were HIRED to destroy. (JON WHITE, "CORTEZ AND THE DOWNFALL OF THE AZTEC EMPIRE", 1971, pages 93-94).

The AZTEC philosophy of life is STILL active and alive to this day, in OUR society. i.e. "Life is essentially APPROPRIATION; INJURY; OVERPOWERING OF WHAT IS ALIEN AND/OR WEAKER; SUPPRESSION (via discrediting or force); HARDNESS; IMPOSITION OF THE CONQUER'S OWN WILL/FORM; INCORPORATION; EXPLOITATION". (FRIEDERICH NIETZSCHE, "BEYOND GOOD AND EVIL" 1886).

The coming of the AZTECS was a JUDGEMENT on the SUPERSTITIONS and MAGIC-LADEN MEXICANS. All of them were fond of HUMAN SACRIFICE and other BARBARIC practices. The AZTECS came and gave the MEXICANS a belly full of there OWN medicine. On one occasion, the AZTECS sacrificed TWENTY THOUSAND human hearts in four days. The black robed priests spelled each other off as their arms became too weary to make the gash in the victim's chest, with the obsidian knife, to cut out the heart.

Today, the AZTECS and their fellow pagans, the MAYANS, are being dug up, cleaned up, and PROMOTED LIKE CRAZY. Many "NEW AGE" prophecies are based on the AZTEC and MAYAN CALENDARS. "NEW AGERS" claim to be CHANNELS for AZTEC/MAYAN WARRIORS.

There is an AZTEC exhibit at Disney World, and the tour talk is all about the ADVANCED CIVILIZATION and AMAZING ACHIEVEMENTS of the NOBLE AZTECS.

Before HISTORICAL ILLITERACY set in, we used to know that the AZTECS/MAYANS had two of the BLOODIEST, MOST DISGUSTING AND CRUEL, so-called CIVILIZED SOCIETIES in the history of the earth. If anything, the AZTEC/MAYAN tribes were WORSE than the ASSYRIANS. The ASSYRIANS used to TORTURE and KILL their enemies; the AZTECS/MAYANS did it to their OWN people, and in UNBELIEVABLE numbers!

"AZTEC society, like the MAYAN and TOLTEC societies

before it, was FILLED with UNSPEAKABLE CRUELTY. TORTURE, HUMAN SACRIFICE, and CANNIBALISM, ABOUNDED on an UNPRECEDENTED scale. The scale on which HUMAN SACRIFICE was practiced is MIND-BOGGLING...20,000 VICTIMS SACRIFICED IN FOUR DAYS DURING THE DEDICATION OF THE GREAT TEMPLE IN TENOCHTITLAN. 50,000 were sacrificed ANNUALLY". (J. STEVEN WILKINS, "AMERICA: THE FIRST 350 YEARS", 1988, page 5).

In months when rain was sought, a band of children were DROWNED, or WALLED UP IN A CAVE, or EXPOSED ON A MOUNTAIN-TOP; and the more they cried, the better the AUGURY for rain. At harvest time, victims were thrown into a FIRE or FURNACE, and their bodies pulled out with hooks, before they were consumed by the fire, so that the precious HEARTS could be extracted in the usual way, i.e. by cutting the heart, still beating, out of the victims chest. At periods when GROWTH and FERTILITY were required, the commonest practice was to behead a priestess and flay her, and for a priest to insert himself in the SKIN and lead a ritual dance. (JON WHITE, "CORTES AND THE DOWNFALL OF THE AZTEC EMPIRE", 1971, page 129).

THE AZTEC "NEW AGE": What makes the VICIOUS AZTECS and MAYANS so terribly attractive to the "NEW AGER"??? Well, THEY were "NEW AGERS" themselves.

Like the NAZIS, who would, centuries later, REVIVE the doctrine of "A NEW COSMIC AGE" of the AZTECS/MAYANS, (the NAZIS called it the THIRD REICH) figured, like the AZTECS/MAYANS, the NAZI'S OWN unique position as the ENLIGHTENED VANGUARD of a "NEW AGE", entitled the NAZIS to throw their weight around.

The AZTECS, as the NAZIS, urged on by their DIVINE MISSION, migrated further away from their original territory, towards traditional MEXICAN cultural centres, the AZTEC CULTURE was increasingly affected. Alien (MEXICAN) influences, both religious and social, were adopted; many MEXICAN gods were admitted into the AZTEC pantheon...there was CONSIDERABLE INCREASE in human sacrifice by the AZTECS, and their MILITARY MEN gained in power, taking over from the priests, more and more ADMINISTRATIVE functions, within their society. To live was to fight. The AZTEC Military had early come to believe that the gods had appointed THEM their legionaries, on earth, and to them had been given the DIVINE DUTY, AND PRIVILEGE, OF FIGHTING ON BEHALF OF THE gods, AGAINST THE COSMIC FORCES OF DESTRUCTION.(PARRINDER, "WORLD RELIGIONS FROM ANCIENT HISTORY TO THE PRESENT", page 77).

The people of MEXICO were crying out under the oppressive yoke of the AZTEC BARBARITY. To the MEXICAN'S, the SPANISH CONQUISTADOR, HORNANDO CORTES, WAS A SAVIOUR.

UP FROM BABYLON: The AZTEC/MAYAN empires are closer to OUR time, than to the ancient empire of BABYLON. From the AZTECS/MAYANS we can learn about the original pagan religion of BABYLON…the AZTECS/MAYANS **CAME FROM BABYLON**. (SYLVANUS MORLEY, "THE ANCIENT MAYA", 1956, page 24).

MEXICO'S ancient civilization is a transplant from MESOPOTAMIA. Christians know that the BIBLE refers to a time when "THE EARTH WAS DIVIDED". (GEN 10:25). We can look at any world map, or globe, and see that the continents OBVIOUSLY once fit into one great land-mass, with Central America quite close to BABYLON. Once the migrating BABYLONIANS settled down in Central America, they had enough leisure time to make use of the ARTS, SOCIAL SETUP, and RELIGION, they brought from BABYLON. So what we have in the AZTECS and MAYANS, is an example of almost pure BABYLONIAN religion, uncontaminated by any contact with BIBLICAL RELIGION, until the time of CORTES.

If ever any group of people on earth had the chance to show how NOBLE men NATURALLY ARE, WITHOUT THE NASTY FETTERS OF BIBLICAL CIVILIZATION, it WAS the AZTECS and the MAYANS. That is why "NEW AGERS" and their followers are sweeping the FACTS about those tribes, 'under the rug', and why we need to know more about them.

HIGHLY ADVANCED BARBARIANS: Perhaps the greatest lesson of ancient MEXICO is that cultures DO NOT evolve away from SUPERSTITION; WITCHCRAFT; and HUMAN SACRIFICE. These things simply become integrated into the governmental structure, then the JUSTIFICATIONS are more elaborate and "SCIENTIFIC". This pattern can be seen in BABYLON; EGYPT; GREECE; and ROME, but even MORE clearly with the AZTECS and MAYANS, who were CULTURALLY ISOLATED.

The apparent CONTRADICTION between the fantastic gardens of MONTEZUMA (which rivaled, and resembled the HANGING GARDENS OF BABYLON), and their utterly debased WITCHCRAFT and BLOOD-RITES, takes one's breath away.

These diametrically opposed attitudes toward LIFE and the UNIVERSE, existed side by side...a situation similar to that of NAZI GERMANY in OUR time, where a MYSTICO-MILITARISTIC WORLD VIEW, and a genuinely humanistic philosophy and literature COEXISTED. Such a mixture of HUMANISM and BARBARISM seems to be an INHERENT quality of the so-called rational animal. (MIGUEL LEON-PORTILLA, "AZTEC THOUGHT AND CULTURE", 1963, page 177).

The SAME conditions existed in all major pagan RELIGIONS/ EMPIRES...JUST BEFORE THEY FELL. Their HUMANISM (i.e. philosophy that makes man into a god), leads to their BARBARISM. "HUMANISM" is merely another face of PAGANISM. It was the PAGAN base of the AZTECS' civilized efforts, that DISTORTED their culture.

ONLY THE STRONG SURVIVE: They carefully cultivated their "MYSTICO-MILITARISTIC WORLD VIEW". Their children were steeped in the teaching of EVOLUTION, (in my opinion, DARWIN STOLE THIS THEORY FROM THE BABYLONIAN/AZTEC THEORY), a system in which only the strong survived. Children were sent to public school, where they learned of the "AZTECS' DESTINY IN THE "NEW AGE" OF THE FIFTH SUN". (in my opinion, the NAZIS OF GERMANY STOLE THIS PHILOSOPHY/'DESTINY' (the THIRD REICH), FROM THE BABYLONIANS/AZTECS). The children were ALSO INDOCTRINATED in the need to participate in the "WAR OF THE FLOWERS"; campaigns waged for the specific purpose of OBTAINING CAPTIVES TO SACRIFICE. This "RITUAL WARFARE" was touted as a means to prevent DECADENCE in the young. Any 'decadent'/weak AZTEC children/youths found themselves to be "CAPTIVES", to be SACRIFICED. The children were also taught that the gods needed CONTINUAL SACRIFICES as a bribe for continued blessings. Aside from that, the AZTECS could believe whatever they wanted to.

The AZTEC children/youths, boys as well as girls, were INDOCTRINATED with these fundamental principles, and their set of CONNECTED values, as long as they were at school, (from their seventh to their twentieth year), either by priest/priestesses at scientific/religious boarding-schools, or by Army Officers at less strict military and vocational schools. (PARRINDER, "WORLD RELIGIONS FROM ANCIENT HISTORY TO THE PRESENT", 1985, pages 82-83).

The ASSUMPTION was that strong people improved the nation, and the weak deserved their fate. (the handicapped and sickly also). (KARMA???). An AZTECS position in life depended ENTIRELY on their accomplishments in arms.

The strength of the AZTEC empire was a result of what can only be described as a WARRIOR CULT. This has now been revived by "NEW AGERS", ('fighting for THEIR rights), in spite of the fact that the AZTEC/MAYAN warriors FAILED, when faced with SPANISH CATHOLICS. (WILDE, "ON THE WARRIOR SAGE", 1988, VOL 1, #10, page 13). And NOT because the SPANISH had superior weapons, either. The SPANIARDS' edge in armament was ENTIRELY nullified by the size of the tiny expeditionary force CORTES led, compared to the VAST HORDES MONTEZUMA could and did mount.

"There is no question here of an urban and sophisticated society attacking a society that was merely agricultural and primitive. They were two virile peoples. It must be remembered how thoroughly saturated the AZTEC state was with the IDEAL OF

MILITARISM...the AZTEC nation was PERMANENTLY in arms, like SPARTA, or the GERMANY of the HOHENZOLLERS, or NATIONAL SOCIALISTS". (WHITE, "CORTES AND THE DOWNFALL OF THE AZTEC EMPIRE",1971, pages 83 and 114).

The central MEXICANS were NOT weak through lack of numbers or armament. They were weak MORALLY. The SPANIARDS, who were no Boy Scouts, were simply ASTOUNDED at the PERVERSITY of the AZTECS/MAYANS.

The religion of post-classic MEXICO, was shot through with WITCHCRAFT; SORCERY; and the baser forms of SUPERSTITION; it was a religion in which FEAR and CRUELTY were primary ingredients. The AZTECS/MAYANS did not look forward in a mood of serenity and expectation; they inhabited a world which threatened constantly; AN ANXIOUS PLACE. (WHITE, "CORTES AND THE DOWNFALL", page 151).

THE DEAR, SWEET MAYANS: The MAYANS were no better than the AZTECS. Recent archaeological and linguistic break throughs are significant; according to the new evidence, the MAYA also waged war to acquire captives, and were in the business of sacrificing human beings, long before the AZTECS.

JUST LIKE "NEW AGERS" today, who talk about blood "FEEDING THE PLANET", the MAYA believed that "BLOOD NOURISHED THE gods AND KEPT THE UNIVERSE IN ORDER". Blood was the mortar of MAYA ceremonial life. Their priests/priestesses devoted much of their time to pagan ASTRONOMY, that the "NEW AGE" people of today try to pass off as "ANCIENT WISDOM". (HESTER, "BLOOD AND SACRIFICE: A NEW LOOK AT THE MAYA", 1987, WORLD YEAR BOOK, page 190).

About all you can say for the MAYA, is that they were victims of the AZTECS. The "BIG BULLY" on the block, had got himself into the grip of a BIGGER "BULLY". Now the two of them were about to get the thrashing of their lives.

JUDGEMENT ON THE MAYANS: The SPANIARDS were not the first JUDGEMENT to hit the central MEXICAN TRIBES. SPANISH BISHOP LANDA, writing in 1566, detailed seventy-five years of progressive Judgments.

The last plague is rather interesting. The first white men to visit YUCATAN were survivors of a shipwreck. Five of them were sacrificed and EATEN by the MAYA. Four years later, the plague of 1515 arrived, the MAYACIMIL or 'easy death", COULD be traced to that CANNIBAL FEAST. If the Indians of North America could catch disease from white men, just by trading with them, the Indians of South America certainly had a better shot at catching something by EATING the white men. (MORLEY, "THE ANCIENT MAYA, page 97, 100-101).

The MAYA set the seal on their fate when their king and his court attempted to make their pilgrimage to offer human sacrifice at the "WELL OF SACRIFICE" at CHICHEN ITZA, in 1536. A t that point, no SPANIARDS were in MAYA territory. The SPANIARDS had tried twice to conquer the region, and gave up. (MORLEY, "THE ANCIENT MAYA", page 98).

The MAYAN king arranged for a safe-conduct through the territory of a hostile ruler. The king was a bit worried about his safety, because his great-grandfather had been involved in the killing of the great-grandfather of the hostile ruler of that territory. The king and his court were feasted well, but on the last day of the banquet, their hostile hosts rose up and SLAUGHTERED them.

"This pitted the two most powerful tribes in the northern peninsula AGAINST each other. This slaughter/massacre, coming so shortly before the third and final phase of the SPANISH conquest, SEALED THE FATE OF THE MAYA. The massacre revived OLD HATREDS, and EFFECTIVELY prevented a united stand against the SPANIARDS, when they returned to YUCATAN. (MORLEY, "THE ANCIENT MAYA", page 99).

JUDGEMENT ON THE AZTECS; The AZTECS had a chance to repent...and blew it. HERNANDO CORTES was a POWERFUL lay PREACHER. "In every city where he passed, CORTES called the priests and 'CACIQUES' together, and delivered a no-nonsense, proconsul type of speech. In the words of DIZA: "He told them as best he could, through our interpreter, that if they wished to be our brothers, they must throw their idols out of the temple, for they were very evil, and led them astray. He said they were not 'gods', but abominations that would bring their souls to hell".(WHITE, "CORTES AND THE DOWNFALL...", page 163).

CORTES described his preaching before MONTEZUMA and his officers and priests/priestesses in these words: "I made them understand by the interpreters how deceived they were, in putting their hope in idols made of unclean things by their own hands. I told them that they should know there was but one God, the Universal LORD OF ALL, who had Created the Heavens and Earth and ALL things, them and us, who was without beginning and immortal; that they should Adore Him and Believe in HIM, and not in any creature or thing". (WHITE, "CORTES AND THE DOWNFALL...", page 214).

CORTES and his men did everything they could to persuade the AZTECS to abolish human sacrifice and idolatry. Their preaching met with no success. When CORTES chided MONTEZUMA for his idolatry and bloody ways, after being taken on a tour through the largest temple, (where the SPANISH were DISGUSTED by the sight of FRESH HUMAN HEARTS, laid before the idols), MONTEZUMA replied that "it would take MORE sacrifices and blood to wash away the INSULTS to the gods, caused by CORTES'S words!"

The AZTECS decided to kill the SPANISH visitors; these men who had blasphemed the gods. But through a SERIES of AMAZING MIRACLES, CORTES'S tiny band WON. Time after time, they were surrounded by HUGE bands of warriors, and the SPANIARDS situation seemed hopeless, but EACH TIME THE SPANISH WERE DELIVERED OUT OF THE HANDS OF THE AZTECS.

In this JUDGEMENT, God was most THOROUGH. MONTEZUMA'S capitol city, more beautiful than any of the cities of Europe, was DESTROYED in house to house fighting. The AZTEC became the SPANIARD'S SLAVES.

From this JUDGEMENT OF GOD, the tribes of central MEXICO have NEVER RECOVERED. The descendants of the mighty AZTECS and MAYA are STILL second-class citizens in the land of their fathers. MISGUIDED attempts to REVIVE pride in ancient bloody empires is NOT what they need, but a pure faith in Jesus Christ...THAT they need. The faith their ancestors REJECTED, and by REJECTING, THEY LOST ALL.

THE IN-BETWEEN AGE
GREECE: THE BEAUTIFUL SIDE OF EVIL: DAN 8: 15, :16, :19, :21-22. "HI! I'M ZEUS, AND I'M HERE TO HELP YOU". Words to strike terror into the heart of any GREEK!

GREEKS liked to tell the story of two weary travelers that came into a town at sunset. From house to house they wandered, begging for a place to sleep and a bite of food, but the unfriendly householders turned them away. Finally, an old couple invited them in and fed them.

THEN CAME THE REVELATION! Up from the traveler's tattered robes, arose the figures of the gods ZEUS and HERMES. As the old couple fell on their knees before them, the two gods told them that they were going to destroy the entire town, as a punishment for its lack of hospitality. The old couple, however, would get a handsome reward for their kindness. They would be turned, that very minute, into TWO TREES, that would be the pillars for a new temple of ZEUS!

Hobnobbing with the GREEK gods was like playing Russian roulette with a totally loaded gun. No matter what happened, sooner or later the gods were 'gonna git ya'. Whether you were turned into a tree, or allowed to live forever (but not remain young), or simply deserted after the gods landed you in an impossible position, life wasn't going to be simple. If your great-grandfather had done something once, to anger a god, the FATES could be pursuing you for the rest of your life. (Ad Deum qui laetificat juventutem meam. [a note to myself]). And then there was that miserable afterlife to look forward to; roaming drearily around the underworld as a shadow…IF you were lucky enough, and managed to escape that portion of afterlife devoted to troublemakers and miscreants…they were tormented night and day forever. When an ancient religion has all this going for it, WHY do we find people trying to revive it in our day ??? Whatever else the "NEW AGERS" may be, they are most INDUSTRIOUS collectors of FAILED RELIGIONS.

The word GREECE evokes pictures of a sparkling blue AEGEAN SEA, and green hillsides, dotted with white columned buildings. HISTORIANS admire it as the "CRADLE OF DEMOCRACY"; PHILOSOPHERS remember "PLATO'S REPUBLIC", and the tragic death of SOCRATES; ARTISTS pine for the days of exulted PATRONS, supporting the SCULPTORS and THESPIANS…and EVERYONE seems to be surrounded by BEAUTY. However, that was NOT the REAL picture.

GREECE AS IT WAS: The ancient GREEK city-states were NOT bastions of FREEDOM, overflowing with COMMUNITY SPIRIT; they were ENFORCED REGIMES from INFANCY to DEATH. Citizenship was CONFERRED, and only on a small ELITE. The NOBEL'S of these "DEMOCRACIES", were the "VOICES OF THE gODS".

The WINNOWING process started at birth. Unsightly babies were SACRIFICED, or EXPOSED TO THE ELEMENTS, AND FODDER FOR THE WOLVES. HUMAN SACRIFICE and RITUAL DISMEMBERMENT **ABOUNDED** IN GREECE. Others, with PHYSICAL DEFECTS; those who were CRIPPLED or MUTILATED, were EXCLUDED from the life of the POLIS…(the city-state).

If one managed to avoid all these pitfalls, he would simply be a member of the "SERVING" class/caste…A SLAVE…unless he was CHOSEN for a higher purpose. The ELITE, those with proper breeding and blood, could reach down and select some SLAVES as ADMINISTRATORS. This 'ADMINISTRATION' class/caste KEPT ORDER. They were the GUARDIANS who CARRIED OUT THE WISHES OF THE "ELITE".

Even PLATO'S famous UTOPIA was only a VARIATION on this entire theme, but it was a bit more ORGANIZED and RUTHLESS. PLATO recommended that the STATE choose which couples will be ALLOWED to mate. Infants were to be taken IMMEDIATELY from their mothers, and "NO PARENT IS TO KNOW HIS OWN CHILD" (KAPLAN, "THE DIALOGUES OF PLATO", 1951, page 316).

PERMANENT day-care was a STATE responsibility, and the mother went back to work IMMEDIATELY after delivering. ALL religions and religious DOCTRINES were STATE-CONTROLLED. EDUCATION was pure INDOCTRINATION for STATE GOALS. MUSIC and LITERATURE were CENSORED so that the STATE'S PLANS would not be CORRUPTED. ALL THINGS, including WIVES, and CHILDREN, would be IN COMMON. There were to be NO PRIVATE MARRIAGES or PROPERTY.

The similarities between PLATO'S "UTOPIA", and the "UTOPIA" proposed by today's "NEW AGE" pagans, in their dreams of a ONE-WORLD GOVERNMENT; ONE WORLD CHURCH etc., are NOT COINCIDENTAL. In the midst of "NEW AGE" literature at their book stores, you find a copy of "THE DIALOGUES OF PLATO".

PROSTITUTION OF BOYS AND GIRLS: PLATO'S REPUBLIC did not have the young girls initiated into temple service as prostitutes; nor were young boys snatched up into institutionalized homosexuality, as they WERE in the REAL GREEK POLIS. But families in the REAL POLIS, HAPPILY SOLD their boys and girls into these PERVERSE relationships…IT WAS SEEN AS AN ADVANCEMENT IN SOCIETY. (W. BURKERT, "GREEK RELIGION", 1985, page 261).

Much like today's West, the GREEKS had a STRONG HOMOSEXUAL / LESBIAN MOVEMENT. In time, it VIRTUALLY captured the ELITE and the REINS OF GOVERNMENT, just as happened in CANADA, when the "NEW AGE" **PAGANISM** WAS

REVIVED, in CANADA. It seems the Canadian "NEW AGERS" stumbled on, and adopted, the GREEK model modus operendi. Homosexuality/lesbianism, the GREEKS TAUGHT, "WAS A HIGHER FORM OF LOVE THAN THE PRO-CREATIONAL LOVE OF A MAN AND WOMAN". This was a CLEAR denial of what THE BIBLE taught...that GOD made them MALE and FEMALE, (not Adam and Steve); NOT PART MALE AND PART FEMALE. There was no ANDROGYNY, HOMOSEXUALITY, or LESBIANISM in **GOD'S** CREATION or RELIGION, but there WAS in **LUCIFER'S** DESIGN and RELIGION.

In today's "NEW AGE" literature (out of satan's realm), HOMOSEXUALITY/LESBIANISM is once AGAIN labelled more loving than RIGHTEOUSNESS. They even argue that HOMOSEXUALITY/LESBIANISM is more loving to MOTHER EARTH, since they do not add to the "population" problem.

In ancient GREECE the trend of homosexuality/lesbianism continued until the reign of the homosexual TYRANT, ALEXANDER THE GREAT, after which the GREEK empire COLLAPSED.

GREEK SCIENTISM: An excellent example of the OUT-WORKINGS of "SCIENTIFIC GREECE" is the description of 'GREEK ALCHEMY", by LUTHER H. MARTIN, 1987.

In GREECE, "The transformative growth of seed grain into cereal grain was MYTHOLOGIZED as a natural growth "from the womb of MOTHER EARTH". The transformative growth of base metals into the nobler metals of silver and gold, was MYTHOLOGIZED as a growth deep within the "ORE-WOMB OF MOTHER EARTH. Through the techniques of 'cultivation', (ancient Greek genetic engineering, revived for us in THIS day and age???), the earth could be INDUCED to produce a greater cereal yield, and more quickly; similarly, ALCHEMICAL PRACTICES SOUGHT TO HASTEN AN ASSUMED NATURAL TRANSFORMATIONAL growth of base metals into PRECIOUS metal. (LUTHER MARTIN, "HELENISTIC RELIGIONS", 1985, page 44).

The FACT that science has DISPROVED the assertions of "SYMPATHETIC MAGIC", does NOTHING to dissuade "NEW

AGE" claims. The "NEW AGERS" simply shift gears and say that SYMPATHETIC POWER comes through "CHANNELS" (there's that word again) other than the PHYSICAL. THIS EFFECTIVELY removes empirical and experimental science from the field, since nobody can weigh and/or measure the SPIRITUAL plane. Thereby, MAGIC is asserted to be 'scientific', and then EXEMPTED from scientific scrutiny...just as in ancient GREECE. (MARTIN, "HELLENISTIC RELIGIONS",1985, page 52).

OUT OF THE MOUTHS OF CAVES: The ancient GREEKS had an enduring respect for certain forms of unexplained PHENOMENA. The DELPHIC ORACLE was one of these. (the "NEW AGERS" love THIS one). It was 'discovered' that ANYONE peering into a certain chasm in DELPHI, would be IMMEDIATELY seized by a "PROPHETIC SPIRIT"; and begin to utter HIDDEN TRUTH. It was not long before the path to the cliff was obstructed by a temple, and priestesses were assigned to risk the danger... (for a fee) of SPEAKING THE ORACLE. Other forms of random 'prophecy' were also held in esteem.

A "CLEDON", (an OMEN contained in a WORD or SOUND), was most reliable when uttered by those least capable of calculating their effect, such as FOOLS or CHILDREN. (MARTIN, "HELLENISTIC RELIGIONS", page 46).

"NEW AGE" pagans LOVE to appeal to the "WISDOM" of children, as a form of GUIDANCE for daily life. A woman put such stock in the random sayings of her children, that she made IMPORTANT decisions based on these words. (she died broken and babbling).

Most often in the West, we hear partial quotes of "OUT OF THE MOUTHS OF BABES", and "A LITTLE CHILD SHALL LEAD THEM", used to justify FOOLISHNESS. But the Scripture says "PRAISE FOR GOD" comes "FROM THE MOUTHS OF BABES", not "WISDOM", and that the child in Scripture is leading NOT THE NATION, but the ANIMALS; and that only during the "MILLENNIUM".

TRANCE "CHANNELLING" also takes advantage of the MYTH

that those people with the least control of their minds are the BEST "CHANNELS" for granting wisdom from the gods. Yet, we do NOT see "NEW AGE" pilgrimages to MENTAL HOSPITALS, where such wisdom SHOULD, according to the theory, ABOUND.

HERE COME DE gODDESS: None of this 'ANCIENT' GREEK pagan corruption would have been complete without the goddess and her perverse companions. 'Ancient' Greece hosted two great mystic religions. 1. The adoration of the "great goddess CYBELE (also spelled SIBYL); and 2. The DIONYSIAN BACCHANALIA, a transplanted OSIRIS worship. In BOTH CASES, THE 'FEMININE' WAS SOVEREIGN; priests who wished to serve CYBELE, along-side her priestess, were clothed and made up as women. They engaged in a FRENETIC initiation dance, in which they cut their own arms, and bled before the goddess, then CASTRATED themselves; a BIZARRE, ANCIENT equivalent of the SEX-CHANGE OPERATION"(MARTIN, "HELLENISTIC RELIGIONS", page 83).

As for the BASIC feasts, they were first exclusively for women, but later expanded to initiate men. The combination of WINE and SEX at these services, led to greater and greater DEBAUCHERY (a word derived from BACCHUS...who loved it). Men that did not keep this a SECRET, were tortured and killed. Then stories were spread that they were "CARRIED OFF BY THE gODS" (MARTIN, "HELLENISTIC RELIGIONS", page 97).

Today, pagan books SERIOUSLY suggest we should REVIVE the GREEK PANTHEON. (D. L. MILLAR, "THE NEW POLYTHEISM: REBIRTH OF THE gods AND goddesses", 1974). There was a float, DEDICATED to the GREEK goddesses, covered with college girls, dressed in flowing GREEK goddess robes, parading down the streets of St. Louis, MO. They distributed "NEW AGE" literature, especially of the FEMINIST variety, inviting OPEN WORSHIP of APHRODITE, and other goddesses.

But the "NEW AGERS" who want to bring back the GREEK gods/goddesses, have a strange habit of NOT telling us the REAL FACTS about 'ancient' GREEK RELIGION. Here is a BRIEF recap of the "GLORIES" of 'ancient' GREEK **PAGANISM**.

NATURE POWER: The GREEKS worshipped NATURE, but they did not love it. (A. H. NEWMAN, "A MANUAL OF CHURCH HISTORY", 1899 & 1933, 1:20). "For the Greeks, all of nature was instinct with life. A mountain was the SKY-gOD'S THRONE; worshippers went to the HILLTOP to pray for RAIN; EVERY tree had it's DRYAD; and the OAK was sacred to ZEUS; the OLIVE to ATHENE; the BAY to APOLLO; the MYRTLE to APHRODITE; the POPLAR to HERCULES...each SPRING had it's NYMPH; each RIVER it's god".

Those who stayed in the country might encounter GOAT-FOOTED PAN, or the SATYRS and CENTAURS (half man and half beast). The SEA was the home of POSEIDON and of PROTEUS, with his MAGIC changes of FORM, and the SEA-GREY spirit GLAUCUS, and of exquisite NEREIDS, and of monstrous TRITONS, and of DEADLY SIRENS.

"This affects our understanding of a number of passages in GREEK LITERATURE. There is little appreciation of NATURAL BEAUTY for its own sake; The Greeks did not climb their mountains to look at the view. NATURE was USEFUL, or she was AWESOME and DESTRUCTIVE. But basically, NATURE meant LIVING POWER. The goddess DIOTIMA, in her catalogue of beauty, "THE SYMPOSIUM", does not mention beauty in NATURE". (PARRINDER, "WORLD RELIGIONS FROM ANCIENT HISTORY TO THE PRESENT", 1985, page 149).

A study of the names in the BIBLE shows that SEVERAL VERY ANCIENT HEBREW PATRIARCHS were the SOURCE of certain gods. TUBAL-CAIN, for example, who is said to be the first man to forge TOOLS OUT OF BRONZE and IRON, is undoubtedly, the origin for the SMITH-gOD, VULCAN. And JAVAN, one of the sons of JAPHETH (the eventual ancestor of the GREEK NATION), could very well have been, (via the power, might, grace and blessings of satan, via his angels, spirits, demon saints, instruments and servants), transformed into the CREATOR-gOD JOVE. We can see how LITERALLY the BIBLE means it, when it says men turned aside from worshipping THE CREATOR, to worshipping what HE CREATED; i.e. ATTRIBUTING TO NOTABLE ANCESTORS, THE VERY DEEDS OF GOD, THE TRUE DIVINE CREATOR.

EUHEMERUS, an ancient GREEK writer, who studied this matter, came to the conclusion that **ALL** the "gods" had once been ANCIENT FAMOUS RULERS OF THE HEBREW RELIGION. This theory came to be named "EUHEMERISM", after him. This theory does not fit every god, but it DOES explain the ORIGIN of a fair number of them. Probably, in my opinion, the gods that DO NOT fit, were thrown in, for good measure, via followers of the ones that DO fit. (via... you know who). Other gods are accounted for by the attempt to personify natural processes.

In my opinion, many pagan religions were founded by 'mysterious' individuals, who wandered into a territory, and simply plagiarized the HEBREW RELIGION, passing those teachings off as their OWN, and, of course, changing those teachings to their OWN way of empirical thinking, via the help and grace of satan, and founded pagan religions of satan's realm. "It has LONG been KNOWN, that the worship of the god JOVE, spread much further than the worship of merely local deities". (PARRINDER, "WORLD RELIGIONS FROM ANCIENT HISTORY TO THE PRESENT", page 19).

"The original CREATOR-gOD of the ARYANS, was WELL KNOWN among the INDO-EUROPEAN NATIONS. His first name was DYAUS PITAR (divine father), which is the same as the GREEK god ZEUS PATER; the Latin JUPITER or DEUS; the early GERMAN god TIU or ZIU; and the NORSE god TYR. Another name was "the heavenly one" i.e. the SANSKRIT god VARUNA; the GREEK god OURANOS; or "the friend", SANSKRIT god MITRA; and the PERSIAN god MITHRA". (ROBERT BROW, "RELIGION: ORIGINS AND IDEAS", 1972, page 14).

When we collect all the versions of the god JOVE, and

stick them together, we begin to see just how UNINVENTIVE, (remember; satan CANNOT be 'original'), pagans really are. The god JOVE bears a strong resemblance to the nastier type of a MODERN TYCOON, somewhat like J. R. EWING, in the TV show "DALLAS", right down to the cheating heart. No wonder none of his follower wanted to meet the gods they had created.

NO LOVE OF THE GODS: It was no fun to meet a god. In fact, much of GREEK pagan religion was designed to PREVENT, or at least MITIGATE the evils of such a meeting.

"In HOMER'S poems, no 'hero' confessed to ELATION when a god revealed his presence. The 'hero' did not court the gods, or strive to meet them. When a 'hero' chanced upon a god, and as the first TERROR left him, he might beg for practical, earthly favours. It took a very SPECIAL 'hero', (a child of one of the gods), to DARE TO PROTEST to a god face to face. Other 'hero's' who were more restrained, and mere mortals, naturally, would observe the greatest restraint. The experience of emotional WARMTH and REASSURANCE, and a SENSE of UNITY with surrounding nature, were NOT the hallmarks of an encounter with DIVINITY, (or god), in early pagan GREECE. (R. L. FOX, "PAGANS AND CHRISTIANS", 1987, pages 110 and 113).

SYNCRETISM: The GREEK pagans loved to hear NEW things, and follow NEW religions. GREEK pagan religion soon resembled our "NEW AGE" book racks, in our local "NEW AGE" bookstores, in the way it LUMPS TOGETHER **ALL** kinds of pagan spirituality. The GREEK pagans would travel over land and sea, to bring home a single strange, new teaching.

"Pagan Greek MAGIC has been influenced from time immemorial by ORIENTAL belief. No nation welcomed foreign ideologies more warmly than the HELLENES. Their priest/priestesses, philosophers, and historians ROAMED FOREIGN LANDS. Their quest for 'knowledge' led the wonder worker APOLLONIUS of TYANA to the shores of INDIA. PLATO tells of "CULTURAL TIES" with EGYPT and CRETE. Pagan GREEKS accompanied the pagan PERSIANS, DARUS and XERXES on their expeditions. Mythical figures and gods of the ORIENT, have been HELLENIZED. The DELPHIC CULT originated in CRETE; the god ADONIS, sprang from the HEBREW ADONAI; the god APHRODITE is the embellished and pacified god ASTARTE; the god ISIS became the god ATHENE; and DIONYSUS hardly veils his ALIEN origin". (KURT SELIGMAN, "THE HISTORY OF MAGIC AND THE OCCULT", 1975, page 48).

The ONLY religion the pagan Greeks REFUSED to borrow from was JUDAISM. Although they had MUCH contact with the land of PALESTINE, the pagan Greeks were simply too PROUD to believe such a SIMPLE and MORALLY DEMANDING doctrine as that of the GOD OF ISRAEL. It left no room for their love of TECHNIQUE and RITUAL. It gave the poor as much access to God as the rich, and the simple as much chance of spiritual enlightenment as the wise. Worst of all, the ISRAELITES had a MORAL LAW, that did NOT endorse all of the pagan Greek's favourite kinds of SEXUAL PERVERSIONS and DIVERSIONS.

NO SIN: The idea of SIN as an OFFENCE against a Holy God, and as involving GUILT was almost WHOLLY ABSENT among pagan GREEKS. Sin was conceived as "IGNORANCE"; A FAILURE TO UNDERSTAND. (blameless). (NEWMAN, "A MANUAL OF CHURCH HISTORY", 1:21).

The pagan Greeks had holy PLACES, but no holy MEN. (FOX, "PAGANS AND CHRISTIANS", page 253).

The pagan Greek MORALS, such as they were, were derived from human nature, rather than from the BEING, and MIND OF GOD. (HAROLD LINDSELL, "THE NEW PAGANISM: UNDERSTANDING AMERICAN CULTURE AND THE ROLE OF THE CHURCH", 1987, page 49). Anyone who understands HUMAN NATURE, realizes what an ABSOLUTE mother lode of DEGENERACY, this idea opens up.

The pagan Greeks considered themselves VERY WISE, and had a horror of "SIMPLISTIC" teachings. This led them to tolerate everything EXCEPT the belief that there was an OBVIOUS right and wrong in DOCTRINE or PRACTICE. As R. L. FOX points out: "IF the supreme God was UNKNOWABLE, who was to say which one of the many cults, of different people, was RIGHT or WRONG??? At its heart, therefore, pagan theology could extend a peaceful coexistence to ANY worship which, in turn, was willing to coexist in peace. In pagan "religiousness", there was no fear of heresy, no urge to orthodoxy and Clerical "control". The Greek pagans' fear was a fear of the RANDOM anger of their gods". (FOX, "PAGANS AND CHRISTIANS", page 253).

"APHRODITE MADE ME DO IT": How can there be no RIGHT and/or WRONG??? It is because the gods move you to do WRONG, just as often as they move you to RIGHT. Among the pagan Greeks, "APHRODITE MADE ME DO IT", was a LEGITIMATE excuse for ANY sexual perversion or outrage. "APHRODITE 'puts desire' into animals, as well as into men, women, and gods. She leads astray "EVEN THE REASON OF ZEUS"; it is SHE who "easily makes ZEUS mate with mortal women, unknown to HERA, the SISTER/WIFE of ZEUS. EMPHASIZING the IRREDUCIBLE and IRRATIONAL character of CONCUPISCENCE, **JUSTIFIES** the amorous adventures of ZEUS (and ANY other, for that matter, including the gods); 'adventures' that will be INDEFINITELY repeated, OVER and OVER AGAIN, by gods, heroes, men, women, and animals; there is a RELIGIOUS JUSTIFICATION for perverted, outrages, sexual activities; (**ANYTHING GOES), ALL incited by APHRODITE**, THEREFORE, sexual excesses and outrages perversity, MUST be recognized as of **DIVINE ORIGIN**". (ELIADE, "A HISTORY OF RELIGIOUS IDEAS", 1978, VOL 1, page 283).

Acts of BRUTAL violence/slaughter could be blamed on the "INSPIRATIONS, COUNSELS, and/or URGINGS of the god MARS; acts of thievery on the god HERMES (the patron god of thieves), and SO ON. As long as it's O. K. with the gods, it CANNOT be wrong.

PERVERTED HEROES': As it turned out, almost EVERYTHING was O. K. with the 'gods'. The "HEROES", BELOVED of the gods, and whom "MODERN" "NEW AGERS" tend to think of as GENUINELY HEROIC, acted more like **DEPRAVED** men and women. The REAL pagan Greek myths were definitely NOT bedtime stories for children. Together, the 'HEROES' perpetrated just about EVERY disgusting, perverted deeds the human mind has ever invented/perpetrated.

'HEROES' USUALLY fell victims to INSANITY. (ORESTES, BELLEROPHON, even the exceptional HERCULES, when he slaughtered his sons). As for their sexual behaviour, it is EXCESSIVE or ABHORENT PERVERSITY. "HERACLES impregnates the FIFTY daughters of THESPIUS in one night; THESEUS is famous for his NUMEROUS rapes (HELEN, ARIADNE, etc.); ACHILLES ravishes STATONICE. The 'HEROES' commit INCEST with their daughters and/or their mothers, and indulge in MASSACRES from ENVY or ANGER, or often, for NO REASON AT ALL, they even slaughter their fathers, mothers, children or relatives. (ELIADE, "A HISTORY OF RELIGIOUS IDEAS, VOL 1, page 288).

SUPERSTITIONS: Pagan Greek life was an absolute MASS of SUPERSTITIONS and FEARFUL ATTEMPTS TO PLACATE THE 'gods'. Only later, when schools such as EPICUREANS and STOICS began to challenge the existence of the gods, did a few upper-class Greeks begin to shake free of a lifestyle bound by HUNDREDS of COMPLICATED rituals and taboos. (SUPERSTITIOUSNESS is generally defined as a kind of COWARDICE, when confronted with the super-natural).

Even a pagan like THEOPHRASTUS can see that such behaviour is "RIDICULOUS". Yet, today's "NEW AGE" thinkers are FEVERISHLY attempting to 'DISCOVER' all such ancient superstitions, so they can COPY them! Superstition is supposed to get you 'EXTRA POWER', and you don't DARE to omit them for fear of losing your place in the 'UNIVERSE'.

FEARFUL MAGIC: Pagan Greeks could not evade the GRIP of MAGIC and RITUALS. MAGIC WAS USED TO PROTECT yourself from the EVIL SPIRITUAL WORLD, not as a way to put an extra tiger in your spiritual tank. Only today are people foolish enough to believe in the "GREAT SPIRITUAL POWERS OF MAGIC".

ALL the philosophers of pagan Greece believed in the reality of MAGIC. HERACLITUS, THALES, PINDAR, XENOPHON, even SOCRATES, were unable to elude the "ENCHANTED CIRCLE"! The later Greek philosophers, like PORPHYRY (A.D. 233-303), were ENTIRELY devoted to MAGICAL POWERS. Their ceremonies were initiated NOT to please the gods, but solely to repel devils. (SELIGMAN, "THE HISTORY OF MAGIC AND THE OCCULT", 1975, page 48).

MISERABLE LIFE AFTER DEATH: Life after death for the pagan Greek was an unmitigated disaster. Although they did not believe they would have to suffer through endless existences on earth, as did the HINDU ARYANS, the pagan Greek afterlife was a dreary, hopeless place resembling the "SHEOL OF THE BIBLE", from which their gods were unable to save them.

For HOMER'S contemporaries, death was a diminished and humiliating post-existence in the underground darkness of "HADES", (ancient HEBREW?) peopled by pallid shadows, without strength and without memory. (ACHILLES, whose ghost ULYSSES succeeded in calling up, declares that he would choose to be on earth, the slave of a poor man, "rather than to reign over the dead". (ELIADE, "A HISTORY OF RELIGIOUS IDEAS", VOL 1, page 260).

WHOSE GOD IS TOO SMALL ? The main appeal of the pagan Greek gods, remains their INDULGENCE OF HUMAN SIN, so APPEALING to the worst in human nature. The gods are CARICATURE, UNLOVABLE, even downright NASTY specimens. They wield their power like a three-year-old might wield a blowtorch, scorching everyone around. They cannot save their followers in THIS life, or in the NEXT.

All this does NOT stop today's "NEW AGE" pagans from trying to make the pagan Greek gods sound BIGGER and NOBLER than the CHRISTIAN GOD. One such "NEW AGE" writer, JOHN HOLLAND SMITH, at the close of his book "THE DEATH OF CLASSICAL PAGANISM", 1976, page 249, has the EFFRONTERY to say "But the gods remain. And what they (the Christians) say is: "YOUR GOD IS TOO SMALL" I say there is divinity in generosity, in tolerance and compromise, and acceptance of differences, though none in narrowness and exclusivity". My question is: is John Smith asking for TOLERANCE and COMPROMISE and ACCEPTANCE from Christians??? Does he not know that MANY Christians erroneously **DO** give TOLERANCE and COMPROMISE and ACCEPTANCE to pagans of the religions of Lucifer's realm??? However, let's juxtapose what J.H.SMITH says, with the observations of R.L. FOX - "The pagan gods come in pocket-sized models, so that anyone could travel with them and keep them handy". Now, really, WHOSE god is too small???

GOD'S JUDGEMENT ON PAGAN GREECE: Pagan Greece, like EVERY other pagan empire before it, was destined for a plot in the graveyard of history. Even while ISRAEL languished under the iron rule of BABYLON, the PROPHET DANIEL predicted that pagan Greece would rise to world power under ALEXANDER THE GREAT...and subsequently be divided, diminished, and finally overthrown. DAN 8: 5-22.   This prophesy was fulfilled...TO THE LETTER.

Pagan Greek INFLUENCE, however, lingered long after its fall from power. The pagan ROMAN empire drew HEAVILY from pagan Greek ideals and culture. It wasn't until the downfall of pagan ROME, that pagan Greece was FULLY submerged.

Purely UTILITARIAN attempts at order, destroys GOD'S order. Science, CORRECTLY used, REVEALS GOD'S WISDOM IN CREATION, and leads to HIS praise. But 'science' that IGNORES God's EXISTENCE, and seeks to justify human ENDEAVORS and MOTIVES, become a MONSTROUS machine. RATIONALISM, without FAITH is DEADLY...as dead as the gods of pagan Greece, and among ALL other pagan societies.

ROME: CHRISTIANS AND PAGANS TAKE OFF THE GLOVES: DAN 2: 39, :40, :44. "HI! I'M JOVE, AND I'M HERE TO CONQUER YOU". Or, as JULIUS CAESAR PUT IT…"I CAME, I SAW, YOU'RE HISTORY".

This PROUD pagan empire, one of the greatest in WORLD HISTORY, was the FIRST TO BOW THE KNEE IN ADORATION, TO JESUS CHRIST. Pagan laws and practices were exchanged for CHRISTIAN laws and practices. Emperor's gave their fond approval, (and money), to Christian Church efforts in EVANGELISM and RELIEF WORK. EVERYTHING, from art to zoology was affected by the coming, WITH POWER, of the GOSPEL OF CHRIST.

Pagan Roman religion, was VERY LIKE PAGAN Greek religion, therefore we don't need to look at it separately in any detail. Pagan Rome shared the SAME "NEW AGE" claim, and emphasis on DIVERSITY, TOLERANCE, and COMPROMISE; the SAME interests in ASTROLOGY/ASTRONOMY, DIVINATION, MAGIC, SEXUAL PERVERSITY, AND THE REST OF PAGAN GREEK PRACTICES AND RITUALS. And even with the same pagan Greek gods; with BAAL, (now known as SATURN), and a few other MESOPOTAMIAN gods thrown in. (DAVIES, "HUMAN SACRIFICES", 1981, pages 50-51).

The pagan Romans were, at first, cooler than the pagan Greeks about their religions; more interested in the priest/priestesses PRECISELY following the CORRECT RITUALS, than interested in EMOTIONAL HIGHS, however, ECSTATIC mystery cults became 'TRENDY' during the first centuries A.D., for those who SOUGHT a religious "HIGH/JOLT". The pagan Romans were also EXTREMELY concerned that religion serve the ends of the godlike STATE. They were also aware of the DANGER, an UNAPPROVED CULT could bring to their highly regimented society. WORLDLY-WISE pagan Rome, was an UNLIKELY CANDIDATE to be taken by SURPRISE, by a NEW religion.

TODAY, 'Christians' often expect the GOSPEL to triumph ONLY in UNSOPHISTICATED areas, while EXPECTING to CONTINUE to LOSE GROUND in HIGHLY DEVELOPED cultures. Yet, pagan

Rome had WEALTH and SOPHISTICATION **TO BURN.** Two thousand years ago, WEALTHY pagan Rome had INDOOR PLUMBING, and some of the roads and bridges pagan Romans built, endure to this day. Pagan Rome trade and commerce encompassed the civilized world, AND BEYOND. And pagan Rome MANAGEMENT SKILLS, allowed pagan Rome to RULE PROVINCES separated by THOUSANDS OF MILES. Pagan Rome WAS a THOROUGHLY pagan society TO BEGIN WITH; a society PROUD of its traditions. PAGANS controlled the ARTS; the SPORTS; the GOVERNMENT, and the BUREAUCRACY. WHOLE INDUSTRIES were built on supporting the PAGAN TRADITIONS, such as the CRAFTSMEN. (who make statues of the gods).

Against this MIGHT OF PAGAN ROME, were pitted a few hundred Disciples of a JEWISH carpenter named JESUS. SOON in pagan Rome, it would be required, BY LAW, and perfectly LEGAL, to INFORM on Christians, and to KILL them in the GLADIATOR RING.Further, there was an INCENTIVE to inform on Christians; the informer could CLAIM and would RECEIVE all of the PROPERTY and BELONGINGS of the CHRISTIANS he turned in.

Governors were REQUIRED to ferret out the Christians, and DESTROY them. Pagan priests/priestesses would WHIP Christians with a FRENZY. Christian BASHING and KILLING was the order of the day. The Christians were blamed for EVERY disaster, from bad weather to a Barbarian uprising anywhere in the empire.

Under such conditions, the "new" Christians would have NO SOCIAL STANDING. WISE, WEALTHY, or INFLUENTIAL pagan Romans would NOT join them. The Church of Christ, with it's COMMITMENT to care for the POOR, would find itself MOSTLY made up of the POOR and the DREGS of pagan Roman society. In LOS VEGAS, the "ODDS' would have EASILY been a thousand to one AGAINST the Christians.

All the same, THE CHRISTIANS WON. How did THIS happen???

THE *BLOOD* OF THE MARTYRS IS THE BLOOD OF THE MARTYRS: Sentimentalist like to quote TERTILLIAN'S phrase:

"THE BLOOD OF THE MARTYRS IS THE SEED OF THE CHURCH", as an explanation of how a RAG –ATAG band of Christians managed to GROW, THRIVE, and TAKE OVER THE PAGAN ROMAN EMPIRE.

All this loose talk about the benefits of 'MARTYRS BLOOD' sidesteps the REAL reason for how Christians took over the pagan Roman empire.

Christians of today are NOT under the same strange DISADVANTAGE, because there is a shortage of lions that like to eat Christians. We can find, and put into practice, the same strategies that delivered pagan Rome into the Christian camp, to put CANADA back into the Christian camp.

CHRIST VERSUS CAESAR: But first, what exactly were the pagan Romans and the Born-again Christians contending about??? Today, we tend to think that they were arguing over which religion was TRUE...CHRISTIANITY or PAGANISM. In a sense, that was the issue.

But Christians were NOT thrown to the lions for believing in Jesus. In pagan Rome, you could believe in JESUS, or MITHRA, or ISIS, or YAHWEH, or ANY gods, or combination of gods, without fear of REPRISAL. Christians were thrown to the lions for believing that JESUS **IS** LORD OF ALL.

Pagan Rome had RELIGIOUS FREEDOM. You could believe anything you wanted to, as long as you upheld the right of other people TO BELIEVE ANYTHING THEY WANTED TO, **_AND_** acknowledged **CAESAR IS A GOD**.

Why did the early Christians DIE rather than offer a pinch of incense before a statue of Caesar??? THEY WOULD WORSHIP NO GOD BUT THE CHRISTIAN HOLY TRINITY. THAT is fairly obvious and simple. But what is NOT so obvious and simple, is WHY THE PAGAN ROMAN GOVERNMENT **INSISTED** THAT THE

CHRISTIANS SACRIFICE TO CAESAR. What did THEY care who the Christians worshipped??? What did it matter to them???

The answer is **TREMENDOUSLY** important for **US** today. Pagan Roman leaders did not want Christians "IMPOSING THEIR MORALITY ON **THEM**. For Caesar to be god, meant that CAESAR made the LAWS; he could NOT be judged by any "HIGHER" Law. CHRISTIANS believed in a HIGHER LAW by which ALL MEN, including RULERS, were to be Judged. THIS struck at the very HEART of the pagan Roman SECULAR STATE.

This belief in the absolute RIGHT of the Ruler to do whatever he wants, is the ESSENTIAL underpinning of any tyrant that has EVER EXISTED on the face of the earth. NO TYRANT can afford to acknowledge the existence of a higher Lord than himself, TO WHOSE LAW he is accountable.

The early Christian Leaders KNEW this. That is why the FIRST recorded prayer of the APOSTLES, in THE BOOK OF ACTS was for **BOLDNESS** TO SPEAK OUT FOR JESUS **IN SPITE OF** THE OPPOSITION OF THE CIVIL RULERS. ACTS 4:24-31.   I n this Prayer, the Apostles quoted PSALM 2:1-2.   The NEXT verse :3, goes on to explain WHY the pagan Roman rulers are so **ANGRY**... "LET US BREAK THEIR CHAINS" they say, "AND THROW OFF THEIR **FETTERS**". Pagans HATE God's ABSOLUTE, NON-NEGOTIABLE LAWS. The pagans want to be gods and make their OWN laws, without ANY restraint on them at all!

Bible HISTORY is the story of GOD'S MEN confronting rulers with the **MESSAGE** that RULERS CANNOT DO JUST WHATEVER THEY LIKE. Think of the Prophet NATHAN telling DAVID off for his adultery, and the constant stream of Prophets who CONFRONTED the KINGS and LEADERS of both ISRAEL and JUDA.H.

Remember how DANIEL warned NEBUCHADNEZZAR to repent of his evil deeds, and how GOD subsequently humbled NEBUCHADNEZZAR in order to IMPRESS that **MESSAGE** on him??? Remember how JOHN THE BAPTIST met his end as a result of telling KING HEROD it was WRONG for him to have his brother's wife??? We could MULTIPLY examples.

Recognizing JESUS as the "KING OF KINGS" means that RULERS, AS WELL AS THEIR PEOPLE, are called to bow the knee before HIM. The Christian **MESSAGE** was that the 'LAW' was **NOT** just whatever CAESAR said it was, JUST AS **TODAY**, the **MESSAGE** must be that the 'LAW' is **NOT** just whatever the **SUPREME COURT** says it is.

This might appear to be a **DANGEROUS MESSAGE; AND IT IS.** However, GOD can use even "THE WRATH OF MEN" to praise HIM. (PSALM 76:10).

Strangely, the very SUCCESS of the pagan Greek, and the pagan Roman **TOTALITARIANISM** HELPED PREPARE THE WAY FOR THE **GOSPEL**.

Pagan GREECE provided a UNIVERSAL pagan language known throughout the pagan Roman empire...It ALSO provided the pagan conceptual frameworks of GREEK PHILOSOPHY...The pagan ROMANS provided STABLE GOVERNMENT; a system of ROADS, superior to any before it; and the PAX ROMANA. (travel around the pagan Roman empire was SAFE). (HAROLD LINDSELL, "THE NEW PAGANISM: UNDERSTANDING AMERICAN CULTURE AND THE ROLE OF THE CHURCH", 1987, page 14).

CERTAINTY OF TRUTH AND INTOLERANCE OF ERROR: Today, as in pagan Roman times, "WAFFLING IS IN". Christians "DIALOGUE" about all sorts of previously **NON-NEGOTIABLE** issues. Church Councils meet to "DEBATE" the advisability of female priests/priestesses or elders; and homosexual/lesbian ordination; marriages etc; "PUNDITS" PONDER **WHICH** parts of the BIBLE are TRUTH; while feminists take an x-acto knife to BIBLE HISTORY (the record of PATRIARCHAL BIAS); and DOCTRINAL TEACHINGS ("our mother who art in Heaven"). This Religious TOLERANCE, ACCEPTANCE and COMPROMISE, that is so WELL known THIS DAY, was JUST AS WELL KNOWN in the first centuries after Christ, among the CHRISTIANS and the PAGANS.

NEVER was there a more tolerant/compromising age, than

that into which CHRISTIANS appeared...SYNCRETISM was the religious hall-mark of the time. There were no clear lines of demarcation among the foreign cults, which showed a MARKED HOSPITALITY IN RELIGION. Different gods agreed to be housed in the same temple. The same priests/priestesses could officiate for half a dozen deities/gods. Men/women were willing to try every religion and/or philosophy in the field.

It was now just as fashionable to owe allegiance to the gods of the NILE; SYRIA; PERSIA; SAMOTH; GREECE and ROME, as it had been in the previous 'EPOCH', to acknowledge only one national PANTHEON. POLYTHEISM is naturally tolerant; and the spirit of the age, only INCREASED religious tolerance. (S. ANGUS, "THE MYSTERY RELIGIONS", 1975, pages 277, 278, 281).

Christians did not share in this 'FEEL GOOD' spirit of UNIVERSAL TOLERANCE. Christians had **TRUTH**, and were in no mood to trade it for the supposed **INSIGHTS** of pagans. While pagans patted each other on the back, and affirmed each other's SELF-WORTH, Christian Preachers talked of SIN and a JUDGEMENT TO COME. The New Testament Epistles STRONGLY DENOUNCED error, and WARNED Church Leaders to BOUNCE OUT the HERETICS who were BOUND to SNEAK IN.

God **HIMSELF** took a hand in ENFORCING Church DISCIPLINE...witness the sudden deaths of ANANIAS and SAPPHIRA, ACTS 5:1-11, and the JUDGEMENTS threatened against the false prophetess JEZEBEL. REV 2:20-23. The areas for TOLERANCE and GENUINE DISAGREEMENT were spelled out...matters of which days to CELEBRATE UNTO THE LORD; of WHAT KIND OF FOOD AND DRINK TO CONSUME. The NATURE OF CHRIST; THE NECESSITY OF REPENTANCE; THE ROLES OF MEN AND WOMEN; SEXUAL MORALITY; among OTHER things, **WERE *NOT* NEGOTIABLE**.

CHRISTIANITY, unlike the PAGAN CULTS based on MYTHS, WAS A HISTORICAL RELIGION. The early Christian **KNEW** that Jesus Christ **ACTUALLY LIVED, DIED,** and **WAS RESURRECTED**. Instead of sitting around, picking at the Gospels, trying to locate the "HISTORICAL JESUS", they **_KNEW_** the "HISTORICAL JESUS". The earliest Christian had **SEEN** Christ **in person**; those who came later, not only had a PERSONAL relationship with Christ in their **spirits**, but also had the documents of MATTHEW, MARK, LUKE and JOHN to consult.

"Where the BACCHIC societies offered a MYTH of their gods, Jews and Christians offered HISTORY; the pagan mysteries conveyed a secret experience, whereas the Jews and Christians offered a **_REVELATION_**, based on texts" (R.L.FOX, "PAGANS AND CHRISTIANS", 1987, page 94).

"The Christians could cite PROPHECIES…they knew EXACTLY who God was, in an age of discreet uncertainty; THEIR GOD WAS A GOD of HISTORY, proven in events; after all, He sent a SON, to redeem men by actions of TOTAL SELFLESSNESS". (FOX, "PAGANS AND CHRISTIAN", page 261).

The Christian "CERTAINTY" spilled over to matters of MORALS and PHILOSOPHY. Pagans tried, and failed, to REASON out answers about the origin of the world, and the PROPER conduct of human beings; Christians KNEW the answers. They were written down in God's book, the B I B L E. (**B**asic **I**nstructions **B**efore **L**eaving **E**ARTH). And, unlike pagan teachings, the **B I B L E WAS NOT SUBJECT TO CHANGE.** ANYONE who ADDED TO, or TAKES AWAY FROM the **CANONICAL WRITINGS**, would come under **ALMIGHTY JUDGEMENT.** The Bible ITSELF said so. REV 22:18-19.

This INTOLERANCE preserved the fledgling Christian Church, from the wasting disease of SYNCRETISM with which the pagan Roman empire languished. In seeking to make the gate WIDE, and the road BROAD, that led to religious acceptance, the pagan Roman CULTS succeeded only into finally blending together, and losing their collective credibility.

In the matter of **INTOLERANCE**, Christianity differed from ALL PAGAN RELIGIONS, and **SURPASSED** JUDAISM; in THAT respect, Christianity stood in direct opposition to the spirit of the "NEW AGE". TOLERANCE which results from INDIFFERENCE or INDECISION. The HOSPITALITY and SYNCRETISM of the pagan competitors of Christianity, while greatly enhancing their POPULARITY, ultimately COMPASSED their DOWNFALL. (S. ANGUS, "THE MYSTICAL RELIGIONS", 1975, pages 277, 278, 281).

People did not join the Church in order to experience 'WARM FELLOWSHIP'; to get A RELIGIOUS 'HIGH/JOLT'; to reach their 'FULL POTENTIAL'; or to solve their 'PSYCHOLOGICAL PROBLEMS'. They joined the Church because THE CHRISTIAN MESSAGE WAS **TRUE.**

BOLDNESS: The first recorded prayer of the Apostles after Christ's return to Heaven (ASCENSION), (to reiterate), was a prayer for **BOLDNESS IN CONFRONTING** the JEWISH and PAGAN AUTHORITIES. (ACTS 4:24-31 (PSALM 2:1-3)). The first Christians **KNEW** the world was **NOT** prepared to WELCOME them with **OPEN ARMS.** However, instead of bemoaning the evilness of those "END TIMES", and using their OBVIOUS **WEAKNESS**, as an **EXCUSE** for **INACTION,** THEY GOT BUSY **ATTACKING** PAGAN SPIRITUAL STRONGHOLDS. The funny thing was, **IT WORKED.**

It must have come as a SURPRISE, to the VIGILANT pagan Roman authorities, that a NEW RELIGION, with apparently no past, should appear on the scene, PROFESSING to be a **UNIVERSAL** Religion, and **DISPUTING the pagan Roman Empire CULT.** Christianity waxed STRONGER, while opposed by the STATE, (and OTHER popular pagan religions), and their parent faith in the 'SCIENCES' and 'PHILOSOPHIES' of the pagan times. (S. ANGUS, "THE MYSTIC RELIGIONS", page 272).

Christians of that time, did not believe in presenting Christian Claims, in RELIGIOUSLY NEUTRAL TERMS. Their Leaders would tell ANYONE, from the lowest slave, to the Emperor himself, that certain things were RIGHT, and certain things were WRONG, because **_GOD_ DECLARED THEM RIGHT OR WRONG.** They were NOT ashamed to speak of SIN and REPENTANCE; HEAVEN and HELL. It did not occur to them to protect the crowds' FRAGILE

SELF-WORTH; when PETER had an opportunity to Preach to his fellow Jews in Jerusalem, he told them STRAIGHT OUT, that they were ACCESSORIES in Crucifying Christ. (ACTS 2:23 & :36).**THIS** kind of Preaching brought RESULTS: sometimes STONINGS, and BEATINGS; sometimes LASTING CONVERSIONS.

SELFLESSNESS: In contrast with both TODAY'S and YESTERDAY'S "NEW AGE" emphasis on "WHAT CAN THE gODS DO FOR ME"???, the Christians asked **THEIR LORD, "WHAT CAN I DO FOR YOU???"**, and those, whether rich or poor, who performed NOTABLE service for their fellow, were HONOURED by the Christian Church, as an EXAMPLE for OTHERS to FOLLOW.

In looking over the stories of early Christian Saints, it is FASCINATING to see what a **DIVERSE** bunch they were. Some are rich, some are poor; some are old, some are young; some are beautiful, some are homely; some are slaves, some are free; some are Jewish, some are Gentiles; some are male, some are female; some are single, some are married, some are virgins. NONE of them were honoured for their image. MOST of them would not be HONOURED, WELCOMED, or even be treated RESPECTFULLY, IF THEY ATTENDED many Churches TODAY. WE seem to have room for only ONE Mother Theresa. But the early Church had THOUSANDS.

BILL PRIDE has written a book, "FLIRTING WITH THE DEVIL", 1988, in which he points out, among other things, WHY, and HOW, the Church today actually DISCOURAGES SAINTLINESS, by an OVER-PREOCCUPATION with NOT making the UN-SAINTLY feel UNCOMFORTABLE. The early New Testament Church had no such preoccupation. Christian Leaders of THAT day were anxious to hold up every good example they could find, in order to SPUR the others on to more good works. Instead of spending its efforts on trying to "CURE" sins, they put their weight behind getting people to work, doing GOOD DEEDS.

HUMILITY: The sin of PRIDE was the hallmark of the pagan CULTS, as it is the hallmark of paganism today. "YOU SHALL BE

LIKE GOD", was the ORIGINAL temptation in the Garden of Eden, and early Christians avoided it like the PLAGUE.

The ideal Christian did not PUSH; did not SHOVE; did not BOAST; did not consider himself ABOVE other people, or above HUMBLE duties or service. He also did not spend long HOURS, or even long MINUTES, thinking about how WONDERFUL he was, or trying to think of himself as WONDERFUL. Poor response and/or behaviour was not attributed to POOR SELF-ESTEEM...Christians were not to have ANY self-esteem at all. LOVING ONESELF was not only low on the 'priority' list, it was OFF the list entirely. Loving GOD and loving OTHERS, was what counted. The IDEAL scenario was provided by Jesus Christ, who had turned His Back on His OWN NEEDS and DESIRES, for the sake of His MISSION; TO SAVE HIS PEOPLE.

All this totally CONFUSED the pagans; HOW could the Christians be so dead to a sense of their OWN HONOUR??? Their OWN WORTH??? How could they bear to turn the other CHEEK??? Or go that EXTRA MILE??? Or serve the UNGRACIOUS and the UNGRATEFUL??? And LOVE their ENEMIES??? Pagans knew that HUMILITY was the mark of SLAVES, and the DEGRADED POOR...pagans saw no POINT in it; it DISGUSTED them.

Among pagans, "HUMILITY" had almost NEVER been a term of COMMENDATION. Men were born "sons of the gods", said the STOICS, and therefore, they should NOT cherish "HUMBLE" or "IGNOBLE" THOUGHT ABOUT THEIR NATURE. The HUMBLE belonged with the ABJECT; the MEAN; the UNWORTHY. Christianity, however, ascribed HUMILITY to GOD'S OWN SON, and EXALTED it as a VIRTUE of man. (R. L. FOX, "PAGANS AND CHRISTIANS", 1987, page 324).

The pagans would have understood the HUMBLE Christians better, if they had known JESUS' teaching, that the MEEK would inherit the earth.

HOPE: The biggest difference between the early New Testament Church, and the 'MODERN' Church of today, are in the areas of HOPE and VISION. Today, when Christians talk of

WORLD EVANGELISM, they do so, in terms of winning a few souls out of every tribe and nation, not in terms of Christian victory over the TRIBES and NATIONS. The hope of many is to be RAPTURED out of the earth, not to be found faithfully WORKING when Jesus comes. The real GAINS Christians of the past made, in establishing Christ's LORDSHIP in EDUCATION, LAWS, and MEDICINE, and so on, are treated like accidents, and ignored, rather than HELD UP, as examples to INSPIRE US, TO GO OUT INTO THE WORLD AND DO LIKEWISE.

For several generations we have been told to expect TOTAL DEFEAT in THIS world. The result has been APATHY, and DISINCLINATION to leave the COZY Christian fortress, which is fast becoming LESS cozy, as its territory radically DIMINISHES. Such thinking was TOTALLY foreign to the early Christians.

People ARE willing to deny themselves, and perform heroic feats, **IF** they are working to FULFILL A VISION they BELIEVE IN, in order to win the VICTORY for THEIR side. The early New Testament Church shared this MILITANT SPIRIT. They remembered the Prophesy of DANIEL that "A ROCK CUT OUT, BUT NOT BY HUMAN HANDS" would grow to fill the whole earth, and they KNEW that this "ROCK" was the Church. (DAN 2: 34-35, and :44-45). They HAD a mission; they INTENDED to fulfill it; and they DID fulfill it.

All the might of "NEW AGE" religion, backed up by the FULL power of the State, was UNABLE to prevent a Christian TAKEOVER of the pagan Roman empire.

PAGANISM A.D.: THERE WILL BE TERRIBLE TIMES IN THE LAST DAYS...BUT THEY WILL NOT GET VERY FAR BECAUSE...THEIR FOLLY WILL BE CLEAR TO EVERYONE. (2 TIM 3:1-4 & :9).

So far, I have been concerned with, and ATTEMPTED TO PROVE three main facts:

(1) THE "NEW AGE" SCENARIO IS NOT "NEW", IT IS CENTURIES OLD. (the "NEW" age we are hearing about in THIS day and age, predominately came from BABYLON, ASYRIA, THE PAGAN GREEK EMPIRE, AND THE PAGAN ROMAN EMPIRE, and there is NOTHING "NEW" AT ALL, WITHIN IT;

(2) THAT LUCIFER CAN DO ALMOST ANYTHING GOD CAN DO VIA his POWER, BECAUSE LUCIFER IS A SUPER-NATURAL PROFESSIONAL DECEIVER; THE father OF ALL LIES; AND A PROFESSIONAL COUNTERFEITER AND DUPLICATOR. LUCIFER ALSO HAS ANGELS; SPIRITS; DEMONIC SAINTS; INSTRUMENTS, AND SERVANTS; LUCIFER CAN (and does) PROVIDE 'GRACE', 'BLESSINGS', 'URGINGS'; 'COUNSELS'; 'DISCERNMENTS' AND 'STRENGTH', FOR his ANGELS, SPIRITS, DEMONIC SAINTS, INSTRUMENTS AND SERVANTS.

(3) THERE EXISTS ONLY TWO DISTINCT REALMS AND RELIGIONS IN OUR UNIVERSE; GOD'S REALM AND RELIGION; and LUCIFER'S REALM AND RELIGION; AND THAT LUCIFER HAS FAR MORE INSTRUMENTS AND SERVANTS IN his REALM, THAN THE LORD GOD OF ALL CREATION HAS IN HIS REALM.

But REMEMBER, "GREATER IS HE THAT IS IN YOU, THAN he THAT IS IN THE WORLD". 1 JOHN 4:4.

Now I intend to prove something else that is ALSO important; that the "NEW AGE" has **ALWAYS** been with us!

Christian books on the "NEW AGE" often make it sound as if the "NEW AGE" is an absolute unprecedented phenomenon, (just as the "NEW AGERS" of this day and age tell us they have JUST RECENTLY discovered THEIR "NEW" INSIGHTS), and as if it's arrival must be PROOF that "THIS IS THE END TIMES"

The TRUTH, however, is that ever since the MONTANISTS (a PHZYGIAN CULT) proclaimed THEY were bringing in a "NEW AGE", in AD 160, (R. L. FOX, "PAGANS AND CHRISTIANS", 1987, pages 404-407), "NEW AGERS" HAVE BEEN 'A DIME A DOZEN'. Even before THEN, the early Christian Church was flooded, (by guess who), with an influx of GNOSTICS, who honoured the idea of "ELITE "HIDDEN" REVELATION". And in all times, and in all places, everywhere the Christian Church displaced paganism, a few were found, who tried to hang on to the pagan traditions of their ancestors, while claiming to be 'Christians'. Here I speak of 'paganism' in the early Christian Church. (actually, 'paganism' originally, reared its ugly head in the Garden of Eden) (where EVE ate ADAM out of house and home).

The real difference between THEN and NOW is not the **PRESENCE** of "NEW AGE" teachings, but the **OPENNESS** of "NEW AGE" teachings. While "NEW AGERS" of the past were usually careful to stay UNDERGROUND, today's "NEW AGERS" appear on NATIONAL TELEVISION. Let's follow the uneven progress of UNDERGROUND PAGANISM in the Western world. We will find WHY the "NEW AGE" has broken from cover.

MISSIONARIES SWEEP AWAY THE "NEW AGE": Throughout the Christian Church age, Missionaries have gone into TOTALLY pagan regions, and have seen the pagans CONVERT to Christianity. For all but the most MODERN, LIBERAL Missionaries, this also meant sweeping changes in the formerly pagan CULTURES.

When GREGORY THE ENLIGHTENER, Christian Missionary to ARMENIA, in the third and early fourth century, succeeded in converting the ARMENIANS' king, the king LEVELLED the temple of the goddess ANAHIT, rather than preserving it as an "IMPORTANT CULTURAL ARTEFACTS". BONIFACE, "THE APOSTLE OF GERMANY", chopped down the "SACRED OAK OF THOR" at GIESMAR, in HESS, thereby PROVING that THOR could not even defend his own tree. The GERMANS were INSTANTLY convinced the God of BONIFACE really WAS STRONGER, and let him take the wood to build a Chapel in honour of ST. PETER.

One of the first things ST. GALL did when he arrived in northwestern SWITZERLAND, was to LEVEL the local pagan sanctuary. Even GREGORY THE GREAT, the accommodating Bishop of Rome, admitted that, although pagan temples could sometimes be turned into Christian Churches, and pagan festivals turned into Christian Holy Days, the IDOLS and pagan RITUALS had to go.

For the early Missionaries, there was no such thing as

RELIGIOUS NEUTRALITY. Cultural practices were either Christian or pagan; Christians buried their dead; pagans burned them up (often accompanied by their wives and servant, (and often burned alive)). Christians married one wife for life; pagans had WIVES, CONCUBINES, and sometimes BOYS/MEN and BEASTS as well, for their sexual gratification. Pagans revelled in DRUNKENNESS, Christians did not. Even one's dress, or the way a field was plowed, could reflect pagan beliefs about honouring the gods; and if so, they would have to be changed.

Wherever Missionaries had the chance, they INFLUENCED, or ENTICED, PERSUADED, or even FORCED, their CONVERTS to replace pagan LAWS; CEREMONIES; SEXUAL PRACTICES; BUSINESS PRACTICES; AND SO ON, with what they considered the proper CHRISTIAN WAY TO DO THINGS. For THIS, the Missionaries incurred the COLD, HAUGHTY SCORN of 'MODERN' Western HISTORIANS, that tend to IGNORE the difficulties of allowing TOTAL FREEDOM OF RELIGION, to people who sincerely BELIEVED in INFANT SACRIFICE and CHILD PROSTITUTION.

While the memory of paganism was green, Christian Missionaries were in no hurry to ALLOW IT BACK IN. So the remaining pagans went UNDERGROUND, conducting their rituals with much SECRECY, in the DEAD OF NIGHT. If caught, they were subjected to SEVERE PENALTIES. Pagan influence only remained in UNCONVERTED regions, or in SUPERSTITIOUS FOLK PRACTICES, and PERVASIVE TALES OF TROLLS, GOBLINS, IMPS and FAIRIES; AND ALL TYPES OF SPIRITS FEARED BY THE PAGAN ANCESTORS. Even the fairy stories, although, now TROLLS, scurried off at the sound of CHURCH BELLS, or THE SIGHT OF THE CROSS.

ARE WITCHES PAGAN ???: At one time, it was thought that WITCHCRAFT was the remnant of an old pagan religion. The NEW ENCYCLOPEDIA BRITANNICA VOL 25, page 95, DISPELS **THAT** NOTION: "These 'MODERN' so-called WITCHES claim to be adherents of an ancient religion, the religion to which Christianity is regarded as a COUNTER-RELIGION, and in THIS

WAY, the 'WITCHES' seek to secure PUBLIC RECOGNITION of their ECCENTRIC ACTIVITIES, by appealing to the cherished 'MODERN' value of RELIGIOUS TOLERANCE".

'Modern witches' usually turn out to be entirely sincere, but MISGUIDED PEOPLE, who have been directly, or indirectly influenced by MARGARET MURRAY'S article, "WITCHCRAFT", 1929, that put forth, in its most popular form, HER THEORY, that the 'witches' of Western Europe, were the lingering adherents of a once great pagan RELIGION, that has been DISPLACED, though not completely, by CHRISTIANITY. This HIGHLY IMAGINATIVE, but now DISCREDITED theory, gave a new respectability to 'WITCHCRAFT', and, along with the more practical influence of such 'modern' practitioners as ALEISTER CROWLEY and GERALD GARDNER, contributed to the emergence of SELF-STYLED 'WITCHES', that are sometimes featured in the sensationalist press".

In all probability, (in my opinion), **MODERN SATANISM** is the child of MEDIEVAL WITCHCRAFT, that is, ITSELF, the leftovers of all the worst parts of ancient religions. The 'witches' did not INVENT human sacrifice, or perverse sexual rituals, after all, these go back to the ancient empire of BABYLONIA. Pure naked devil-worship, however, is somewhat UNUSUAL in ancient religion. Generally, the ancient pagans were aiming for some BENEFIT; GOOD CROPS; VICTORY IN BATTLE; etc…not just trying to throw the most EVIL PARTY they could. The only reason for hanging on to old-fashioned paganism, was because they enjoyed the BLOOD and SEX. This theory would adequately explain both the presence of 'WITCHES', and their lack of the better features of ancient pagans.

But medieval "WITCHES" were not the only pagan force Christians had to deal with. More significant, were the SECRET SOCIETIES. These started as individuals interested in the practice of "WHITE MAGIC". In their OWN way, they considered themselves as "SCIENTISTS", searching out the ancient spiritual laws that would enable them to "PERFORM WONDERS".

Most numerous where the "ALCHEMISTS", of whom PARACELSUS was the most known. ALCHEMY had its practical materialistic side. Allied with the practice of ALCHEMY, was the eternal desire for "HIDDEN KNOWLEDGE", and "SPECIAL POWERS", which, since the Garden of Eden, has ALWAYS led to PAGANISM.

SECRET SOCIETIES: In time, ALCHEMY had produced enough interest, that an attempt was made, to gather men of this frame of mind together

"In 1614 AD, there appeared a pamphlet, written in GERMAN, entitled "THE REFORMATION OF THE WORLD". The brief satirical treatise used the god APOLLO as spokesman, assisted by the wise men of antiquity, and the 'modern' world, and proposed an attempt to reform the UNIVERSE; or rather, it maintained that APOLLO had made such an attempt, in vain. It appealed to many 'intelligent' people of various countries, and was reprinted, and translated, MANY times. It is safe to say, that the originator of the text was an ITALIAN, TRAJANO BOCCALINI, whose book had appeared two years earlier, in VENICE. He was murdered in the following year. The GERMAN version, contained, in addition, a MANIFESTO: "FAMA FRATERNITATIS, OR A DISCOVERY OF THE FRATERNITY OF THE MOST LAUDABLE ORDER OF THE ROSY CROSS" (KURT SELIGMAN, "THE HISTORY OF MAGIC AND THE OCCULT", 1975, page 253).

This book recounted the MYTHICAL adventures of the "ILLUMINATED FATHER AND BROTHER CHRISTIAN ROSENCRUTZ", as he roamed around the world, obtaining "SECRET WISDOM", from the 'SAGES', near and far. Once home, he spent his time studying, and training his three disciples. The book ended with an AFFIRMATION that the BROTHERS were CHRISTIANS, and an appeal to others to join them...although the BROTHERS had neglected to tell who they WERE, or WHERE they might be found.

KURT SELIGMAN says, "Ever since, "SECRET SOCIETIES" have exerted their attraction upon men". This is not terribly accurate, since the ROSICRUCIANS were simply following in the footsteps of ancient MYSTERY CULTS, such as the early A.D. CULTS, of MITHRA and ISIS. NOTE their appeal to "HIDDEN WISDOM", and their use of the god APOLLO, as spokesman for their cause.

Next on the scene were our old friends, the "FREEMASONS", (today, known simply as the "MASONIC SOCIETY"). The "MASONS" had been around since the eighth century or so, and you can find any number of books ACCUSING them of "PLOTS TO RE-ESTABLISH PAGANISM IN CHRISTIAN COUNTRIES". Be that as it may, the OCCULT ROSICRUCIANS formed the BACKBONE of the new MASONIC revival.

"It was through VALENTINE ANDRAE, (a Lutheran Pastor who (AUTHORIZED several TREATISES and BOOKS, PROMOTING ROSICRUCIANISM) that FREEMASONRY, which probably originated in the eighth or ninth century, gained NEW IMPETUS. In 1645, a few ENGLISH ROSICRUCIANS met, for the purpose of organizing their efforts...They justified their SECRECY, with the claim that, the general INTOLERANCE of their wicked epoch would not otherwise ENDURE them, and that they had to find ways of gaining new members, despite their concealment. ELIAS ASHMOLE found the SOLUTION. As every Londoner was obliged, by custom, to be a member of a Corporation, ASHMOLE registered himself as a STONEMASON; the others followed his example, and under the sign of the MASONS, they met freely, in the assembly hall of the Corporation. From this group of ASHMOLANS, originated the CEREMONIAL of the freemasons." (SELIGMAN, "THE HISTORY OF MAGIC AND THE OCCULT", pages 294-295).

FREEMASONRY was NOT the friendly DO-GOOD organization that it's 'modern' followers claim it was. Christians of that day already had hundreds of Monasteries, Convents, Charitable Orders, Missionary fields, and so on, that they could have joined, if they wanted to help their fellow man. Rather, the FREEMASON'S ROOT INTERESTS were IN REVIVING PAGAN TEACHINGS.

"The FREEMASONS, and especially the MARTINIST, shared

the ancient ideal of raising man from SIN to FELICITY. Initiatory was reminiscent of paganism. The CANDIDATES' ordeal was inspired by GREEK and EGYPTIAN precedents. The MASONS were to be regenerated, like the initiates of ELEUSIS, to ASCEND to a higher realm, and thus acquire KNOWLEDGE, REVELATION, and SECRET WISDOM". (SELIGMAN, "THE HISTORY OF MAGIC AND THE OCCULT", page 311). In 1738 POPE CLEMENT XII, EXCOMMUNICATED ALL THE FREEMASONS OF EUROPE; LOUIS XV INTERDICTED MASONARY IN FRANCE.

MAGIC and PAGAN gods WERE extremely IMPORTANT TO ALL THESE SOCIETIES. They were SECRET societies, for the very good reason that the average man in the street was OPPOSED to such HEATHEN goings-on.

FRANCE GOES PAGAN: The first mass introduction to paganism began, strangely, with the death of a Christian Deacon. In the first quarter of the eighteenth century, a young man, the Deacon FRANCOIS De PARIS, (1690-1727), a JANSENIST, lived in PARIS, in PIETY and SECLUSION. After his death, strange events took place at his tomb in the St. MEDARD cemetery...the cemetery resembled a 'WITCHES' sabbath. The aspect of the frenzied crowd, the display of hideous disease, the howls and the MACABRE surroundings, bore little resemblance to that elegance and refinement we ordinarily associate with the eighteenth century. But the scenes were enhanced by the AURA of the marvellous. The disregard of the rigid, classic, APOLLONIAN IDEAL, and the acceptance of the DIONYSIAN frenzy, (the uncontrolled), is significant in the EPOCH following the death of the DOMINATING LOUIS XIV, who BELIEVED, that he WAS the STATE, and who called himself the "SUN KING" APOLLO. There developed a tendency toward SELF-TORTURE; instead of HEALING, the Saint now spread SUFFERING. (snared).

While the happenings at ST. MEDARD CEMETERY mostly interested the peasantry, the NOBLES also had their OWN version of PAGAN AWAKENING. Fifty years after the pagan outbreak at St. Medard, PARIS was ROCKED by a gruesome scandal, involving ranking members of the NOBILITY. Higher born men and women had become involved with an INFANT-SACRIFICE CULT, run by CATHERINE LA VOISIN.

"LA VOISIN told fortunes with coffee grounds, and a magical crystal; but this divination trade was only a FACADE for larger enterprises. She evoked the dead and the devil, and solemnized magical rites in her back-chambers. She had many assistants, among them, two hangmen of Paris, who brought her horrible 'gifts' from the gibbet. ABBA GUIBOURG, a priest of noble descent, sixty two years old, performed BLACK MASSES. MADAME DE MONTESPAN offered herself as the "ALTAR CLOTH" for the BLACK MASSES. She lay naked on the altar; the chalice was placed on her belly; the priest GUIDBOURG slit an infant's throat, and let the blood run down into the chalice. Many other equally dreadful acts were committed.

LA VOISIN was burned at the stake in 1680; others committed suicide. Thirty six were executed; five were sent to the galley's; one hundred and fourty-seven were sentenced to prison; several of them died in prison. Among the indicted were the flower of the French nobility. However, the NOBILITY WERE SPARED; to the COUNTS and the DUCHESSES, THE WHOLE INDICTMENT SEEMED LIKE A BAD JOKE. When the Counsellor of State asked the Duchess of BOUILLON if she had seen the devil during those evocations, she answered, "I see him right now; he is disguised as a Counsellor of State, and he looks rather ugly!" Everybody in the court room laughed. Yet, during the BLACK MASSES, these witty people, had WITNESSED the slaughter of two thousand, five hundred babies ". (SELIGMAN, "THE HISTORY OF MAGIC AND THE OCCULT"). 1975.

These pagan outbreaks coincided with the BEGINNING

of the so-called "AGE OF REASON", also known as "THE ENLIGHTENMENT".

"We have already gathered, from the happenings at St. MEDARD, the so-called "SKEPTICAL PERIOD" ushered in by the eighteenth century, was "less skeptical" than had been supposed. The number of occult publications DID NOT diminish, but rather INCREASED. The old pagan prophesies were revived and reprinted, along with the "NEW AGE" ones, for an expanding public. Secret societies found leaders, and grew QUICKLY. "MAGI" and "SEERS" attracted public interest; MAGICAL CURES; ALCHEMY; DIVINING RODS; PHYSIOGNOMY; MYSTICAL SECTS; were the talk of the town. LOUIS XV was fond of working in his ALCHEMICAL laboratory; and the Royal Example ENCOURAGED many gentlemen at court, as well as the citizens of Paris. Ancient MAGICAL TEXTS were systematically complied ". (SELIGMAN, "THE HISTORY OF MAGIC AND THE OCCULT", pages 300-303, under the chapter title "REVOLT AGAINST REASON").

As students of History know, this new French FANATICISM, culminated in the bloody FRENCH REVOLUTION. The revolutionaries dressed up an OPERA SINGER, as the goddess of LIBERTY, and held worship services devoted to her. They OUTLAWED every form of CHRISTIANITY, and even tried to ABOLISH the SEVEN DAY WEEK, as ESTABLISHED at CREATION. Secret Police roamed everywhere, accusing thousands of innocent people of plots against "THE gODLIKE STATE". Before things settled down, FRANCE had experienced such HORRORS as had never before been seen in a CHRISTIAN NATION. All under the guise of bringing in a "NEW AGE" of FRATERNITY, EQUALITY, and LIBERTY.

At the early stages of the Renaissance (1345 AD), JOHN WYCLIFFE (1320 – 1384 AD), a megalomaniac, was snared by Lucifer, to be the 'MORNING STAR' of the REFORMATION, as part of Lucifer's plan to fragment the Church of Jesus Christ.

Wycliffe was a self – appointed English religious reformer, and is annoted as the "FIRST PERSON" to begin a systematic translation of the Bible (Latin VULGATE) into the English language, in defiance of REV 22: 18-19, written by hand, and completed in 1382 AD. Wycliffe's hand written version was printed in 1456 AD by Gutenberg.

What was ACTUALLY happening, Lucifer was laying the foundation for the REFORMATION; the birth of Protestantism; and the birth of the church of education, via ARROGANCE, DISOBEDIENCE, DEFIANCE, and REBELLION, whereby the Renaissance may be further fuelled and energized, and laying the foundation for the King James version of the Bible (1611 AD), at the same time, via Lucifer's St. Wycliffe, and Lucifer's other servants and instruments.

Actually, The Vatican produced the only approved and sanctioned version of the VULGATE (405 AD), in the English language, named by The Vatican as the "DUAY – RHEIMS" version, and was produced to correct the ERRORS and OMISSIONS contained Wycliffes's version (1382 AD, and the King James version (1611 AD), for the BENEFIT of the Roman Catholic Church in England, at that time.

Wycliffe was WELL known because of his protests against the Roman Catholic Church. (He criticized MUCH about the Roman Catholic Church. He studied at Oxford University, where he became master of Balloil College about 1361 AD. (the conception – time of the Renaissance, and the church of education).

Thanks to Lucifer, Wycliffe believed the Roman Catholic Church exercised too much control over civil affairs, and was too wealthy. He proposed that the Roman Catholic Church property should be taken over, and managed by the Government of England. Wycliffe supported the anti – Papal policies of his COLLEAGUE John of Gaunt. They denied the authority of The Pope.

Wycliffe's work won the favour of King Edward III. In 1374 AD, the King sent Wycliffe to meet representatives of Pope Gregory

XI at Bruges, Belgium, to settle disputes between the English Government and the Papacy, over the question of CHURCH AUTHORITY, which Wycliffe vehemently opposed..

Soon after Wycliffe returned to England, Wycliffe began to lay the foundation for the CHURCH OF ENGLAND, by attacking the doctrines, and the established order AND hierarchy of the Roman Catholic Church. (The Church of Jesus Christ MATT 16:18).

Wycliffe claimed that the Bible (his/Lucifer's translation of course), (REV 22 : 18 – 19), was the highest source of truth, and that IT contained all that was necessary for man's Salvation.

More than 100 years later, in Germany, Martin Luther echoed Wycliffe's beliefs, particularly Wycliffe's emphasis on his version of the Bible.

The Vatican (Roman Catholic Church), pronounced Wycliffe a HERITIC. In 1377 AD Pope Gregory XI issued five Papal Bulls (decrees) attacking Wycliffe, and demanding Wycliffe's imprisonment. But the English Government refused theses demands of the Vatican.

Wycliffe's entire translation was issued in 1382 AD. (Wycliffe and his followers were NOT members of the Clergy). About 1387 AD, Wycliffe's followers became known as LOLLARDS, and their teachings gave birth to the Church of Education, via the lay PR FLAKS of that day.

Through those same, and other saints, servants, and instruments of Lucifer, Lucifer spawned and executed his Reformation plans, and completed Lucifer's programmes for the Renaissance, the birth of the church of education, and the Reformation. AGAIN, LUCIFER HIT 'PAY – DIRT'.

Wycliffe died in 1384 AD. In 1428 AD, at the order of Pope Martin V, Wycliffe's body was exhumed and burned; his ashes were scattered on the River Swift.

ENGLAND GOES CHRISTIAN: Across the channel, Englishmen watched with HORROR as the FRENCH nation covered itself with BLOOD. Although the English lower classes had been DECIMATED by DRUNKENNESS, and their 'social superiors' looked upon them as subhuman beings, social friction never erupted into open battles. The difference was that while FRANCE was giving itself over to PAGANISM, ENGLAND was experiencing a CHRISTIAN REVIVAL.

ENGLAND, too, had its SECRET SOCIETIES. A group of YOUNG LORDS had named themselves the HELLFIRE CLUB, and were engaged in EVIL PAGAN RITUALS. MASONS and MARTINISTS could be found in ENGLAND, as well as in FRANCE. But in ENGLAND, a small group of young CHRISTIAN UNIVERSITY STUDENTS, had been led by THE HOLY SPIRIT, to ATTACK EVIL SPIRITUAL STRONGHOLDS IN ENGLAND. Labeled THE HOLY CLUB, (and later called "METHODISTS") by their DETRACTORS, they REFUSED to let LORDS or BISHOPS; DRUNKEN THUGS; or SCORNFUL PHILOSOPHERS **SLOW THEM DOWN.**

When they were DENIED the use of the CHURCHES, they Preached in the FIELDS. GEORGE WHITEFIELD, the most accomplished Preacher of the group, even ventured to take up his stand in the English equivalent of TIMES SQUARE (New York), Preaching to the people gathered for amusement shows at KENSINGTON COMMON.

"KENSINGTON COMMON was an area of about twenty acres, and lay south of the THAMES RIVER. It was especially notable as the scene of hangings. If the people at Moorefield were rough, those of Kensington were brutal, for here the lowest of London's citizens congregated in teeming numbers. Here were vicious sports and drunken brawls. Here the harlot and pick-pocket sought the victims of their trades, and here the mob assembled, ready for any act of violence. Moved with COMPASSION, WHITEFIELD walked out upon Kensington Common and proceeded to take the enemy's citadel by storm ". (ARNOLD DALLIMORE, "GEORGE WHITEFIELD: THE LIFE AND TIMES OF THE GREAT EVANGELIST

OF THE EIGHTEENTH -CENTURY REVIVAL", 1970, VOL 1, page 288).

Nor were WHITEFIELD'S (1714 – 1770 AD) colleagues, among whom were JOHN and CHARLES WESLEY, (1703 – 1791 AD) and the indefatigable Welshman, HOWELL HARRIS, any less courageous. They ALL were BOLD; CERTAIN OF THE TRUTH OF THEIR MESSAGE, and INTOLERANT OF ERROR; SELFLESS, ADMIRERS OF HUMILITY; LOVERS OF HOLINESS; AND BELIEVED THAT GOD COULD DO GREAT THINGS. These were not men to sit around bemoaning the EVIL OF THE TIMES. They GOT UP, and went on the OFFENSIVE, Preaching the GOSPEL to the dissolute nobility, as well as to the degenerate coal miners, passionately urging them to change their practices, as well as their beliefs. And this was in an age when ANY kind of religious fervour was labelled "ENTHUSIASM", and the fashionable belief was TO BELIEVE IN NOTHING.

As a DIRECT result of the METHODIST REVIVAL, slavery was abolished in Britain, (**WITHOUT** A CIVIL WAR); Labour laws were changed to prevent factory owners from exploiting women and children; Sunday schools were started to teach the children of the poor, Christian Doctrine; and how to read; the "GIN CRAZE" ended; the London mob disbanded; debtor's prison was abolished; pornography disappeared off the book-stands; mental hospitals were formed; nursing societies were started; and the great Missionary movement of the nineteenth century began. (Lucifer **MUST** disrupt THIS scenario, by snaring (suckering) people out of God's Realm, and into his realm).

Yet, at the same time THIS mighty work of God was going on, ANOTHER movement was beginning to roll, that would eventually, IF NOT STOPPED, undo every bit of good the REVIVAL had brought about. It did not appear to be a pagan movement on the surface, yet it has led DIRECTLY to every "NEW AGE" book, video, TV show, public school class, law, medical practice, and so on, that you have ever seen, or will see. It CAN be stopped; the METHODISTS in ENGLAND challenged it HEAD-ON, as it was just beginning, AND STOPPED IT COLD. But Christians today, not RECOGNIZING it, have actually ENCOURAGED it to take over OUR Canadian Culture...**PAGAN "NEW AGE" EMPIRICAL THINKING; GROSS THEOSOPHY; AND SPURIOUS SPECULATION, COMPLETE WITH THE TOLERANCE AND COMPROMISE OF THE NON-NEGOTIABLE.**

May God help us as we look at the ***REAL*** power of the "NEW AGE" in Canada today.

'CHRISTIANS' MAKE SOME MISTAKES: Soon after GUTENBERG (1395 – 1468 AD) invented the process of printing with movable type, printers were made available, to "SCHOLARS and PEOPLE ALIKE; Greek and Roman classics that were steeped in PAGANISM".

"CLASSICAL STUDIES", meaning the study of PAGAN AUTHORS, became the rage. The 'educated' man knew classical Greek and Latin, and was ACQUAINTED with the pagan writers and pagan MYTHOLOGY. OVID, SENECA, and CICERO replaced AUGUSTINE and CHRYSOSTOM in the curriculum. School boys still studied the BIBLE, but they also studied HOMER; Greek history was as important as English history. Greek and Roman styles were revived in DRAMA, SCULPTURE, PAINTING, LANGUAGE, and especially ARCHITECTURE.

All of this would only have historical interest, if it had not been for several other MAJOR CHANGES, that occurred around the same time. One was the PROTESTANT REFORMATION. HAROLD LINDSELL, former editor of CHRISTIANITY TODAY, himself a Protestant, plainly states "The Reformation was a major factor in opening the door, WIDE, to "THE ENLIGHTENMENT" of the eighteenth century. Once the Protestant Churches claimed their freedom to DISSENT, and FREEDOM to believe other than what was taught by ROME, they opened the door to WIDER DISSENT, and to IRRELIGION as well. The very notion of RELIGIOUS

FREEDOM, of necessity, **INCLUDED** the right to DISSEMINATE, and PROPAGATE religious ideas of EVERY sort, whether they were in accord with the Commandments, Oracles, Precepts, and community standards or not. This DANGEROUS PRECEDENT had its roots in the REFORMATION, and was to bring forth its OWN FRUIT, in the years to come. Since RELIGIOUS FREEDOM has implications in the fields of ECONOMICS, *POLITICAL, and SOCIAL LIFE, and RESPONSE, and BEHAVIOUR PATTERNS, there was no Church that could render COMPELLING DECISIONS, to determine what the CIVILIZATION of a people should be ". (LINDSELL, "THE NEW PAGANISM", 1987, pages 40-43). * (Webster's) POLITIC: characterized by shrewdness in managing, contriving, or dealing; sagacious in promoting policy; shrewdly tactful; ("malicious cunning if necessary"...Einstein) (the chicanery of Party politics).

In other words, the REFORMATION eventually led to a theory of RELIGIOUS TOLERANCE and COMPROMISE, and to NEGOTIATE THE **NON-NEGOTIABLE** PRECEPTS, ORACLES and COMMANDMENTS; and to re-write Scripture to accommodate the ROLE YOUR OWN RELIGION concept, ignoring REV 22:18-19. Since the COMPETING religions were all BRANDS of CHRISTIANITY, no real need was seen for setting bounds on which religions could be TOLERATED. THAT led, in turn, to a philosophy of **COMPLETE** religious TOLERANCE, COMPROMISE, and FREEDOM FROM RELIGION. And COMPLETE RELIGIOUS TOLERATION, and COMPROMISE, taken to its logical conclusion, means that PAGANISM CANNOT BE OUTLAWED. This led to **UNEXPECTED** results in FUTURE CENTURIES. AGAIN Lucifer "hit pay dirt".

ANOTHER result of the REFORMATION was that THE CHURCHES LET GO OF EDUCATION. As LINDSELL also mentions, "EDUCATION, BEFORE THE REFORMATION HAD BEEN A CHURCH FUNCTION; THERE WAS NO EDUCATION TO SPEAK OF, THAT WAS NOT INCLUDED WITH RELIGION". Concerned with fighting TYRANNY in the Church, the Reformers sometimes went overboard in handing power over Religion to the State. With the Church no longer the guardian of education, PAGANS were handed a BRAND-NEW OPPORTUNITY to PROMOTE THEIR IDEAS TO THE YOUNG, VIA THE **GOVERNMENT**. (That Lucifer is one smooth cookie).

It was not long before "FREE-THINKING", formally the exclusive province of the SECRET SOCIETIES, became a MOVEMENT in its OWN right. CLAIMING to be motivated SOLELY by LOGIC, philosophers such as VOLTAIRE and ROUSSEAU in FRANCE, and LOCKE and HUME in ENGLAND, began to develop THEORIES of MAN, RIGHTEOUSNESS, and GOVERNMENT, that DELIBERATELY were **NOT** based on the BIBLE, but rather VIA THEIR **OWN** EMPIRICAL THINKING. They ACCUSED their opponents of "UNINTELLIGENT FANATICISM, and A MERE WILLINGNESS TO BELIEVE, **NOT** BASED ON **REASON**". This MOVEMENT, was called, by it's founders and followers, "THE ENLIGHTENMENT", but, this MOVEMENT, more aptly, should have been called "THE ENDARKMENT", because it is at the root of the PAGAN REVIVAL OF TODAY.

"By the middle of the eighteenth century, there was a clearly defined, and significant movement in process that has been called The Enlightenment. This movement, in two centuries, was to do what took the Church at Pentecost three centuries to do. It would reverse what the early Church had done, and bring to Europe and to the West in general, the "NEW PAGANISM"; this new paganism has dislodged the Church from its KEY religious and cultural position.

While the victory of "THE ENLIGHTENMENT" did not erase the Church from history and the West, it DID UNSEAT the Church from its primary position in WESTERN CIVILIZATION, and worked to break the hold of the Church, by installing a new WESTANSCHAUUNG (world view) that stood in opposition to Christianity, and THAT, in turn, brought the West under the control of a new ZEITGEIST (literally "time-spirit"), (I would call this "moral climate" or even "lifestyle"), that was SECULAR and ANTI-CHRISTIAN ". (LINDSELL, "THE NEW PAGANISM", page 45).

Some might ask "how can this be???" Good question; and here is the good answer...

In order to REASON and use LOGIC on a question, one has to develop a hypothesis, in order to start somewhere. One such as ROUSSEAU, might start from the proposition, "NATURE IS GOOD AND WE SHOULD LEARN FROM HER".

Another might start from the idea, "SURVIVAL IS THE HIGHEST DUTY OF THE HUMAN RACE".

Still another might begin by arguing, as B. F. SKINNER does, that "A SMOOTH WORKING SOCIETY IS THE HIGHEST GOOD".

None of these people can prove that his (hypothesis) starting point is correct, by using LOGIC, especially when he is utilizing the empirical thinking process, compounded and complicated via gross theosophy and spurious speculation.

We could well argue that: NATURE IS CRUEL, AND MEN ARE NOT ANIMALS, SO WE NEED NOT TO IMITATE NATURE AND/OR THE ANIMALS.

SURVIVAL IS NOT THE HIGHEST DUTY. TO KNOW, SERVE, AND LOVE GOD, WITHIN THE CONFINES OF GOD'S LAW, (Precepts, Oracles, and Commandments), IS THE HIGHEST DUTY.

IF WE ARE ALL MACHINES (as B.F. Skinner says), WHO CARES IF SOCIETY RUNS SMOOTH OR NOT??? IF MAN IS BUT A MACHINE, HE HAS NO CONTROL OVER ANYTHING, AND CAN DO NOTHING ABOUT ANYTHING.

"THE ENLIGHTENMENT" philosophers had a **NAÏVE** belief in the power of human REASON to produce a LOGICAL hypothesis. They **GRIEVOUSLY** underestimated the contribution that a shared Christian heritage made, via their OWN empirical thinking. The whole question of RIGHT and WRONG, for instance, is NOT found in HINDU thinking, yet those 'philosophers' spent HOURS arguing which form of society was RIGHT, and which was WRONG. Their conclusion was "RELIGIO DELENDA EST"...**RELIGION MUST BE DESTROYED**. It BOGGLES THE MIND, that MOST people CHOOSE to follow a bunch of LOSERS like them; demon saints, servants, and instruments, of Lucifer.

They also **GRIEVOUSLY** UNDER-ESTIMATED the EFFECT of their **OWN** empirical WISHES and DESIRES on **THEIR** logical philosophical systems. A man that WANTS to commit adultery, has a vested interest in PROVING the ILLOGIC of monogamous marriage.

Men need SCRIPTURE, (God's NATURAL LAW, and the PRECEPTS, ORACLES, and COMMANDMENTS, that are TOTALLY NON-NEGOTIABLE), to PROVIDE the ABSOLUTE PRINCIPLES, that men CANNOT reason out by pure logic.

"ENLIGHTENMENT" 'thinkers/philosophers also UNDER-ESTIMATED the SPIRITUAL SIDE OF MAN: THE GOD BLANK; his CONSCIENCE; SENSE OF ETERNITY; SUBCONSCIOUS MIND; and NEED FOR GOD. However, they DID manage to TRAP THE CHURCH, (via the church of education) into a FUTILE effort to PROVE the TRUTH OF THE BIBLE, FROM LOGIC ALONE. The EMPIRICAL thinking of the Church also contributed to their ENTRAPMENT, even though the Bible itself dictates RELYING ON THE POWER OF THE HOLY SPIRIT; the TESTIMONY OF THE WRITTEN WORD OF God; and the POWER OF GOD'S GRACE and BLESSINGS. The DIALECTIC thinking process would have served the Church people, much more effectively, and would have produced TRUTH.

What the Church DID, (and has kept on doing), ERRONEOUSLY, was to CONCEDE the point that TRUTH COULD NOT BE PROVED ABSOLUTELY; and they were WRONG. (Lucifer hit pay – dirt AGAIN!)

"THE ENLIGHTENMENT" 'philosophers' said that NOBODY should be taught truth at all; (in opposition to the Book of Proverbs); that each person should be left free to "DECIDE FOR THEMSELVES" what to believe. They said "ANYTHING ELSE WAS SHEER FANATICAL INDOCTRINATION". However,

INDOCTRINATING young children into "THE ENLIGHTENMENT" beliefs, was simply, they said, "teaching the children to THINK and REASON, on their own". And guess what??? MOST OF THE CHURCH PEOPLE BOUGHT IT. ANYONE that functions within the confines of the Precepts, Oracles and Commandments, CANNOT be brain-washed via the propaganda of the PR FLAKS.

People have NATURAL Spiritual needs, and "THE ENLIGHTENMENT" could not OBLITERATE these. i.e. the God blank. What it **DID** accomplish, was to "MAKE A BELIEF IN ABSOLUTE TRUTH UNFASHIONABLE, AND GUESS WHAT??? THE PEOPLE BOUGHT IT. This, of course, was no bar at all to believing in, or amusing oneself, with, PAGAN gods, whose religion never claimed to be the ONE TRUE WAY.

As HAROLD LINDESLL noted, "THE ENLIGHTENMENT" steeped itself in the writings of the GRECO-ROMAN pagan world, into which Christianity entered at Pentecost". This was the spirit of classical paganism: tolerant of all beliefs, except the belief that there was only one RIGHT belief; PROUD of its ability to REASON and act; totally hostile to all MORAL RESTRAINTS.

The MISSION of the 'ENLIGHTENMENT' was to turn the clock back to EARLY PAGAN ROME...A ROME WITHOUT CHRISTIANS.

FIRST FRUITS OF "THE ENLIGHTENMENT". The "fruit" of "THE ENLIGHTENMENT" was IMMEDIATE and BITTER. Prominent "enlightenment" philosophers/writers got together, and produced the "FRENCH ENCYCLOPEDIE", the first attempt to build a "MONUMENT IN WORDS" to the achievements of men. Needless to say, the ENCYCLOPEDIE was totally ANTI-CHRISTIAN. It's contents ran counter to everything intrinsic to a culture and civilization based on HEBREW/CHRISTIAN tradition and Laws. Based on the ENCYCLOPEDIE and the "enlightenment" writings, the

FRENCH launched their DISASTROUS Revolution. Meanwhile, across the channel, WITHOUT the benefit of any revolution, the common Englishmen got more rights and justice, than the common French worker, thanks to the METHODIST REVIVAL.

But the FRENCH REVOLUTION was just the beginning...

Once the 'ELITE' had closed their minds to BIBLICAL REVELATION, they IMMEDIATELY began falling for EVERY spiritual CON GAME and FRINGE TEACHINGS around, a la Lucifer.

In the United States, it took until the 1840's for 'enlightenment' thinking to make any serious inroads. The people had been so heavily Christianized, that even SECRET SOCIETY members, were more Christian in their outlook, than MANY Christians **TODAY.** George Washington, for example, although a MASON, had a STRONG Christian view of the role of Government.

FAKERS AND FRAUDS: The first big COUP for PAGANISM in the U.S.A. was the SEANCE FAD, started by the FOX family of HYDESVILLE, NEW YORK. The FOX girls, (who, years later, CONFESSED to having FAKED the WHOLE THING), conducted TABLE-RAPPING sessions, during which "GHOSTS" supposedly answered the questions of the people around the table.

In spite of the almost continuous exposes of FAKE MEDIUMS, "it persisted as a mass phenomenon until the 1920's" (TED SCHULTZ, "FRINGES OF REASON", 1989, page 22). And LONGER across the sea in Great Britain and other countries. The 'UPPER CLASS' (the ELITE) were particularly SUSCEPTIBLE to the appeal of the SEANCE. AGATHA CHRISTIE featured SEANCES', and the GHOSTS OF THE DEAD in her books. Even the Humour writer P.G. WODEHOUSE found SEANCE such a prominent feature of the UPPER CLASS (ELITE) SOCIETY, that many of his stories feature batty spiritualistic ladies.

SEANCES were just the kick-off. In the mid 1800's, literally DOZENS of new CULTS would EXPLODE onto the American scene. Founded by mostly women, (see 1 TIM 2:14 and 2 TIM 3:6), these CULTS claimed great "NEW" SPIRITUAL REVELATIONS.(and **AGAIN**, the people bought it). Teaching the same doctrines as the PAGAN SECRET SOCIETIES, these CULTS counted on the American doctrine of COMPLETE RELIGIOUS TOLERATION and COMPROMISE, to ENABLE them to 'come out of the closet' (sound familiar ?) and into the open.. In a few cases, notably that of MORMANISM, the CULT'S doctrines were so violently OPPOSED to Christian practice, that parts of it were OUTLAWED. For example, the MORMANS had to jettison POLYGAMY before UTAH could join the Union.

The CULTS, however, all claimed to fall in the Christian Tradition. The founders were "re-interpreting" or "re-translating" the Bible, or DISCOVERING HIDDEN BOOKS (folklore) of the Bible. Not yet had paganism, as paganism, been seriously promoted in the U.S.A.

THE FIRST AMERICAN "NEW AGE": The THEOSOPHICAL SOCIETY changed all that. Headed by the sombre, heavy-eye-browed MADAM BLAVATSKY, the THEOSOPHICAL SOCIETY in the mid 1800's featured "MAJOR EXPLOITS OF CHANNELLING". MADAM BLAVATSKY supposedly was in touch with "AN EGYPTIAN GROUP OF THE UNIVERSAL MYSTIC BROTHERHOOD" and TIBETAN MASTERS", all through the miracle of "TIME-WARP TELEPATHY" (unbelievable - the people actually bought it; truly, what fools we mortals be).

After some embarrassing years in INDIA, during which the BRITISH PSYCHICAL SOCIETY unmasked favourite THEOSOPHICAL SOCIETY practices as TOTAL FRAUDS, BLAVATSKY headed for ENGLAND, where she spent her time PROMOTING her books, and her organization.

Meanwhile, back in the U.S.A., a series of SCANDALS resulted in the coming to power of ANNIE BESANT, a lady of similar personality and beliefs of MARGARET SANGER, the founder of PLANNED PARENTHOOD. With an AVANT-GARDE ELITIST type in control, the THEOSOPHICAL SOCIETY gained

SOCIAL RESPECTABILITY among the UPPER-CLASS ELITE. A RESPECTABILITY not at all DIMINISHED by the SEX SCANDALS that so freely circulated about IT'S LEADERS. (???).

It was FASHIONABLE to twiddle with CHANNELLING, and to natter about the 'ANCIENT WISDOM OF THE AGES', (meaning the THEOSOPHICAL SOCIETY'S version of HINDUISM). "WE MUST BE OPEN TO THE LEADING OF THE SPIRITS"…etc…etc was GOOD STUFF for cocktail parties, and it fit right in with the INCREASING DEGENERACY OF THE UPPER-CLASS.

Many of us today do not realize HOW DEBAUCHED UPPER-CLASS AMERICANS OF THE 1920's WERE. This was the era when MARGARET SANGER WAS PROMOTING FREE SEX; WHEN THE FIRST MINISKIRTS CAME IN; WHEN GIRLS CAST OFF THE ROLE OF FUTURE HOUSEWIFE, AND PARADED AS FLAPPERS; WHEN COUPLES DANCED ALL NIGHT, AND GOT DRUNK, AT SPEAKEASY JOINTS.

MEN, IN A FRENZY OF GREED, WERE AMASSING HUGE DEBTS IN ORDER TO MAKE A 'KILLING' ON THE STOCK MARKET. Thanks to the "new" crop of PERMISSIVE PARENTS, and the model T ford, the market for BIRTH CONTROL WAS WIDE OPEN. This was when the THEOSOPHICAL SOCIETY successfully introduced REINCARNATION; KARMA; PLANES OF CONSCIOUSNESS; BODILY AURAS; CHAKRAS; and many other PAGAN CONCEPTS…ALL CONCEPTS THAT HAVE BEEN EMBARRASSED, AND ARE PROMOTED, BY "NEW AGE" GROUPS OF **OUR** DAY. "In many cases, books published by THEOSOPHICAL SOCIETY PUBLISHERS, on those subjects, were the first of their kind". (JAY KINNEY, "DEJA VU: THE HIDDEN HISTORY OF THE "NEW AGE"). (a **MARVELOUS** Article, on this subject can be found in "FRINGES OF REASON", TED SCHUKLTZ, 1989, page 30).

The UPPER-CLASS was JADED. It was looking for "NEW KICKS"…they **GOT** them…but NOT in the way they had expected… GOD HAD MERCY ON AMERICA…HE SENT A **DEPRESSION**.

THE DEPRESSION KNOCKS BACK THE "NEW AGE": The FIRST effect of the stock market crash, was a RAPID DECLINE in the market for OCCULT and IMMORAL teachings. Faced with the need to come back from DISASTER, America (and Canada) was not in a mood to play funny mind games. Life had become SERIOUS again. People simply couldn't AFFORD to act like LIBERTINES.

Various minor OCCULT leaders carried on the work of PROMOTING PAGANISM, but it was HEAVY SLEDDING. GUY BALLARD, the leader of the "I AM" movement of the 1930's, died unexpectedly...a HEAVY blow, since he said he wasn't going to die, but "ASCEND". His widow got zapped for MAIL FRAUD the next year, and the mighty "I AM" movement soon became "I WAS". Unfortunately, the "I AM" movement has been resurrected, and is with us in OUR "NEW AGE" scenario.

ALICE BAILEY, and her husband FOSTER kept busy churning out "NEW AGE" books, but she died in 1949, too early to collect the big royalties from today's large sales of these tedious tomes. A few other scattered wierdos did their best, but found it hard to make a living at it anywhere...except in CALIFORNIA.

PROSPERITY RETURNS... AND HERE COMES THE "NEW AGE" *AGAIN*: (WILL WE *NEVER* LEARN ???) Not until prosperity returned, in the 1950's, did the "NEW AGE" paganism pitch hold out reasonable possibilities for a LUCRATIVE career. MARK and ELIZABETH CLARE PROPHET, [{(???)}] picked up where the "I AM"-ers had left off, and managed to make a decent living at it.

SPIRITUALISTS in ENGLAND managed to get the laws AGAINST WITCHCRAFT and OCCULT activity REPEALED, (we sure have come a long way) and various 'WITCHES' crawled out of the woodwork, to go on SPEAKING TOURS. Still, "PAGANISM" was an activity that did not look good on a Business Resume, UNTIL the "YOUTH REBELLION" of the 1960's finally produced a large crop of MONIED YOUNGSTERS, ready to adopt

ANY teaching that FLATTERED THEM, and INSULTED THEIR PARENTS, and SINCERE CHRISTIANS. Many of them, with the help of Lucifer, moved to CALIFORNIA, giving them even GREATER EXPOSURE to the "HEAVY TEACHINGS" of the assorted GURUS, SWAMIS, CHANNELERS, HEALERS, and SO ON and SO ON... recommended by their FAVOURITE ROCK STARS. This group of "SIXTIES" kids, is now the 'backbone' of the "NEW AGE" trash and MOVEMENT of today, such as it is. AND THROUGH THIS SAME GROUP AND EPOCH, LUCIFER MANAGED TO GET RID OF "ETHICS" IN ALL DISCIPLINES, AND SHOVE ACADEMIA WAY OFF BASE, AND OUT INTO LEFT FIELD, IN NORTH AMERICA. **EFFECTIVELY**, THEREBY, COMPLETING THE EFFORTS OF HORACE MANN AND JOHN DEWEY. AND AT THE SAME TIME, ATTESTED TO THE WISDOM OF THEODORE ROOSEVELT, WHO, ON THE 11 NOV 1902, SAID, "TO EDUCATE A MAN IN MIND, AND NOT IN MORALS, IS TO EDUCATE A MENACE TO SOCIETY".

STUDENTS OF **THIS EPOCH**, ARE NO LONGER EDUCATED, THEY ARE SIMPLY GIVEN JOB TRAINING, THROUGH NO FAULT OF THEIR OWN, AND GRADUATE UNEDUCATED, **INDOCTRINATED** TO FUNCTION WITHIN THE EMPIRICAL THINKING PROCESS, AND THEY DON'T EVEN KNOW IT.

"SUCH AS IT IS"..., because the actual CORE of TRUE BELIEVERS of PAGANISM, appears to be much smaller than the number of people WILLING to AMUSE THEMSELVES with "NEW AGE" teachings. JIM and SELENA FOX, who run the largest PAGAN network on the North American Continent, and who publish the quarterly newspaper CIRCLE NETWORK NEWS, need to print only three thousand copies. This 'newspaper' reaches a substantial section of the pagan community, estimated at 50,000 practicing adherents. These are HARD-CORE PAGANS, not the average "NEW AGE" TRIPPER, and the "NEW AGE" influence cannot be measured solely in terms of DEDICATED BELIEVERS. As long as OUTSIDERS ALLOW THEMSELVES TO BE 'LEAVENED' BY "NEW AGE" TEACHINGS, they will find themselves drifting closer and closer, toward CLASSICAL PAGANISM.

THE PAGANS ARE NOW ACCREDITING THE CHRISTIANS:
This would not necessarily be a matter for FULL-SCALE ALARM, **IF** education in CANADA were in the hands of the people. **BUT IT IS NOT!** For the most part, GOVERNMENT is controlled by the EDUCATIONAL CHURCH. Specifically, the TEACHER COLLEGES, **INDOCTRINATE** EVERY SCHOOL TEACHER IN CANADA, **IN THE LATEST "EDUCATIONAL THEORIES"**. (meaning the latest fashionable belief about the nature of man).

Educational Associations are thoroughly committed to ANTI-CHRISTIAN PRINCIPLES, and control most Provincial Legislatures. University faculties are more influenced by FEMINISTS than Christianity; and "NEW AGERS"; and AN EDUCATIONAL PHILOSOPHY GONE AWRY; than Christianity. In practice, under the guise of "RELIGIOUS NEUTRALITY", Public School and University Students are **INDOCTRINATED** in the pet beliefs of the uneducated "ELITE", of the educational church.

This uneducated "ELITE" ARE under the cloud of 2 THES 2:11-12, and are very fond of following their **OWN** law and will, but utterly IGNORE the LAWS and WILL of GOD. For example, they don't KNOW and NEGLECT EXODUS 20:5 (DEUT 5:9), as if THAT LAW OF GOD DOES NOT EXIST, (OR WORSE...DO NOT ACCEPT IT), then ask "WHAT'S HAPPENING" ? When the PENALTIES or CONSEQUENCES GOD'S LAW WILL EXACT, (if violated) COME ABOUT. PROVERBS 1: 22 - 33.   And DANIEL 3: 26-45.

The educational church ELITE would do better to pray DANIEL 3: 52 -90, FROM THEIR HEARTS.

At first, this meant Canadian children were INDOCTRINATED in "NEW AGE" "ENLIGHTENMENT" SECULAR HUMANISM. TODAY, it means, children are PARTICIPATING in HUMANISTIC-WORSHIP RITES, UNDER THE GUISE OF TOLERANCE AND COMPROMISE; LEARNING TO CALL UP DEMONS, THROUGH "STRESS MANAGEMENT" (actually Eastern meditation); and

FINDING THE WISE PERSON INSIDE YOURSELF; LEARNING ABOUT CASUAL SEX; LEARNING ABOUT CONDOMS; LEARNING ABOUT SAME SEX FAMILIES; LEARNING HOW TO PARTY AND USE DRUGS/ALCOHOL; AND MORE ABUSES THAN I HAVE ROOM TO MENTION.

Good parents COMPLAIN, but in VAIN. The educational church ELITE is convinced that it will save the planet by INDOCTRINATING children in "NEW AGE" ideals. If this is ALLOWED to continue, for a few more years, the number of "NEW AGERS" will be swelled by literally MILLIONS of young adults who have been INDOCTRINATED to UNQUESTIONINGLY believe in "NEW AGE" teachings, and this by 'good Christian teachers' who have unsuspectingly and unwittingly, allowed the educational church "ELITE" to brain-wash them via propagandists (PR FLAKS) of the Teacher Colleges, UNKNOWINGLY.

"If the Educational System is not equal to the task, HISTORY will repeat itself, and our CANADIAN SOCIETY, as we know it, WILL collapse, along with the EDUCATIONAL SYSTEM CHURCH…A cold, hard, stark REALITY. I ask you to neither believe nor to contradict; but to simply weigh and consider my views, from a Social Science point of views, via the DIALECTIC THINKING PROCESS. " (R. A. PRATT, Ph.D., F.B.F.S., "LET'S TALK ABOUT SCHOOLS" 1985, 12 pages). THIS HAS NOW COME TO BE.

Believe it or not, this is OUR INHERITANCE from "THE ENLIGHTENMENT" via the pagan discipline/church of psychology/psychiatry; the church of education, and the Grandparents that failed God and their children.

From "THE ENLIGHTENMENT" educational church "ELITE" we got the idea of giving LEADERSHIP to the "LEARNED MAN", meaning the person with a degree from an "ENLIGHTENMENT" APPROVED… INSTITUTION…the beginning of the "NEW AGE" EXPERT.

Academia decided long ago, that we had to have an ACCREDITED DEGREE to do almost ANYTHING, pseudo or otherwise, and THEY decided what was pseudo. This meant that THEY would only degree THEIR guys, then put those guys in charge of the universities, thereby giving themselves a CAPTIVE AUDIENCE for THEIR TEACHINGS. JOHN DEWEY, the famous "educator", was the ORIGINATOR of this "DEDICATED BELIEVERS" PHILOSOPHY. JOHN DEWEY, author of the HUMANIST MANIFESTO, FOLLOWED **EXACTLY** THAT STRATEGY...AND HIS FOLLOWERS, OF HIS "NEW AGE" EDUCATIONAL PHILOSOPHY, TOOK OVER THE ENTIRE AMERICAN EDUCATIONAL SYSTEM.

And what affect did this have on the Canadian Educational System??? Canada now has the BIGGEST, UNACKNOWLEDGED (educational) 'CHURCH', (a 'church' of Lucifer's realm), IN OUR HISTORY. And the majority of Christians SEND their children to it. And the Christians are FORBIDDEN, BY SUPREME COURT LAW, from using the Public Schools to teach Christian Doctrine, whereas "NEW AGERS", and the pagan educational 'church' is **NOT** FORBIDDEN TO TEACH **THEIR** DOCTRINE.

There are only TWO REALMS in our universe: (1) GOD'S REALM (2) LUCIFER'S REALM. These were established BEFORE MAN WAS CREATED.

There are only TWO RELIGIONS in our universe: (1) THE RELIGION OF GOD'S REALM (2) THE RELIGION OF LUCIFER'S REALM. And we may rest WELL ASSURED, that each time GOD "LOOKS INTO THE DEPTHS (this world) FROM HIS THRONE" (PSALM 113:6 & DANIEL 3: 55) HE SEES, VERY CLEARLY, THAT LUCIFER HAS MORE SPIRITS, ADHERENTS, SAINTS, SERVANTS, AND INSTRUMENTS IN THIS WORLD, THAN **HE** DOES. **Now you _KNOW_ _WHY_ the world is in the mess it is.**

The "ELITE" of the pagan educational church know how to make their OCCULT teachings sound "SCIENTIFIC" and "NEUTRAL". 'CHANNELLING' sessions can be recast as "HELPING THE STUDENTS GET IN TOUCH WITH THEIR INNER SELF". Pagan worship rituals are recast as a means to "OVERCOME PREJUDICE AGAINST OTHER RACES, OR AS RELIGIOUS DIVERSITY". On the other hand, there is NO WAY that the Doctrine of CHRIST

COMING TO SAVE SINNERS can be smuggled in as a SELF-HELP DEVICE.

Our educational church "ELITE" even protest the teaching of Christian morality...i.e. THAT MARRIAGE IS BETTER THAN FORNICATION and MASTURBATING IS WRONG; HOMOSEXUALITY/LESBIANISM; and SAME SEX MARRIAGE IS WRONG. While the school doors are wide open to the pagan church of the "NEW AGE", the same doors were slammed shut in CHRISTIANS' FACES LONG AGO.

"ENLIGHTENMENT" "ELITE" educator types also preach MODERNISM...the doctrine that nothing your father, or his father believed amounts to a hill of beans...while CONVENIENTLY ignoring the FACT that the "ENLIGHTENMENT" beliefs came from failed ancient Greek and Roman PAGANISM. Under the banner of PROGRESS, they were able to accomplish AMAZING feats, such as barring CHRISTIANITY and the BIBLE from schools, replacing them with the GROSS THEOSOPHY and SPURIOUS SPECULATION of the pagan educational church.

The end result??? It is easier to teach a class on WITCHCRAFT, or have the students conduct a SEANCE, than to have the student say a Prayer to the God of the Bible, or have God's Book, the BIBLE, read in school. And if the students DO SO, ALL HELL WILL MOST CERTAINLY BREAK LOOSE.

WHAT IS THE ANSWER??? Are Canadians doomed to see the pagan "NEW AGE" educational church "ELITE" take over the reins of POWER, while we are FORBIDDEN to lift a finger???
LET'S SEE!

For Canadians, generally, it CAN be said, our capacity for self-deception; to deceive OURSELVES, and to be deceived by OTHERS; is LIMITLESS. As DIANE FRANCIS, said, in an article that appeared in McLEAN MAGAZINE, 31 MAY 1999, CANADIANS ARE TOO EASY TO SCAM. I agree with her.

EPILOGUE

If the Canadian people do not repent, and turn to God AS A NATION, (see 2 Chron 7:14), then the only alternative is to carry on, as we are, and the Natural Law of God's Realm will grind to it's inevitable end, and Canada, as a Nation, will disappear off the face of the earth, just as Babylon did, and for the same reasons. No Nation in History has ever walked the path Canadians are walking and survived as a Nation, and Canada is not going to be the first.

It will take a Nationwide Revival, by Canadian Pastors and Evangelists, and the Servants and Instruments God has in place RIGHT NOW, to salvage Canada. The outcome of Canada's life, as a Nation, is NOT in God's hands, *IT IS IN OUR HANDS*.

The Book of ISAIAH, *SUCCINCTLY* describes this **ENTIRE SCENARIO! Whether we believe it or not; like it or not; at this point in time, (this epoch), does not matter a WHIT to God; THE CHOICE IS *OURS*, NOT HIS.** God will NOT interfere with our free - will, nor FORCE ANYTHING on us; **THE CHOICE IS *OURS*. God is no respecter of persons.** God's part we CANNOT do; our part God WILL NOT do

There are three GREAT, fundamental MORTAL errors a man can make:

1. To fail to HONOUR and OBEY the dictates of our Soul because of DISSOCIATION between our SOUL and our CHARACTER/PERSONALITY, HEART, SPIRIT, MIND, BODY, INNATE APTITUDES, TALENTS, GIFTS and TRAITS.
2. WRONG TO OTHERS, ACTING AGAINST *UNITY*.
3. SENSUALITY/LUST.

"The REAL primary cause of disease of man are such defects (sins) as: PRIDE; VANITY; CRUELTY; HATE; SELF-LOVE; IGNORANCE; INSTABILITY; INCONSISTENCY; GREED; PRESUMPTION; PRETENSION; HYPOCRISY; FROWARD MOUTH; IMMATURITY; IMPAIRED RATIONALE; REBELLION; ARROGANCE; MALICIOUS CUNNING; DECEIT; DECEPTION;

LYING; CONTENTION; DISSENTION; ANIMOSITY; SENSUALITY/ LUST; LACK OF TITHING.

Dr. Edward Bach, 1937.

GOD JUDGES VIA THE **THOUGHT** BEHIND THE DEED; THE **MOTIVE** BEHIND THE ACTION.

Too many of us WORSHIP OUR WORK; WORK AT OUR PLAY; PLAY AT OUR WORSHIP; AT ENMITY WITH OUR SOUL.

There are three necessary components to effect CHANGE: (1) THE **URGE** TO CHANGE; (2) BELIEF THAT YOU **CAN** CHANGE; (3) THE REALIZATION THAT YOU **MUST** CHANGE.

If we will not ACCEPT the pain of SELF-DISCIPLINE, we will be GIVEN the pain of REMORSE and REGRET.

We MUST learn to THINK; REASON; PONDER; SEE; HEAR; SPEAK; and PRAY; from the HEART, not the head, to be in tune with our SOUL; and to MASTER the DIALECTIC THINKING PROCESS.

I know you believe you understand what you think I said, but I am not sure you realize, that what you heard, is not what I meant.

"Oh boy; Oh joy; WHERE DO WE GO FROM HERE???"

Canadian's have not been TAUGHT, or LEARNED, HOW TO FUNCTION AS A NATION, for too many years. Clarification of our Canadian National thinking is overdue.

Applying doctrines of philosophic indifference, isolation, and 'wait and see' tactics, injustice, deceit and hate, destructive strategy and intrigue, brought such a heavy harvest of agony, and has wrung the hearts and hopes of many un-offending Canadian men and women.

Canadians must come to a sudden discovery of themselves. The Canadian people have not consciously appraised our Nation according to the measure of our capacity; the lack of development of a self-appreciation commensurate with her potential; Canadian's failure to recognize that Canada has already become a near-great Nation; All this contributes to our problems.

Canada has been slow in coming to a sense of herself, as a

National entity, because of the unhappy continuance of a political life that still anchors itself in her colonial history, in spite of what the Politicians tell us. The efforts of opportunist politicians to capitalize on racial and religious differences, and the failure of the Government to teach immigrant's to get in step with the Canadian people, rather than encouraging them to get the Canadian people to get in step with them, and bandying of epithets with little consideration of their TRUE meanings, have caused a lot of damage. We must find new solutions to old problems. Canadian consciousness must be free of out-worn traditions.

The Statesmen and politicians have, for the most part, left only blurred impressions, on the more superficial levels of our existence; thank God the Mother's of the Nation did not have room on their laps for lapdogs.

Our Nation is dying; perishing for lack of Patriotism's vital oxygen; cut off from the very source of her life; slowly dying the death of the asphyxiated; -Laboured breathing - uneven, strenuous, spasmodic. No one even recognized the peril. What chance does our dying Nation have, when her citizens are groggy in slumber??? She languishes in bleak despair; her citizens unaware of the digression of Canada as a Nation, instead of experiencing a spectacular demonstration of growth in productive capacity and power, in any other like period of time.

Canada's political leadership has been more absorbed with the exigencies of Party Politics, rather than with concepts of National Unity and Purpose. Canadian's must develop greater detachment, and learn to discriminate between true Statesmanship and the chicanery of Party Politics. In recent years, there has been a too obvious tendency on the part of Canadian politicians, to adopt some of the less desirable tactics that have been observed elsewhere.

A critical examination of political life in Canada, especially as exemplified in some of the Provincial administrations, would find many illustrations of how things should NOT be done; AND considerable evidence of irresponsible, haphazard, and even venial Political Leadership.

The deeply perturbed National conscience of the present moment; The multiplying of political Party groups; The abortive efforts of minority Governments; the carpings of one locality against other localities; (their virtues and talents; their arts and skills; contribute **MUCH** to the rootage and flavour of our National life), are 'things' the people of Canada must address. For the most part, such citizens desire a fair (deal) distribution of the essentials of a good life among ALL citizens. Neither has there been much effort to assess the relationships between the Canadian peoples', and the domain ON which, and BY which, we live.

The extent, diversity, and latitude of that domain, are significant factors to be reckoned with, since people and the land areas in which they live, constitute the basic assets of a Nation.

All these manifestations of disturbed emotional and political life, and confused thinking, on the part of Canadians, come as a challenge to the great body of **ALL** well-meaning Canadian citizens.

What the average Canadian citizen does not recognize, is his and her PERSONAL OBLIGATION, to seek ever better solutions. A Nation is rooted in the daily lives of it's people. Canadian citizens have been conditioned by our past, to an obsequious frame of mind, that gives, too readily, an ear to the shibboleths of the old, and the catch-phrases of the "NEW AGE".

The possibilities that look like inevitabilities are so important at this time. It is important that we learn to shape our OWN philosophy of Canadian State-craft, and to trust our own judgments on all questions relative to Canadian human progress.

If Canada is to survive the present crisis she is in, then we her citizens must turn to God in repentance, abandoning the paganism of the "NEW AGE", and gather the directives on which to shape the chart of our National life. We must gather the desires and directives of Nation wide planning. Redevelop our old Social and Political theory via constructive thought and achievement, and be DEDICATED to the realization of our plans. And set goals of achievement, conscious of dynamic Government leadership, within the confines of God's Natural Law. (Precepts; Oracles; and Commandments). **REVIVE FRATERNALISM.**

Canadians must re-establish a true Democracy. There is much yet to be learned by Canadians everywhere, as to what a full application of true Democracy can mean. We will find, that the much vaunted political party system of this day, is a very incomplete expression of the Democratic ideal. i.e. Paid lobbyists and PR FLAKS dictating policies and regulations, and duping politicians, for the benefit of their Multinational Corporations, (who pay their exorbitant fees), thwarting Canadian Sovereignty, forcing Canada into **THEIR** own world sovereignty Government. i.e. they don't give a damn about Canada or the Canadian people, thereby thwarting the silent, purposeful human stream of Canadians, by which all Canadian values are determined, and all National attainment is made possible, robbing the Canadians of their capacity to direct their growth and destiny.

Unless we turn our Nation around, taking Canada out of the grip of the educational church 'elite', the Multinationals / Global Corps., and the paganism of the "NEW AGE", our children will remain in the warp and woof of the old dying Canada, and will remain there, until THEIR children rise up, and bring the old Canada down. If we do not turn this nation around, there are two alternatives; our grandchildren will be utilized by God, to fight a revolution, to rebuild Canada, as a judgment against the Parental Incompetence Syndrome the Grandparents caused, by not teaching their children, how to teach THEIR children, to function within the confines of God's Precepts, Oracles, and Commandment; or; Canada will disappear as a Nation.

It is NOT, therefore, to the TEXTBOOKS of our educational church 'ELITE', that we can turn to, for an understanding of what has come to pass, in the land we call Canada.

We must AVOW ourselves to ceaseless effort on behalf of our dying Nation; to cease from the busyness of merely superficial activities, and give ourselves to the true business of going to the aid of our Nation.

There is no indication over the past 50 years, that Canadians have worked together, to go to Canada's aid, to help Canada via serious, sustained, concentrated effort.

Canadian Patriotism (nationalism) is too complex, divided, and diversified to be capable of the necessary sustained effort, without the aid of Almighty God, via a National Revival with Canadian Pastors and Evangelists at the helm.

Many people who begin with a serious concern about mortally wounded Canada, are soon switched off the main issue by unscrupulous paid PR FLAKS, working for the Multinational/Global Corps., deceiving and deluding Canadians into imagining that they are doing just fine.

With undisguised suspicion, based on a crude and childish conception of Canada's Political Parties, we see Canadians resolving themselves into little more than opportunities for fleeting emotional display, at best. i.e. Canada day; Remembrance Day. We suffer, in fact, from arrested development, prompted by immaturity,(a person with a froward mouth, will never mature, as long as he lives), impaired rationale, arrogance, rebellion, double minded and double tongued, stupidity produced by sin, megalomania, deceit /deception, stealing, gouging, etc. Now you know HOW Canada was dealt the mortal blow, that has her mortally wounded.

If MUNDANUS sees a book on Patriotic devotion to Canada, he passes it by just like he would a spelling book, because he remembers that he learned about THAT, playing at his father's knee. MUNDANUS' still lives among us, and may be found by the score, in any Canadian Community, scarcely adequate to the intelligence of a thoughtful schoolboy, playing at his father's knee.

Patriotism, in the final analysis, is worth EXACTLY as much - or as little, as the individual man behind it. If the man has an obstinate, prejudiced, undisciplined mind, his Patriotism will suffer from the same defects. If his Patriotism is limited, gross, and ill-guided, so will be his attitude toward Patriotism.

This does not mean that we can afford to wait, before reviving Canadian Patriotism and Democracy, until we have secured the ideal presuppositions. We must begin at once, ready or not; we CAN learn from each other as we go along. But remember, no one can safely lead, until he has first learned how to follow, via self-disciplined exercise. And one of the first things he must learn, is how to think, reason, see, hear, speak, and pray, from the HEART, not the head, to be in tune with his soul, and to master the dialectic thinking process.

Before we can revive Patriotism and Democracy in Canada, for Canada, there are THREE necessary components to effect that change; you know what they are. (page 271).

Learning, undigested by THOUGHT is labour lost; thought, undigested by LEARNING, is PERILOUS.

We are quite ready to admit the fact that a man's home life and friendships have more to do with his work for his Country, than a whole lifetime of public activity. This is a truism that we wouldn't dream of questioning. But we seem curiously reluctant to measure our Politicians by this same truism; we seem to think that moral perfection is not required of Politicians.

"AMONG US THE WICKED STRUT AND IN HIGH PLACES ARE THE BASEST OF MEN"

GOD gives us **ALL** a WARNING; a LAW; and a PROMISE;... "DON'T BE ***DECEIVED*** (warning), GOD ***IS NOT*** MOCKED (law), WHAT A MAN SOWS, ***THAT*** HE WILL ALSO REAP" (promise). GAL 6: 7-8.

A full scale alarm is sounding. The key to what Christians must do now, is found in ACTS 5: 29. TO OUR **BEST**, **GOD** WILL ADD THE REST. Matt 8: 37-38.

Let the Christians, by God's Help, Grace, Blessings, Power and Might, begin a Canada wide REVIVAL, restoring Canadian Society as a Western Christian based Society, functioning within the confines of PATRIOTISM AND A TRUE DEMOCRACY, WITHIN THE CONFINES OF GOD'S NATURAL LAW, PRECEPTS, ORACLES, AND COMMANDMENTS, with Canadian Pastors and Evangelists at the helm, supported by Saints, Servants, and Instruments of God's realm, that are already in place, via the POWER of The Holy Spirit of God.

1 John 5:4.

Our un-hospitable Nation scourges Christ anew, casting Him out.

Let us take counsel from C. H. Spurgeon: "At first, those within Lucifer's realm will treat us as they treated Him...they will despise us.

Do not expect that the more Holy, and the more Christ-like we are, the more respectfully people will act towards us. They did not prize the Polished Gem; how can they value the jewel in the rough ?

If they called our Master Christ of the House Beelzebub, how much more will they call them of His Household ? (MATT 10:25) If we are more like Christ, we will be more hated by His enemies.

It is a sad dishonour to a child of God to be the world's favourite. It is very dangerous to hear a wicked world (Society) clap it's hands, or pat him on the back, and say "well done" to the Christian. If this IS done, he should begin to look at his life and wonder what has he been doing wrong; or where he has gone wrong, when the servants and instruments of Lucifer give him their approval.

Let us be true to our Master and have no friendship with a blind and evil world which scorns and rejects Christ. Far be it from us to seek a crown of honour where our Lord received a Crown of thorns ". (end of quote).

"The Lord watches over the way of the just, but the way of the wicked He thwarts. Because of our enemies, He guides us in His Justice. All our enemies shall be put to shame in terror; they shall fall back in sudden shame".

In the beginning, do not expect too much help from some of

the Churches, that are steeped in COWARDICE, TOLERANCE and COMPROMISE for and with the enemy. By **GOD'S** Grace, Power, and Might, they will come around. **TO OUR BEST, GOD WILL ADD THE REST.**

It will take COURAGE, but we CAN do it. We must **BOLDLY** attack, with a heart of kindness, compassion, humility, forgiveness, and charity, the bond of perfection, gladly, with a willing, steadfast heart.

At the moment, to our chagrin, Lucifer has more instruments and servant in his Canadian realm, than God has in His Canadian Realm. We must reverse this sad state of affairs.

It must be found, in our great Canadian Nation, that God has more instruments and servants in His Canadian Realm, than Lucifer has in his Canadian realm.

CHRISTIANS MUST BE FOUND **LABOURING**, (UP TO, AND INCLUDING), **ON THAT GLORIOUS DAY.**

R. A. Pratt, Ph.D., F.B.F.S.

27 NOV 2000

The wrath of God is revealed from Heaven against ALL the ungodliness and wickedness of those who, in wickedness, hold back the TRUTH of God, being that what may be known about God is manifested to them, for the Blessed Paraclete has manifested it to them.

Since the Creation of the world, God's invisible attributes are CLEARLY seen - His everlasting Power and Divinity also, being understood through the things that are Created.

Therefore, "they" are without excuse, seeing that, although they knew God, they did not Glorify Him as God or give thanks, but became vain in their reasoning, and their senseless minds have been darkened. While professing to be wise, they have become fools, and they have changed the Glory of the Incorruptible God, for an image made like to corruptible man, and to birds, and four – footed beasts and creeping things.

Therefore, God has given them up, as the Scriptures say,

NOT by impelling them to do evil, but by DESERTING them. God JUSTLY withdraws His Grace from them, in punishment for their idolatry, and being abandoned by God, man follows the bent of fallen human nature, and falls into the degradation of unnatural vice; to the lustful desires of their OWN hearts, to uncleanness, so that they dishonour their own bodies among themselves. ROM 1:11-18 GAL 5:19 EPH 4:19 etc.

"They" had not made use of the PRESCRIBED PRE-SERVATIVES; now "they" must have recourse to the PRESCRIBED RESTORATIVES.

By REPENTANCE we must give Glory to our Creator whom we have OFFENDED, and by FAITH we must give Glory to our REDEEMER who came to "SAVE US FROM OUR SINS".

Both REPENTANCE and FAITH must go TOGETHER; HAND IN HAND. We must NOT think that REFORMING our lives will save us, without trusting in the RIGHTEOUSNESS and Grace of CHRIST; or that trusting in Christ will save us, without the REFORMING of our HEARTS and LIVES.

Christ has joined these two (REPENTANCE and FAITH) together, and let no man think to put them asunder. They WILL mutually ASSIST and BEFRIEND each other.

REPENTANCE will quicken FAITH, and FAITH will make REPENTANCE Evangelical. And SINCERITY of both together MUST be EVIDENCED by a DILIGENT CONSCIENTIOUS SUBMISSION and OBEDIENCE to ALL God's PRECEPTS, ORACLES AND COMMANDMENTS.

So began the preaching of the Gospel, and thus it CONTINUES. The call is to REPENT, and BELIEVE, and LIVE a LIFE OF REPENTANCE and a LIFE OF FAITH.

SO is it WRITTEN; SO it MUST BE. God will NOT get in step with US; we MUST get in step with GOD. There is to be no TOLERANCE or COMPROMISE here. MARK 1:15 ACTS 20:21 HEB 6:1. Our REPENTANCE, FAITH and SELF – DISCIPLINE **WILL** BE IN PRECISE RATIO TO OUR SINCERITY. R A Pratt, 2 July 2001.

GOD'S REALM THINKING

Thinking in the HEART (not the head) via faith in God, together with gratitude, love and adoration for God, for the good of God's Realm, having reverential fear (AWE) and respect for God, on account of His Sovereignty, Goodness and Justice toward man..

SATAN'S REALM THINKING

Thinking in the mind or head via evil, selfishness, ego, greed, deception, or malicious cunning, for the good of satan's realm.

The presuppositional evidence AND argument for this scenario is the fact that satan is a practiced deceiver; a master of duplication and camouflage. It must be remembered that because of this, there are only five things that God CAN do that satan CANNOT do:

Satan **CANNOT:**
1. BE ORIGINAL;
2. CREATE LIFE;
3. BE TOTALLY HONEST;
4. BE JUST, LOVING, MERCIFUL, AND/OR KIND;
5. FORGIVE SINS AND/OR OFFENCES.

Otherwise, satan (it CAN appear), can do anything God can do, THEREFORE is equal to and with God, and to co-reign, not subservient to God. this erroneous thinking was the basis for the rebellion of Lucifer and his angels and spirits (angels and spirits that agreed with, and sided with, Lucifer) on this question, before creation.

Satan will ALWAYS begin with a TRUTH OF GOD, then pervert that truth, to accomplish satan's purpose via malicious CUNNING, LIES, DECEIT and DECEPTION, even to the point of providing 'blessings' and 'grace' for HIS angels, spirits, saints, instruments and servants, subtly, just as God does for HIS angels, spirits, saints, instruments and servants, SUBTLY.

Lucifer, the champion of infamy, and the practiced arch

deceiver, is also a practiced counterfeiter and duplicator, INDEFATIGABLE. Lucifer, in FACT, is challenging God's Religion via his OWN religion...i.e. still trying to get 'even' with God for banishing him, and his angels and spirits out of Heaven, and into hell, which God created for this purpose, at that time. To quote Milton, "Lucifer would rather reign in hell, than serve in Heaven", i.e. taking VENGEANCE on God, with a vengeance.

To reiterate, we MUST be cognizant of, and never forget, the FACT that, for all intentions and purposes, on the surface, it CAN appear that Lucifer can do anything God can do, via counterfeiting and duplication.

The GOOD God DESERVES better treatment than He is receiving from our Nation; the GREAT God CLAIMS it; the JUST God will HAVE it, or He will repay His adversary Nation to it's face, because of the AUDACITY of the Nation's sin.

How MONSTROUS is rebellion against God by ANY Nation; How TERRIBLE A DOOM is prepared for the Nations that treat God the way WE do.

R.A. Pratt; 13 Sept. 2000

STRANGERS ARE COME INTO THE SANCTUARIES OF THE LORD'S HOUSE (JER 51:51)
POLLUTED: SCRIPTURE, PULPIT, SANCTUARY AND TABERNACLE

To quote C. H. SPURGEON on this subject "On this account the faces of The Lord's people were covered with shame, for it was a terrible thing that man should intrude into the Holy Places reserved for the Priest's alone. Everywhere about us we can see cause for sorrow. How many of the ungodly are now being educated to enter into the Ministry! How fearful it is that Ordination would be placed on the unconverted, and that among the more enlightened Churches of our land, that there would be such a laxity of discipline.

We must take this matter before The Lord to avert the evil which will come on His Church. To adulterate the Church is to pollute a well. May we all have Grace to maintain, in our own proper way, the purity of the Church as being an assembly of believers, and not an unsaved community of unconverted man. PSALM 139:23"

AND THEY GAVE HIM TO DRINK WINE MINGLED WITH MYRRH; BUT HE RECEIVED IT NOT. Mark 15:23

This myrrh cup with it's ANAESTHETIC INFLUENCE, Christ refused. He would not pollute the suffering and agony the ATONEMENT would require. Oh, that we would promptly and willingly put away SELF and COMFORT when it interferes with finishing the work which HE has given us to do for HIM. We must NOT obstruct our Soul.

Well – fortified cities have broad walls, just as Jerusalem had in her glory. NEH 3:8

The New Jerusalem must also be surrounded and preserved by a broad wall of NON – CONFORMITY to the world, and separation from it's CUSTOMS and SPIRITS. The tendency these days is to break down the Holy Barrier, and make the distinctions between the Church and the world appear nominal. There will be no pagan mysticism via pseudo Christian cowardice, tolerance and compromise.

Most Believers are no longer STRICT and PURITANICAL. Questionable literature is eagerly read, and frivolous pastimes are indulged. A general relaxation of standards threatens to deprive The Lord's people of those Sacred differences which separate them from the sinners. It will be a sad day for the Church AND the world, when there is no distinction between the children of God's Realm, and the children of Lucifer's realm.

Remember, the friendship of this world is at enmity with God.. (JAMES 4 : 4). We walk at Liberty, because we keep God's

Precepts, Oracles and Commandments; we must walk with God, imitating Jesus Christ.

As FRIENDS meet each other on the city wall, so meet God in the way of PRAYER and MEDITATION. C. H. SPURGEON.

TRIMORPHIC

IN ASSOCIATION – IN UNITY – AS ONE – IN COMMUNICATION.

GUARDIAN
ANGEL

SOUL
    PERSONALITY / CHARACTER
    HEART
    SPIRIT
    MIND, EMOTIONS, & WILL
    BODY
    IMMUNE SYSTEM
    LYMPHATIC SYSTEM
    ALL ORGANS
    ALL GLANDS

<u>TWELVE APOSTLES</u>
1. SOUL;
2. HEART AND SPIRIT;
3. BRAINS & MEMORY;
4. MIND WILL & EMOTIONS;
5. TALENTS & GIFTS;
6. EYES;
7. EARS;
8. MOUTH & TONGUE;
9. HANDS;
10. FEET;
11. TIME;
12. MONEY.

WHAT DOES IT MEAN TO BE "SAVED" ???

It means that a person has acknowledged being as sinner, at enmity with God and God's ways, and decided to deal with this matter.

TO BE 'SAVED' YOU MUST:

(ALL 7 steps are necessary; any missing steps will render the process ineffective)

Step 1. ACKNOWLEDGE YOUR SINS.　　See yourself as a sinner. ROM 3:23 1 JOHN 1:9

Step 2. CONFESS YOUR SINS:　　honestly; openly; manfully; completely. PSALM 32:5 PROV 28:13

Step 3. REPENT OF YOUR SINS:　　Be truly sorry for your sins LUKE 13:3 ACTS 3:19 2 COR 7:10

Step 4. FORSAKE YOUR SINS　　Willingly; be disgusted with sin ISA 55:7

Step 5. DO PENANCE FOR YOUR SINS (ASCETICISM)　　penance is NOT atonement 2 CHRON 6:24 & :47 & 7 : 14 ISA 58:5-7 EZEK 18:21 LUKE 24 : 47

STEP 6. BELIEVE IN GOD'S FORGIVENESS　　believe in the finished work of Christ. ISA 53 : 5 ACTS 10:43 ROM 10 : 9

STEP 7. ACCEPT GOD'S FORGIVENESS　　Christ must be received personally, by faith. IT'S DONE. PSALM 103 : 12 ISA 1 : 18 JOHN 1 : 12

AND BELIEVE that Jesus Christ IS the Son of God, the Messiah; that Jesus died on the Cross bearing our personal sins, paying the price for each of us individually, thereby reconciling us to the Father; That on the third day, Jesus was raised from the dead by The Father; that Jesus ascended into Heaven, and sits at the right hand of he Father, ALIVE; That Jesus is our peace with the Father, and is there, at our disposal, to advocate on our behalf, with The Father, The Holy Ghost, and others. ACTS 16 :30.

WHAT DOES IT MEAN TO BE "BORN AGAIN" ???

MUST be Baptized. Allow Christ to reign supreme on the "throne" of our Heart, (not tucked away in the manger). Yield our ALL to Christ (our 12 Apostles); all that we have and all that we are. To be Christ's follower, servant and instrument. Being indwelt by Christ's Spirit, allowing Jesus to rule our life according to HIS will. We must learn to KNOW, LOVE and SERVE God, with all our HEART, SOUL, MIND, BODY and STRENGTH, walking the path God created us to walk for HIM, as HIS servant and instrument, in association with our Soul, looking forward to the second coming of Jesus Christ, allowing Christ to hold absolute sway over our being.

WE MUST FIRST, COUNT THE COSTS OF FOLLOWING CHRIST AND DECIDE WHETHER OR NOT WE ARE WILLING TO PAY THAT PRICE; WE MUST BE PREPARED TO PAY WHATEVER PRICE IS NECESSARY.

I must look STEADFASTLY toward Christ, IMITATING HIM. I have MY PART to do via REPENTANCE, FAITH and DISCIPLINE. And if this is NOT done, I will NEVER advance beyond the "BABE IN CHRIST" stage, where, unfortunately, many SAVED AND STUCK Christians remain, their ENTIRE lifetime, and EVERYONE loses; God, themselves, and mankind. I must strive to imitate Jesus Christ, at this point, so that Christ can live in me, because I am doing MY part.

The "flesh" must be subdued...CRUCIFIED...[MY CALVARY] via the inner attitude I adopt. I must COME OUT OF THE 'GARDEN', take up MY Cross, and go on to MY Calvary. There can be no compromise here...COUNT THE COSTS.

Toward "the flesh" I must take up such an ATTITUDE of FIERCE RESISTANCE and RUTHLESS REJECTION, that only the word "CRUCIFIED" can describe it. But to the indwelling Spirit of Christ, I must TRUSTFULLY SURRENDER MY LIFE. An INWARD change of MIND and ATTITUDE [through the heart (not the head)] toward sin, that leads to a change in RESPONSE and BEHAVIOUR patterns.

The more I make a HABIT of DENYING the flesh, and OBEYING the Spirit of Christ, the more the ugly works of the flesh will DISAPPEAR, and the lovely fruit of the Spirit of Christ WILL take their place. In PRECISE ratio to my SINCERITY.

I must trust in Jesus Christ; surrender my ALL to Christ; and commit myself to Christ and HIS cause. There can be no FOLLOWING without a previous FORSAKING. No one can safely LEAD until after they have first learned how to FOLLOW.

OUR BUSINESS ???...LIVING FOR CHRIST...Lucifer ALSO can say "my sheep hear my voice, and I know them, and they follow me".

There must be a FREE CHOICE; a DECISION; a RESOLVE; a DELIBERATE ACT; to freely offer ourselves to Christ TOTALLY and ONLY; to be Christ's SERVANT and INSTRUMENT, WILLINGLY and TOTALLY, from the HEART, and with a GLAD HEART.

This must be through REPENTANCE, FAITH and a STRICT SELF-DISCIPLINE, TURNING RESOLUTELY, FROM EVERYTHING WE KNOW TO BE DISPLEASING TO CHRIST.

We must be willing for Christ to do whatever re – arranging He wishes; there must be no resistance, and no attempt to negotiate on our own terms; an unconditional surrender to the Lordship of Jesus Christ; we must FOLLOW CHRIST UNQUESTIONABLY, in OBEDIENCE **AND** SUBMISSION.

WE open the door to admit Christ, the RISEN, LIVING CHRIST, into our HEART / SOUL; we give ourselves to Christ UNCONDITIONALLY. Christ gives HIMSELF to us; now we are FRIENDS. Christ clothes us; touches our eyes into SPIRITUAL sight; enriches us with SPIRITUAL WEALTH; Christ will re – decorate, and re – furnish..

We must be willing that the Trimorphic of our house comes

under Christ's management; we must hand Him the entire set of keys, granting Him free access into every 'room', committing ourselves to Christ, and Christ's cause; WE MUST IMITATE CHRIST.

ONLY if you are WILLING, and SUBMIT IN OBEDIENCE.
ISA 1 : 18 – 19. Otherwise, you will NEVER advance beyond the "BABE IN CHRIST" - "MILK" STAGE. (REPENTANCE... FAITH...DISCIPLINE).

REPENTANCE: Two words are used commonly in the Old Testament for REPENT, n`aham, literally 'pant' or 'groan', and sh`ubh, 'turn / return' (in particular, to God). The New Testament equivalents are metanoia 'change of mind', and epistrephein 'turn'. However, it is God Himself who must create the NEW HEART / SPIRIT PSALM 51 : 10 EZEK 36 ; 25. You do YOUR part, THEN God will do HIS part; YOUR part God WILL NOT do; GOD'S part you CANNOT do.

THE A B C's OF BEING SAVED

PART A - PRE REQUISITES:
GEN 6:5-6 We can REALLY tick God off
EXOD 32:14 We can also prompt God to relent with us
NUM 23:19 We cannot CON God; God does not DECREE, and
    not act on that DECREE, like humans do
1 SAM 15:35 We can make God sorry for helping us
PSALM 51:10-12 We must ASK God regarding our needs
EZEK 24:14 God judges us according to OUR WAYS and
    DOINGS
Mark 2:17 Christ came to heal the sick(o's) and help us
LUKE 4:18 Christ NEEDS us to be HIS servants and
    instruments
"" 15:7 JOY in Heaven IF you TRULY repent
"" 15:10 JOY even among the Angels

"" 15:21 Do NOT play 'HIDE AND SEEK' with God; (hide our sins and seek His forgiveness) be HONEST, OPEN, FRANK, and ABOVE – BOARD with God (He will be with you)
"" 15:24 Dead and back to life; was LOST, but now FOUND
ACTS 5:31 GOD made CHRIST our ADVOCATE, and REPENTANCE possible
"" 17:30 God has 'over-looked' long enough; now HE calls you to repentance
ROM 2: 4 God's goodness to you, is meant to lead you to repentance

PART B GOD'S PART
1 SAM 15:35 Do NOT cause God to regret He helped you
PSALM 51:10-12 AFTER you have done YOUR part re a 'new heart', God will do HIS part re a 'new heart'
JER 3:12 God will not turn away from you, or be angry with you forever; ('relented' stage)
EZEK 24:12 It WILL come to pass 'according to your ways'
EZEK 36:25-27 IF you do YOUR part, God WILL do HIS part
LUKE 4:18 God NEEDS you, and WILL use you, as soon as you are ready
ACTS 5:31 Christ is God's GIFT to you; don't INSULT God via His gift
" 17:30 Enough nonsense; it's time to get serious
ROM 6:1-2 CONTINUE IN SIN SO THAT GRACE MAY ABOUND?
2 COR 7:9 Sorrow from God is meant to produce REPENTANCE
COL 2:12 In BAPTISM we RISE through FAITH in Jesus Christ
HEB 6:1 Leaving the ELEMENTARY teachings of Christ, we pass on to teachings more profound i.e. 'solid food'

PART C – YOUR PART:
LUKE 14:28-30 Count the COSTS; are your WILLING to pay

the price for an ETERNITY in Heaven? Or do your prefer ETERNITY in hell?

1 SAM 15:29 God will NOT spare or be moved to compassion if you play ' HIDE AND SEEK' or any OTHER game with Him

" " 15:35 Do NOT tempt God to SEAR you; if you DO, He WILL. This is a VERY SERIOUS MATTER.

PSALM 51:10-12 You have YOUR part to do towards creating a new heart and a new spirit (attitude) within yourself

ISA 1: 15-20 Clean up your act; learn to do well, THEN go talk things over with God. YOUR part God will NOT do; HIS part you CANNOT do

ISA 55:6-9 Seek God while He may be found; call on Him while He is near; forsake your WAYS and THOUGHTS; turn to The Lord and He WILL have mercy on you. God is bountiful to forgive

Jer 3:12 Turn from your REBELLIOUSNESS; THEN God will turn and Look towards YOU

EZEK18: 30-31 God WILL judge you by the THOUGHT behind the DEED, and the MOTIVE behind the ACTION. Make to Yourself a new heart and a new spirit; why do you prefer Hell?

EZEK 24: 13-14 Your uncleanness is very execrable; God DESIRES to clean you, but YOU will not let Him. God WILL judge according to YOUR ways and doings, whether you like it or not does not matter a WHIT to God

HOS 6:1 COME; turn to the Lord

JOEL 2:12 Turn to The Lord with all your heart; in FASTING, WEEPING, and MOURNING. Rend your heart

AMOS 5:4 SEEK God, and you will live; if not, you will die

MATT 3:2 REPENT...heaven is at hand

" 3:8 Bring forth 'fruits' befitting REPENTANCE

" 4:17 REPENT; Heaven is at hand

" 27:3 Do NOT betray the Blood of Christ

Mark 1:14 REPENT and BELIEVE the Old Gospel Story

" 1:15 The Kingdom of God is at Hand
" 2:17 Christ is here for the SICK(OS)
LUKE 3:8 Don't be over-confident, thinking you don't need Christ
" 24:47 Penance and remission of sin is what GOD wants to see
JOHN 3: 3 MUST be born of WATER and the SPIRIT
ACTS 2:38 Repent and be Baptized
ACTS 3:19 Repent and be converted
ACTS 11:18 God gives room and time for REPENTANCE
ACTS 20:21 Repent and believe in Jesus Christ
" 26:20 DO works befitting REPENTANCE
ROM 2:4 God's goodness to you is meant to lead you to REPENTANCE
2 COR 7:9-10 God's sorrow produces REPENTANCE; worldly sorrow produces DEATH
COL 2 :12-13 When you were dead by reason of your sins, Christ brought you to life via BAPTISM
2 TIM 1:9 Christ calls us according to HIS own purpose
HEB 6:1 YOU must grow in YOUR knowledge of GOD

    MEET CHRIST AT THE THRONE OF MERCY
    AND GRACE; THE MERCY SEAT!

    JUST AS I AM, WITHOUT ONE PLEA
    BUT THAT THY BLOOD WAS SHED FOR ME,
    AND THAT THOU BID'ST ME COME TO THEE,
    O LAMB OF GOD, I COME.

    JUST AS I AM, AND WAITING NOT,
    TO RID MY SOUL OF ONE DARK BLOT,
    TO THEE WHOSE BLOOD CAN CLEANSE EACH SPOT,
    O LAMB OF GOD, I COME!

JUST AS I AM, THOUGH TOSSED ABOUT,
WITH MANY A CONFLICT, MANY A DOUBT.
FIGHTINGS WITHIN AND FEARS WITHOUT,
O LAMB OF GOD, I COME!

JUST AS I AM, POOR, WRETCHED, BLIND;
SIGHT, RICHES, HEALING OF THE MIND,
YEA, ALL I NEED IN THEE TO FIND,
O LAMB OF GOD I COME!

JUST AS I AM, THOU WILT RECEIVE,
WILT WELCOME, PARDON, CLEANSE, RELIEVE,
BECAUSE THY PROMISE I BELIEVE,
O LAMB OF GOD, I COME!

JUST AS I AM, THY LOVE UNKNOWN
HAS BROKEN EVERY BARRIER DOWN,
NOW TO BE THINE, YEA, THINE ALONE,
O LAMB OF GOD, I COME! CHARLOTTE ELLIOT

DID NOT MAKE USE OF THE PRESCRIBED PRESERVATIVES; NOW MUST MAKE USE OF THE PRESCRIBED RESTORATIVES.
1 COR 3:2 HEB 5: 11-14
HEB. 6:1-20 1 PET 2:2

How Urgently I need Your grace, O Lord; without it I can do nothing

HYPOTHESIS

Incorrigible son DEUT 21 : 18 – 21
Commanded to keep the Precepts, Oracles and
 Commandments of God, NOT MAN
PSALM 118 : 4 PROV 19:16 LEV 25: 18 & 26: 15-17 2 PET 3:2
Read Scriptures 2X daily (morning and evening) JOS 1:8
Sin of Onan (birth control) GEN 38:8-10 JOB 31:15 ECCL 11:5
Wandering (11 days – 40 years) DEUT 1:2-3
God will not be mocked; a warning, a law and a promise GAL
 6:7-8
Not tempted beyond our strength 1 COR 10:13
Spiritual Milk (must start at) 1 PET 2:2 1 COR 3:1-4 HEB 5:12
 - 14
Do you believe that there IS a God ? GOOD! Lucifer also
 believes JAS 2:19
Many words…sin not wanting PROV 10:19

Foolishness to them; can't understand 1 COR 1:18 & 2 : 14
Froward mouth PROV 6: 16-19 & 8 : 13 SIR 23:15 JAS 1:26
Hearers of the Word, but not doers of the Word JAS 1: 22 – 27
Need Wisdom / direction ? JAS 1: 5 – 8
Double minded / unstable ? JAS 1 : 7 – 8
Hearing Christ's words, but not acting on them MATT 7: 26

MISCELLANY OF FACTOIDS: story heading "RELIGION: GUNS DON'T KILL PEOPLE, BIBLE STUDIES KILL PEOPLE" (Vancouver Sun Newspaper, 23 NOV 1996) : Gabel Taylor, 38, after winning a debate on Scripture, was shot and killed by the man who lost. Taylor and the suspect were comparing their Bible knowledge outside an Apartment complex, and each quoted a different version of the same passage, (their OWN versions) Police said. When the suspect retrieved his Bible and realized he was wrong, he threatened Taylor, saying: "I'll kill you before the night is out". And he did.

This is an example of what can happen, when WE teach OURSELVES, instead of allowing the PARACLETE to do the teaching, through the **B**asic **I**nstructions **B**efore **L**eaving **E**arth Book.

HOW TO READ THE SCRIPTURES

Urgings, Counsel, discernments, guidance, direction, Truth, Precepts, Oracles and Commandments are to be sought in Scripture, NOT eloquence or subtlety of speech, nor prophetical insights into Scriptures, nor to solve deep and profound mysteries or revelations, nor to satisfy our own ego, pride or vanity.

Read in simplicity, through the HEART, not the HEAD. Our curiosity is often a hindrance to us in reading Scriptures…we want to understand and discuss were we ought to pass on in simplicity. If you are to derive PROFIT from Scripture reading, read with humility and simplicity, and with FAITH… NEVER wish to have the name of LEARNED. Listen in silence to the words, and don't allow the Parables, Precepts, Oracles or Commandments to be DISPLEASING to you...they are not written without a 'cause'.

The parallel to the SPIRITUAL growth is the physical growth... first the MILK, then the Pablum, then the strained foods, then the Junior foods, THEN the meat and potatoes.

You KNOW there is a God ? good; so does satan ...and satan goes one better than us...satan TREMBLES at the thought of God.

Listening (sacrifice) is NOT required...DOING (obedience / submission) is what is required. WHATEVER is to be accomplished, will ONLY be accomplished by DOING...not by LISTENING only.

COMMANDMENT: Divine Command.

ORACLE: Infallible Guide...profoundly wise...tester or indicator.

PRECEPT: Divine Maxim...basic (milk) moral instructions. Will usually indicate the consequences that WILL be paid for violation of the Precept.

SCRIPTURE ADDRESSES ONLY THREE GROUPS OF PEOPLE:
1. The sinner or reprobate;
2. The 'babe' in Christ or seeker;
3. The solid, mature, standing, Follower, Servant and Instrument of God.

We must NOT take Scripture out -of –context by taking something said to one group, then try to apply it to another Group.

If you have no other, an example of a Prayer before each Scripture reading follows: Oh Holy Spirit of God, be Thou now and forever blessed. I thank You for all that You have done for me up to now, the known and the unknown. Oh Holy Spirit of God, Thou who has spoken to others through the Holy and Sacred Scriptures, please speak also to me. Please remove the scales from my eyes; the darkness from my heart, Spirit and mind, and the dullness from my ears, so that in the midst of the day's uncertainties and opportunities, Thy message and instructions may be understood by me. Please grant me the Grace to be free of deluding, or deceiving myself. Please free me from contumacious desire. I ask these things in the Name of Jesus Christ, on the merits of Jesus Christ, and through Jesus Christ, my Saviour, Redeemer, Master, Lord and King who lives and Reigns with You and our Heavenly Father, One God, for ever and ever, world without end. AMEN. JOS 1 : 8

The DIDACTIC or Teaching Books of the Bible are:

LEVITICUS	COLOSSIANS
NUMBERS	1 THESSALONIANS
DEUTERONOMY	2 THESSALONIANS
JOB	1 TIMOTHY
PSALMS	2 TIMOTHY
PROVERBS	TITUS
ECCLESIASTES	PHILEMON
CANTICLE OF CANTICLES	HEBREWS
WISDOM	JAMES
SIRACH (ECCLASIASTICUS)	1 PETER
ROMANS	2 PETER
1 CORINTHIANS	1 JOHN
2 CORINTHIANS	2 JOHN
GALATIANS	3 JOHN
EPHESIANS	JUDE
PHILIPPIANS	

Begin by reading PROVERBS, PSALMS, WISDOM, and SIRACH, in that order. Then read the rest of the DIDACTIC books from the top of the list to the bottom. All reading should be in conjunction with the Gospels, at different times, but each day as well. Try reading the Scriptures for a minimum of 15 minutes each morning, and read the Gospels for at least 15 minutes each night.

After ALL of the DIDACTIC Books have been read, from then on, read the Scriptures cover to cover, (front to back), for the rest of your natural life, DAILY, for a minimum of 15 minutes every morning and evening / night. (2X).

Why start at the Book of PROVERBS ??? As human beings, we ARE COMMANDED, BOUND, AND OBLIGATED, BY GOD, TO KEEP THE COMMANDMENTS, ORACLES AND PRECEPTS OF GOD'S NATURAL LAW. whether we believe it or not; like it or not, does not matter a whit to God. However, we WILL be Judged, by God, according to how we have lived / kept the Precepts, Oracles and Commandments). BELIEVE it or not; LIKE it or not; that IS the bottom line. PROV 1 : 7 & 9 : 10. (most of the "MILK" precepts are in PROVERBS).

"FEAR OF THE LORD" - REVERENTIAL FEAR AND RESPECT (AWE) FOR GOD ON ACCOUNT OF HIS SOVEREIGNTY, GOODNESS, AND JUSTICE TOWARD MEN. This is the foundation of religion.

P L E A S E; DO NOT make the fundamental, mortal error many 'babes' in Christ make, (via urgings, counsels and discernments from Lucifer's realm), i.e. shoving The Holy Spirit (Paraclete) aside, preferring to teach THEMSELVES, rather than allowing the Holy Spirit to do the teaching. (if you DO, you will have a FOOL for a teacher; trying to teach 'you' about a subject the teacher ('you') knows nothing about.

When The Holy Spirit (PARACLETE) teaches, He will start with the "MILK", then on through up to the 'meat and potatoes'...SOLID FOOD. You MUST allow the Paraclete to do the teaching.

In order to accomplish Spiritual Growth, there is a NECESSARY pre – requisite, (under no circumstances to be by-passed), Spiritual Growth must be accompanied with WILLINGNESS...FROM A GLAD HEART AND SPIRIT.

N.B... There is no such thing as INSTANT GODLINESS: Godliness can ONLY be obtained by EXERCISE and PRACTICE, together with the Grace of God, through Jesus Christ.

The parallel to the SPIRITUAL GROWTH, is the PHYSICAL GROWTH: (from the 'babe' in Christ, on up to the SOLID,

STANDING, MATURE, FOLLOWER, SERVANT and INSTRUMENT, of The Lord God of ALL creation). The steps up are :

STEPS	PHYSICAL GROWTH	SPIRITUAL GROWTH
5. solid, standing, mature follower, servant and instrument	solid foods	Intelligence
4.	junior food	knowledge
3.	strained	wisdom
2. Seeker	pablum	understanding
1. Babe in christ	milk	discipline

THE 7 STEPS: LUKE 15 : 11 – 24

DOWN	UP
1. SELF WILL :12	7. REJOICING :23 – 24
2. SELFISHNESS :13	6. RE - CLOTHING :22 SOLID FOOD
3. SEPARATION :13	5. RECONCILIATION :20 JR. FOOD
4. SENSUALITY :13	4. RETURN :20 STRAINED FOOD
5. DESTITUTION :14	3. REPENTANCE :19 PABLUM
6. ABASEMENT :15	2. RESOLUTION :18 MILK
7. STARVATION :16	1. REALIZATION :17

CRAVE, as new-born Babes, PURE SPIRITUAL MILK. 1 PET 2 : 2

1 COR 3 : 1 - 4 HEB 5 : 12 – 14.

Christ came to call the sinners, not the just MATT 9 : 13

Avoid foolish controversies 2 TIM 2 : 23 – 26

DO NOT show God arrogance or rebellion LEV 26 : 14 – 43 DEUT 30: 2 – 3

PSALM 11 : 4 – 5 & 51:6 & 119: 2, PROV 1: 23 – 33 & 8 : 17, JER 24 : 7 & 29:13.

Your 12 Apostles :
1. SOUL;
2. HEART AND SPIRIT;
3. BRAINS & MEMORY;
4. MIND, WILL, EMOTIONS:
5. TALENTS & GIFTS;
6. EYES:
7. EARS;
8. MOUTH & TONGUE;
9. MONEY;
10; TIME;
11. HANDS;
12. FEET.

Your punishment (you fathers) may extend to your children down to the 3rd and 4th generation. DEUT 5 : 9 EXOD 20 : 5

YOUR part 2 PET 1 : 5 – 7 and : 9.

What must our Nation do ? JER 18 : 8 – 9

God says to Jonah "GO", Jonah says to God "NO", God says to Jonah "OH ?"

JONAS 1 : 1 – 16

What we do to/for the least of Christ's, we do to/for Christ MATT 25 : 40

Omission is sin HEB 10 : 26 – 31

Expel the wicked from your midst 1 COR 5 : 11 – 13

If The Lord is not in the home, there will be no home PSALM 126

Doing what you don't want to do ? ROM 7 : 14 – 23

Do you think God doesn't see you ? EZEK 9 : 9 – 10

Dine not with… SIR 9 : 9

We owe kindness even to those who have forsaken God

JOB 6 : 14 & 30 :24

No tattoos LEV 19 : 28

If a person inadvertently commits a sin LEV 4 : 1 & :27 & 6 : 17

Conscience - NOT a guide system ; an ALARM system

Angry with your wife ??? YOUR Prayers are hindered 1 PET 3 : 7

Judgment seat of Christ re Heaven bound 1 COR 3 : 11 – 16 2 COR 5 : 10

ROM 4 : 10 2 TIM 4: 7 – 8 1 PET 2 : 4 – 6

Great White Throne judgment re hell bound MATT 7 : 21 –23 REV 20:11-15

YOU must forgive (and forget) others, or GOD will not forgive (and forget) you MATT 6 : 14 –15 LEV 19 : 17 – 18

Pray 3X per day (morning; noon and night) DAN 6 : 13

God forbids the races to inter-marry NUM 25 :6–9, JOSHUA 23:12, 1 KINGS11:1-11

Not to look on the body of a nude woman / man except for your own husband / wife ISA 3 LEV 1 EZEK 2

The purpose of the Scriptures PROV 1 : 1 – 7 2 TIM 3 : 16 – 17

The Precepts, Oracles, and Commandments are TOTALLY NON – NEGOTIABLE

You must NOT condone secular humanism or atheism in the Church via the cowardice, tolerance, deceit, deception, or compromise of Lucifer's realm

GOD SEEMS FAR AWAY PSALM 139
YOUR FAITH NEEDS STIRRING HEB 11
LONELY AND FEARFUL PSALM 23

YOU ARE BITTER AND CRITICAL 1 COR 13
FEEL DOWN AND OUT ROM 8 : 31

IF YOU ARE NOT AS CLOSE TO GOD AS YOU ONCE WERE, MAKE NO MISTAKE ABOUT IT...WHO MOVED AWAY FROM WHO ??? DID YOU MOVE AWAY FROM GOD, OR DID GOD MOVE AWAY FROM YOU ???

WANT COURAGE FOR A TASK ??? JOSHUA 1

ARE YOU DEPRESSED ??? PSALM 27

POCKETS EMPTY ??? PSALM 37 & 46

LOSING CONFIDENCE IN PEOPLE ??? 1 COR 13

ANXIOUS ??? MATT 6 : 25 –34

PEOPLE SEEM UNKIND ??? JOHN 15

DISCOURAGED ABOUT YOUR WORK ??? PSALM 126

PRIDE TAKES HOLD PSALM 19

FOR UNDERSTANDING OF CHRISTIANITY 2 COR 5 : 15 – 19

HOW TO GET ALONG WITH YOUR FELLOW MAN ROM 12

PAUL'S SECRET TO HAPPINESS COL 3 : 12 – 17

DEALING WITH FEAR PSALM 34 : 7

"AND THE LORD SHEWED ME FOUR CARPENTERS" ZECHARIAH 1:20

"In the vision described in this chapter, the prophet saw four terrible horns. They were pushing this way and that, dashing down the strongest and the mightiest. The prophet asked, "What are these?" The answer was, "These are the horns which have scattered Judah" (Zechariah 1:21). He saw before him a representation of those powers which had oppressed the Church. There were four horns – The Church is attacked from all quarters. The prophet had good reason to feel dismayed; but suddenly there appeared before him four carpenters. These are the men whom God found to break those horns in pieces. God will always find men for His work, and He will find them at the right time. The prophet did not see the carpenters first when there was nothing to accomplish, but first the horns came and then the carpenters. Moreover, the Lord finds enough men. There were four horns, and there must be four workmen. God finds the right men. Not four men with pens to write or four architects to draw plans, but four carpenters to do rough work. When the horns grow troublesome, the carpenters will be found. You need not fret concerning the weakness of the Church. Apostles may come forth from unlikely places, and prophets arise from the thickest darkness of poverty. The Lord knows where to find His servants. He has a multitude of mighty men prepared to ambush, and at His word they will begin the battle. The battle is the Lord's and He will be victorious. Let us remain faithful to Christ, and He at the right time, will raise up for us a defence". C.H. SPURGEON.

LET'S REBUILD!

REPENTANCE; FAITH; SELF – DISCIPLINE; PRESERVATIVES

Be sure to have PRACTICAL FACTS. Before activity, meaningful solitude. After solitude, strong motivation. With motivation… inevitable opposition. Practice spiritual exercises. (Used repeatedly to develop, strengthen, and maintain Spiritual growth). (Milk to solid food). Prayer; Scripture; Meditation; talk to God; Listen to God; via the Paraclete. (NOT yourself).

When David took off the armour of Saul he said "is there a cause?" While everybody else stood around figuring the 'odds', David shouted 'get out of the way'… David picked up 5 smooth stones…you know the rest of the story. You must possess the inner motivation to never surrender or quit.

If you never get criticized, chances are you are not getting anything done.

You can have your eyes in various directions:
1. On some other person; you will be disillusioned or disappointed, because that person will fail.
2. On your own situation; you will become absorbed in self-pity.
3. On yourself, you will become puffed-up with pride or be demoralized by insecurity.
4. Steady your eyes and focus on Jesus; look steadfastly toward Him. Don't take your eyes off Him. Imitate Jesus in ALL things, at ALL times.

The choice is YOURS. Do not permit your eyes to wander aimlessly. Simply look up, and fix your eyes on the Director...The Lord. "BUSY" does NOT mean "SPIRITUALITY".

Positive motivation must be geared to the individual; push the button that says "LET'S GO".

The heart of the habitual critic RESISTS change... to him/her 'change' is a threat. These people are most inflexible and critical of 'change'.

When a LEADER is attacked, he must NEVER retaliate. Leaders are people of very strong WILL. It takes GET-TOUGH; MINDSET; and DETERMINATION to be a Leader.

If you want to stop an argument, CLOSE YOUR MOUTH. If you want to keep the argument going, answer the complaint or criticism with harsh words, in a harsh way.

CRITICS DEMORALIZE... LEADERS ENCOURAGE.

The easiest thing to do when one is criticized, is to GIVE UP. PERSISTENCE in the form of COMMON SENSE must prevail.

It is foolishness to leave your doors and windows unlocked, when you are praying that your home will not be burglarized.

Out of a job? PRAY! But hit the road too... get out and LOOK for a job.

It is impossible to lead anyone without facing opposition. It is essential to face opposition in/with prayer. Prayer is not ALL that is necessary if opposition GROWS. Common sense must be employed. It is not the CRITIC who counts.

No LEADER is exempt from criticism; don't expect to be. But when criticism comes, be ready to BATTLE against DISCOURAGEMENT, which is poised and ready to strike...you can COUNT on it!

Sometimes, when a Leader tries to alleviate a problem, the greater it becomes. You will face SARCASM; MOCKERY; CRITICISM; and CONSPIRACY. Where conspiracy is great, DISCOURAGEMENT WILL set in. And when it does, the problems will get worse right before your eyes. And Lucifer knows this; hence, Lucifer's WHISPER CAMPAIGN (this is where the PR Flaks got the "whisper campaign' from). Lucifer knows that people will believe ANYTHING that is whispered. "where realistic rebuttal is not possible, mud slinging is an excellent substitute", is a precept of Lucifer's realm.

DISCOURAGEMENT is a difficult syndrome to cure...it will take the wind out of your sails quickly and EFFECTIVELY. The ANTIDOTE is OPTIMISM... but it must be of the CONTAGIOUS variety.

One cannot constantly hear negativism without having some of it rub off on you.

There are 4 causes of DISCOURAGEMENT:
1. LOSS OF STRENGTH: The strength of the burden is failing. A loss of strength takes an EMOTIONAL toll on our bodies.
2. LOSS OF VISION: The Burden Bearer's strength was expended and began to fail. In spite of all the work, there is lots of rubbish. Discouragement and rubbish are Siamese twins. We can EASILY begin to lose the whole vision of our work because of the 'rubbish' surrounding us.
3. LOSS OF CONFIDENCE: Perhaps THIS is the most DEVASTATING cause of discouragement.

When we lose STRENGTH, we lose VISION. Then we lose CONFIDENCE, and when we lose confidence, DISCOURAGEMENT is just around the corner.

When we lose CONFIDENCE, we lose HEART, then we lose MOTIVATION.

There is always an EMPTY FEELING... that is overwhelming; a discouraging sense that we are NEVER going to 'catch-up'.

4. LOSS OF SECURITY: The final cause of discouragement, causes the work to cease. When we least expect it... WHAM! The labour suddenly slumps into discouragement when we lose our security.

There are many areas in life that we hang onto for tangible SECURITY... our jobs... close friends... familiar circumstances.

Some think that discouragement is only for those not walking with God... THAT IS NOT TRUE! I have seen that times of discouragement have been signals from God, announcing a whole new direction and plan.

Strange as it may be, discouragement, brought on by a removal of our tangible securities, have been known to usher in incredible achievements. I have seen this many times.

Have you ever wanted to run away? What a desire to escape we have from time to time... to get away from life's demands. But if we will endure the discouragements, we will probably find we are being lead to an opportunity offering unbelievable fulfillment.

Maybe you are right now standing before the door of opportunity or change. You've lost your strength... you've lost your confidence... you've lost your vision... you've lost your security. There's that feeling down deep within you that says "IT ISN'T WORTH IT".

BUT WAIT! You could be on the verge of the greatest years of your ENTIRE LIFE...

How can we deal with discouragement???

For Nehemiah, building that Jerusalem wall was no easy feat; Lucifer was having a 'field day'. But Nehemiah did NOT ignore the discouragement.

We can't ignore discouragement either... that would be like ignoring a trashed flat tire that rolled off the rim. Pray all you want... drive all you want; you'll NEVER get back into that tire. You've got to SOLVE the problem. That's the way it is with discouragement.

Nehemiah used 5 techniques that still work to this day:
1. UNIFY YOUR EFFORTS TOWARDS A GOAL: Nehemiah unified the people around the goal... stationed men in the lowest parts of the space behind the wall, the exposed places. He stationed the people in families with their swords, spears and bows. Nehemiah united them according to families, and gave each one a common goal – FAMILY PRESERVATION.

He turned their attention from THEMSELVES to the ENEMY. From the discouragement of self-pity, to the goal of self preservation... he tightened the ranks, and thereby encouraged the disheartened.

The home should be a basic source of ENCOURAGEMENT... he brought them together as units. NOTICE WHAT HAPPENED; IN THE PROCESS OF UNITING THE PEOPLE, HE STOPPED THE WORK.

When discouraged, take some time off. A Greek motto says "you will break the bow if you keep it always tight". How tight is YOUR BOW??? When was the last time you loosened the 'bow' and got away for a couple of days??? Nehemiah stopped the work and said "Let's pull together as families". THAT will do a lot to stop discouragement.

2. DIRECT YOUR ATTENTION TO THE LORD: Next Nehemiah directed their attention to the Lord. They were looking at the RUBBISH... they needed to be looking at The Lord. Nehemiah TOOK CHARGE... that's a basic job of the Leader. Nehemiah unified them... he had to stop the work process and get them alone... Nehemiah turned their attention to The Lord.
3. MAINTAIN A BALANCE BETWEEN YOUR THOUGHTS AND YOUR ACTIONS: Nehemiah encouraged the people

to maintain a balance; fight for your brothers, your sisters, your sins, your daughters, your wives, and your houses. Guard against the teaching that suggests God does everything, and we step back and do nothing. We must balance faith with action.
4. DETERMINE A RALLYING POINT: What was the rallying point? First of all it was a PLACE, but it also suggests a PRINCIPLE... DON'T TRY TO FIGHT ALONE.

We need a 'Rallying point'... a close friend... somebody we can attach ourselves to whenever the 'attack' comes... don't try to fight alone. Rally 'round' God for sure, but remember, God gives you a "buddy" with whom you can be accountable (That's very important); bare your soul; share your hurts; and relieve your loneliness.

Do you have someone like that? If not, cultivate someone. Look for, long for, pray for such a friend; someone in your area who cares about you.

5. DEVELOP A SERVING OTHERS MINISTRY: Nehemiah occupied his people in a Ministry of serving others. He said - "Hey... we need help... serve and assist each other... we can't handle this alone.

How involved are you in OTHER'S lives? Serving others? Or are you only wrapped up in yourself?

Retirement seems to be 'don't bother me... I've no time for others'.

Think of the Ministry of ENCOURAGEMENT God could give to YOU when He releases you (through retirement) and uses YOU as a servant and/or instrument.

Nehemiah seems to say "Let's not sit around and lick our own wounds... we need help from one another... let's get at the business of caring... let's serve... let's minister... isn't that what the raw edge of Christianity is all about???

Discouragement starts with SELF-DOUBT... through fear and negative exaggerations it begins to grow and multiply... soon we lose our way... we weaken, and run and hide. As it continues, we become virtually useless and downright defeated. It can happen almost overnight.

Discouragement may be tough to handle... but remember, IT IS NOT A TERMINAL DISEASE.

SELF-CONTROL is a virtue a leader CANNOT afford to be without.

If you are a leader, you spend your time either on the top or on the bottom, not in between... hero or villain... it's at the 'outhouse' times we show our true colours. This is true especially within God's Spiritual Realm.

INPUT vs INSIGHT. Insight is essential for leaders... he MUST see the 'BIG PICTURE'... he must see the results of his "NOW" ahead of time.

To gain insight takes time... it takes the right people... it takes the right attitude... there is no such thing as instant insight... like sponges, we get bigger and bigger SPIRITUALLY... it takes an open, teachable mind.

PUTTING FIRST THINGS FIRST

Thinking is hard work... thinking includes praying and quietness... thinking calls for projection.

DOCUMENTING THE PRIORITIES:
1. serious thought precedes ANY significant change.
2. Written plans confirm right priorities.
3. A loss of distinction and conformity to the world go hand in hand.

DEVOTION OF THE NAMELESS; DEEDS OF THE NAMELESS:
1. PREPARATION: Integrity... honesty... faith
2. PERSPECTIVE: look at God; not at the giants. No panic

or emergency meetings in Heaven. Only plans; God is Bigger.
3. PURPOSE: There IS a cause. Deal with the sinister spirit of fear. You will be laughed at... laughed to scorn. Discouragements of and by the pseudo 'experts', (who boasting of cutting off the Lion's tail with a pen knife; [but the Lion's head had been cut off first; but they don't want you to know that]). (And/or like the woodpecker that found a large tree that had been split in half and fell to the ground via a powerful lightning bolt, and brought 9 other woodpeckers back to the tree with him, to show them what he did),
4. PROGRESSION: Small victories at first. Then from larger to larger.
5. PROTECTION of God will be invisible.
6. POWER: In the Name of Jesus, via the Authority of God, to God's Glory.

DEVELOP, AND HAVE A GOOD SELF-IMAGE that:
You can live with:
Is acceptable to YOU;
Is wholesome;
You can trust and believe in;
not ashamed to be;
feel free to express creativity;
not to hide or cover up or be ashamed of due to inadequacy;
that corresponds to / with reality;
functions effectively in a real world;
know your strengths (Be honest with yourself)
know you weaknesses (be honest with yourself);
reasonable approximation of 'you'
neither more than you actually are, nor less than you actually are;
when intact and secure, you feel good;

when threatened, you feel anxious and insecure; when adequate, and you can be wholesomely proud of it, you feel self-confident; you feel free to 'be yourself', and express yourself. You function at your optimum. When it is an object of shame, you attempt to hide it rather than express it. Creative expression is blocked. You become hostile and hard to get along with.

Since we CAN re-shape ourselves, WE are responsible for the shape we are in. The outcome of my life is NOT in God's Hands; it's in MY hands.

Via our THOUGHTS we choose to follow in the Realm of God, or in the realm of Lucifer. Set your mind on the things of the flesh/ world, and you will be dead to the things of God's Realm. (mind set). Set your mind on the things of God, and you will be dead to the things of Lucifer's realm. (mind set).

But remember... never forget; Lucifer's evening wolves are engaged in a CONSTANT tug of war for our mind/ conscience, to devour our good/ HOLY intentions and practices. If WE provide them with the opportunity to do so, they WILL devour the good intentions and practices that WE failed to accomplish as we SHOULD have, in keeping with OUR resolutions and practices, i.e. our BAD. GUARANTEED! NEVER neglect our spiritual exercises/duties i.e 2X 3X etc.

Provide those ravenous evening wolves with GOOD to eat, not BAD, (From a Christian prospective), to BURST their stomach, and destroy THEM!

GOD'S SERVANT AND INSTRUMENT ???
OR
LUCIFER'S SERVANT AND INSTRUMENT ???
DID WE CHOOSE JESUS OR BARABBUS ???
DID WE GIVE JESUS THE KISS OF JUDAS ???

TO PROMOTE UNITY

A HEART OF MERCY
KINDNESS
HUMILITY
MEEKNESS
PATIENCE
BEAR WITH ONE ANOTHER
FORGIVE ONE ANOTHER
IF YOU HAVE A GRIEVANCE, FORGIVE IT
CHARITY, THE BOND OF PERFECTION
COL 3: 12-14

<u>LOVE IS:</u> PATIENT
    KIND
    NOT JEALOUS
    IS NOT SNOBBISH
    NEVER RUDE
    NOT SELF-SEEKING
    NOT PRONE TO ANGER
    DOES NOT BROOD OVER INJURIES
    DOES NOT REJOICE IN WHAT IS WRONG
    REJOICES WITH TRUTH
    NO LIMIT TO FORBEARANCE
    TRUST
    HOPE
    POWER TO ENDURE
    NEVER FAILS
    1 COR 13: 4-8
  Control your thoughts!

    We are not what we think we are, but what we think, **THAT** we are.
    Pain the picture; Rehearse the part; Play the role.
    Do NOW what you would do THEN!